AF479129

Arthur Landt
Leica R7

Arthur Landt

LEICA **R7**

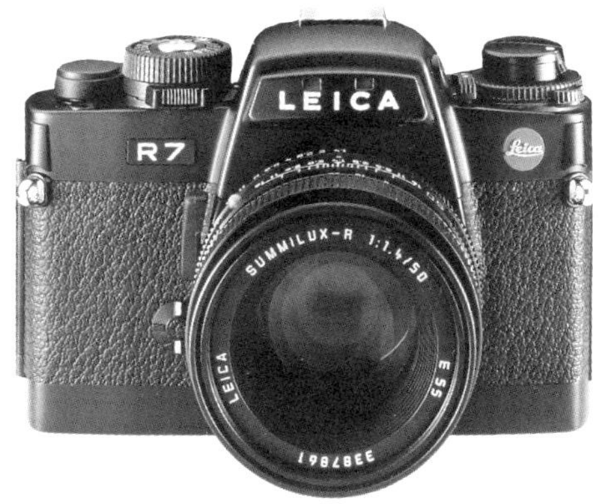

Hove Books

First English Edition January 1993
Hove Books
34 Church Road, Hove
East Sussex BN3 2GJ

British Library Cataloguing-in-Publication Data
A catalogue record for this book is available from the British Library
ISBN 1 897802 00 5

Copyright © 1993
English Language version by Hove Books.

Copyright © 1992
German Edition by Verlag Laterna Magica Joachim F. Richter, Munich.

English translation: *Petra Kopp*
Editor: *Dennis Laney*
Design and typesetting: *Facing Pages*
Printed in England by Hartnolls Ltd., Bodmin.

Distribution in U.S.A.
The Saunders Group
21 Jet View Drive
Rochester, N.Y. 14624-4996
Fax: (716)328-5078

Distribution in Canada
Amplis Foto Inc.
22 Telson Road
Markham, Ontario L3R 1ES
Fax: (416)477-2502

Contents

Acknowledgements

The author and publisher would like to thank the Leica Camera Group for permission to use their registered trademarks.

The following Leica trademarks appear in the book:
ABSORBAN
COLORPLAN
ELMAR
ELMARIT
ELPRO
FOCOMAT
FOCOTAR
LEICA
PHOTAR
REPROVIT
SUMMICRON
SUMMILUX
TELYT

and combinations thereof (e.g. MACRO-ELMAR); also the following Schneider trademarks:
PA-CURTAGON
SUPER-ANGULON
PC-SUPER-ANGULON

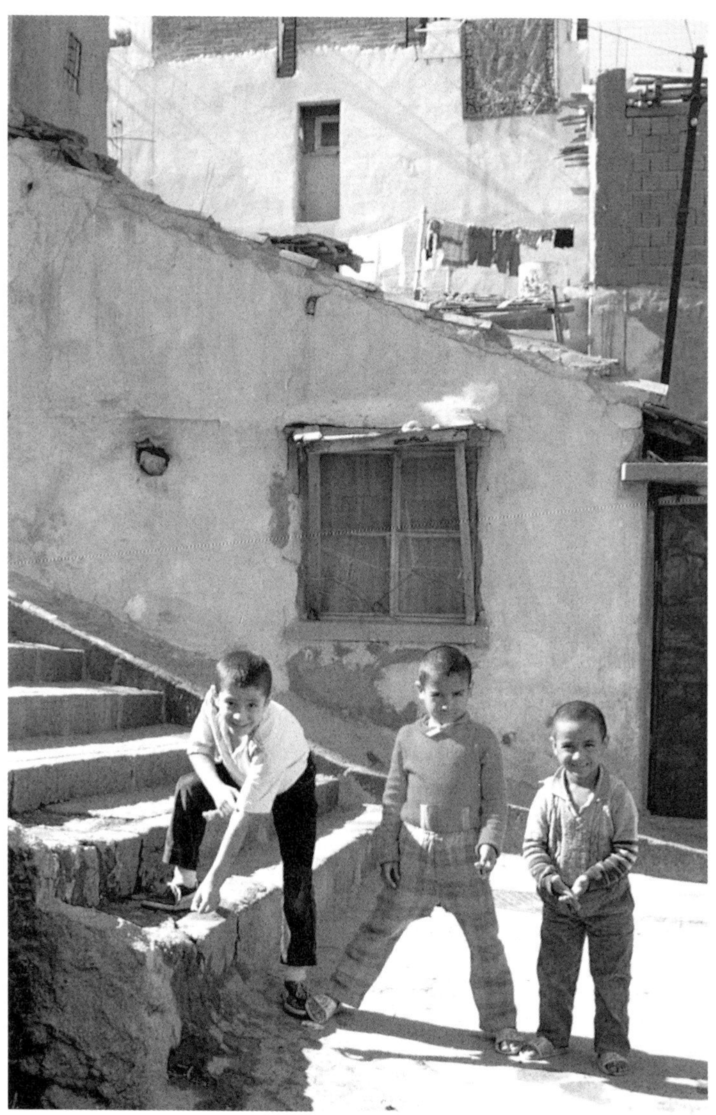

All the Leica R lenses, not just the rapid-focusing ones, enable you to shoot quickly

Introduction – the Leica R7

Experienced Leica users will no doubt be expecting at this point the obligatory effusive retrospective about the Leica tradition, starting with Carl Kellner, or at least with Oskar Barnack and his 'Ur-Leica' of 1913. It is also traditional in Leica books to establish the connection with today's cameras. But the Leica R7 deserves to be presented in its own right: it has about as much in common with Leica's historical cameras as a Mercedes 600 SEL has with Daimler's motor carriage of 1886.

The R7 is presented in the well-known inconspicuous Leica-guise, often called 'timeless' by connoisseurs. But behind the deliberately understated exterior you will find modern high technology in its most sensible and practical form. Happily we are not subjected to the grandiose 'feature show' of the high-tech festival staged by Japanese camera manufacturers, but the Leica R7 still impresses with a good technical presence. The new camera, one of the top models in the Leica range, is the product of thoughtful design. The technical features are not an end in themselves, but guarantee sensible and practical operation. There is nothing showy on the R7, even its shape is functional. This is why the Leica R7 isn't just a camera for wealthy amateurs and ambitious would-be professionals, but for everyone who takes 35mm photography seriously, and particularly for those who have to earn their living by it.

You won't find anything superfluous on the Leica R7, but neither will you have to go without important features. It has everything the discerning photographer needs for sensible photographic work. The functions are controlled by an eight-bit microprocessor. The two exposure metering modes (integral and selective) are combined in a practical way with program mode, shutter priority and aperture priority modes, as well as manual exposure mode. Thanks to sophisticated TTL flash metering and TTL flash control the Leica R7 offers professional flash techniques such as fill-in, flash exposure compensation, and slow shutter speed sync. Exemplary viewfinder displays, DX coding, exposure compensation, manual shutter speed selection in half-step increments, and independent mirror release are further features of the camera.

In this high-tech age the Leica R7 is the best example of the quintessential electronic camera. It gives the impression of being a photographic tool like no other electronic 35mm SLR camera. This book is intended to provide you with a guide to working with it, starting right at the beginning. It is written from the viewpoint of the practical photographer. Technical and theoretical issues are covered where necessary against the background of their practical application, which is given the most emphasis, but I have omitted subjects such as 'photographic practice'. We could not do without technical terms altogether, but enthusiastic photographers, even beginners, will probably be familiar with most of the technical terms we have used.

I hope you enjoy reading the book, and using the camera.

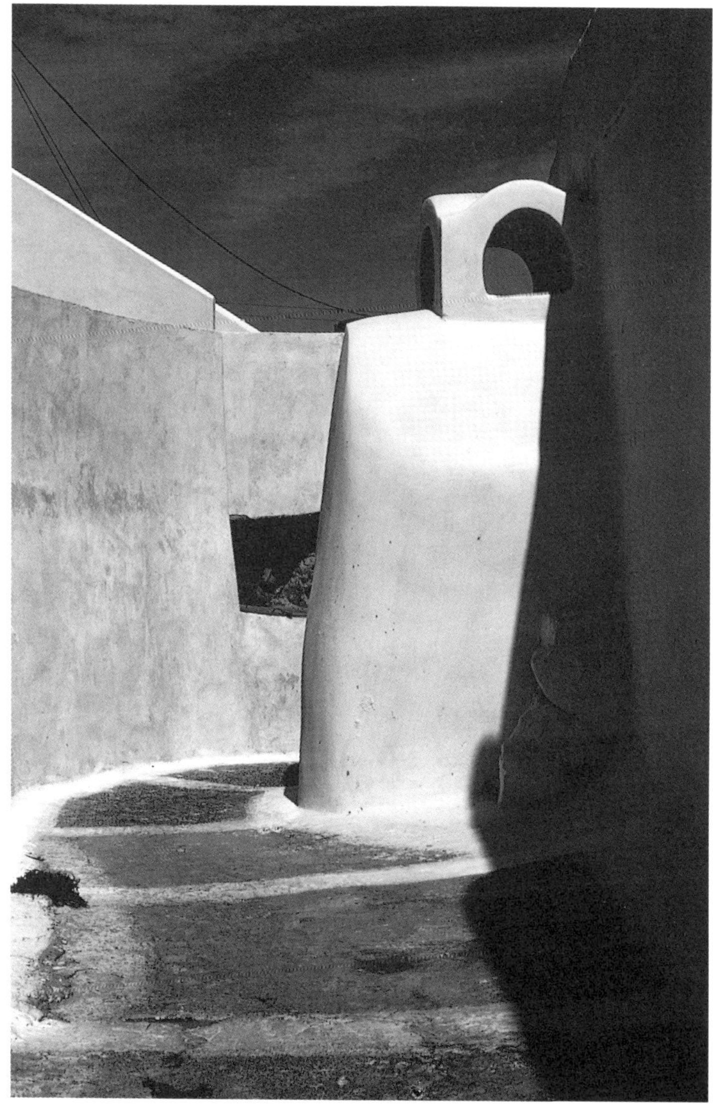

With the selective metering system of the Leica R7, careful, creative exposure is no problem.

A Short Tour of the Leica R7

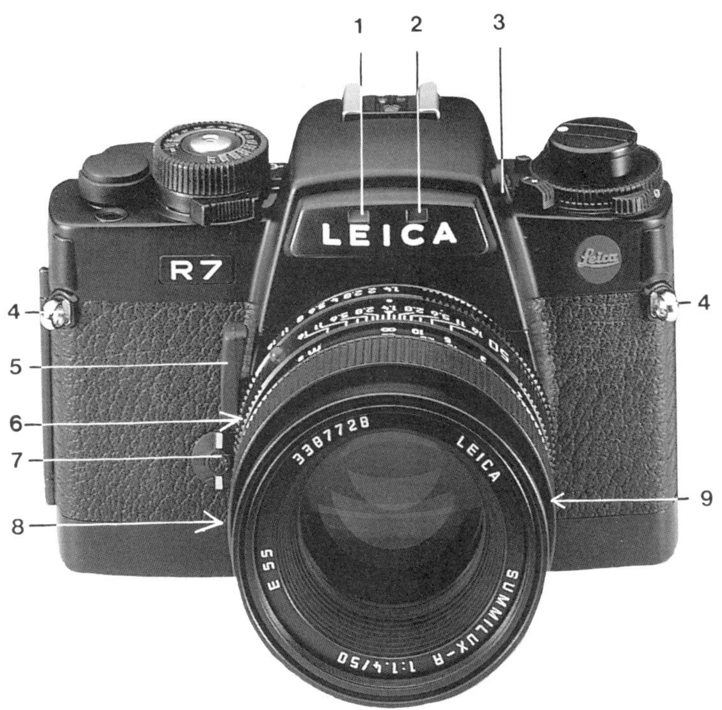

1. Window for illumination of the aperture scale
2. Self-timer LED
3. Coaxial flash-cable contact
4. Carrying strap eyelet
5. Depth of field lever
6. Bayonet lock
7. Electronic self-timer
8. Connection for independent mirror release
9. Aperture scale illumination switch

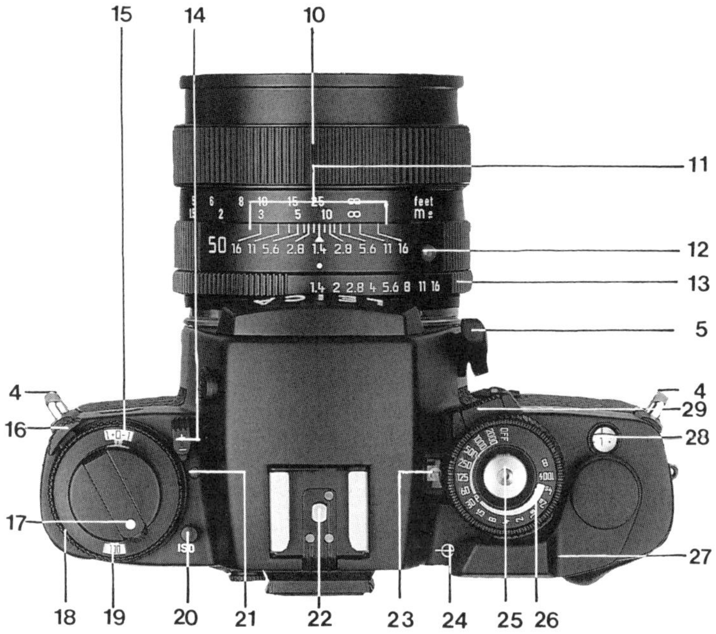

10 Focusing ring
11 Depth of field scale
12 Red dot for alignment of interchangeable lenses
13 Aperture setting ring
14 Release button for exposure compensation lock
15 Exposure compensation viewing window
16 Exposure compensation lever
17 Fold-out rewind crank
18 Film speed setting ring
19 Film speed control window
20 Release button for film speed setting
21 LED
22 Accessory shoe with central hot-shoe and control contacts for SCA adapters
23 Display window for mode selected
24 Film plane index
25 Shutter release, with screw socket for cable release
26 Shutter speed setting dial
27 Rapid wind lever to wind film and cock shutter
28 Automatic frame counter with magnifying window
29 Mode selector with locking button

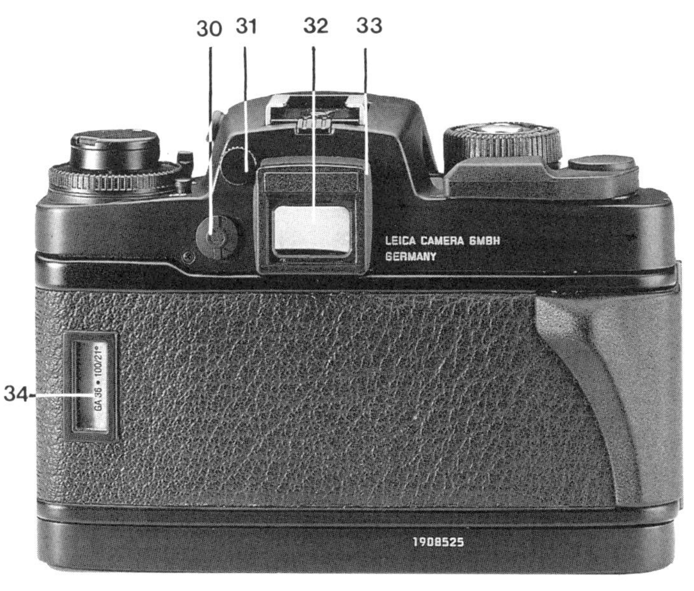

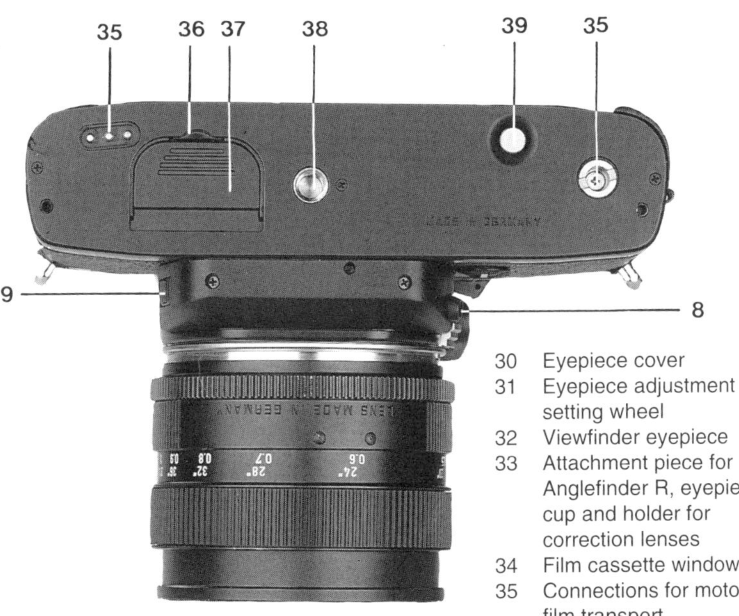

30 Eyepiece cover
31 Eyepiece adjustment setting wheel
32 Viewfinder eyepiece
33 Attachment piece for Anglefinder R, eyepiece cup and holder for correction lenses
34 Film cassette window
35 Connections for motorized film transport
36 Battery cover release
37 Battery compartment cover
38 Tripod socket, A-type
39 Rewind release and double exposure button

13

1. Getting Started

Like any other expensive camera, the qualities of the Leica R7 are only revealed in the work of photographers who are thoroughly familiar with its handling and functions. Gradually getting acquainted with the technology of the Leica R7 – which involves getting to know the camera, finding out how to get started and how to go about your first 'dry runs' – is essential if you want to achieve technically perfect pictures.

The numbers in brackets refer to the names of the operating controls as shown in the illustrations.

Attaching the carrying strap

A simple system for attaching the carrying strap provides maximum security against its accidentally coming loose and maximum protection against rubbing or scratching the camera's surface. Unless you are using a tripod, you should leave the carrying strap attached to the Leica R7 and keep it over your shoulder or round your neck when carrying the camera. This will allow easier lens changing and ensure that you don't drop the camera accidentally.

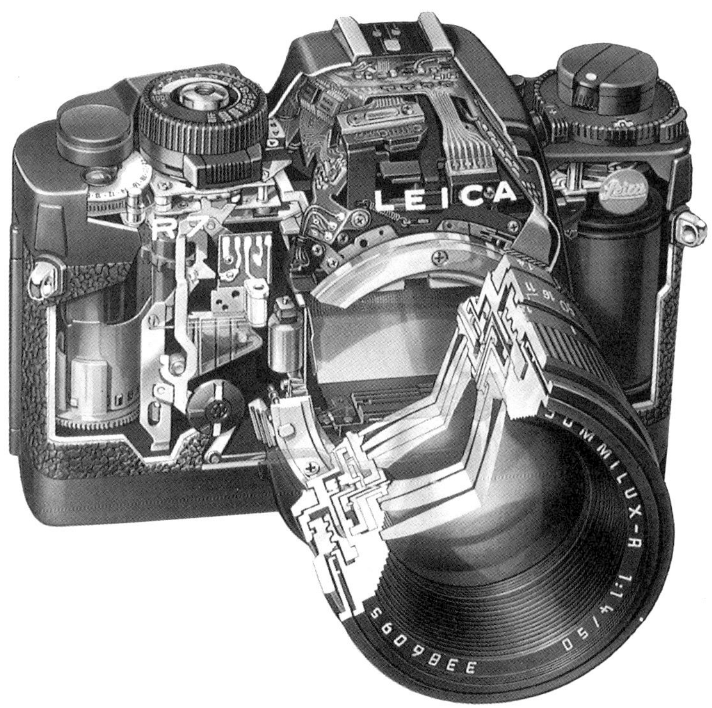

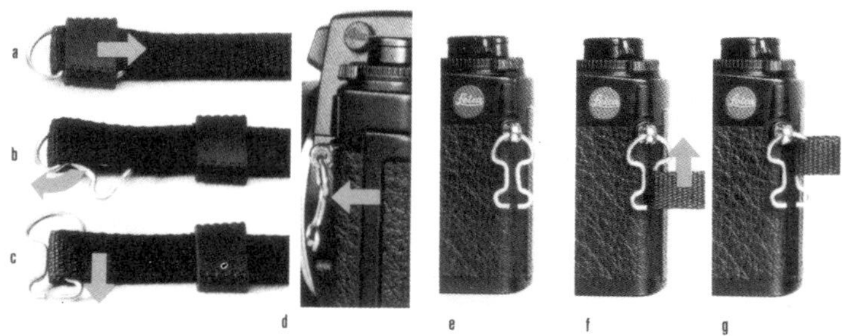

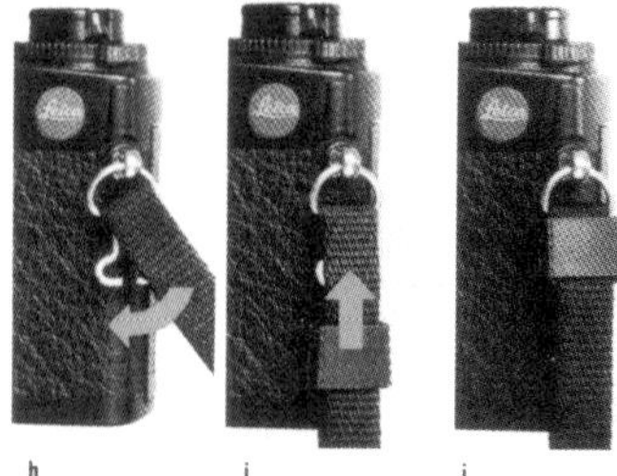

Figures a-j demonstrate how to attach the carrying strap

The carrying strap is attached to the eyelets (4) on the camera as follows: slide back the securing loop (Fig a) and remove the metal hook from the strap (Figs b, c); slip the slightly angled metal hook into the eyelet (4) with the opening pointing downwards and the angled curve pointing towards the camera (Figs d, e). Then insert the carrying strap through the opening of the hook and turn it slightly to place it above the waist of the hook (Figs f, g, h). Finally, slide the securing loop over the metal hook as far as it will go (Figs i, j).

Changing lenses

All lenses with control cams for Leica R cameras can be mounted on the Leica R7. Older Leicaflex lenses without the Leica R control cam (third cam) must first have one fitted at the factory.

Remove the body cap by pressing the bayonet lock (6) on the camera body whilst turning the cap to the left (if the camera is upright in front of you). Regardless of the distance and aperture setting, Leica R lenses are attached as follows: grip the lens by the fixed ring (11) which has the raised red dot and the depth of field scale on it; align the red dots on the lens and on the bayonet lock on the camera; engage the lens with a slight turn to the right. The lens will engage with an audible and noticeable click. To make sure the lens is properly engaged grip the fixed ring and gently try to turn it to the left. If it is engaged properly the lens will

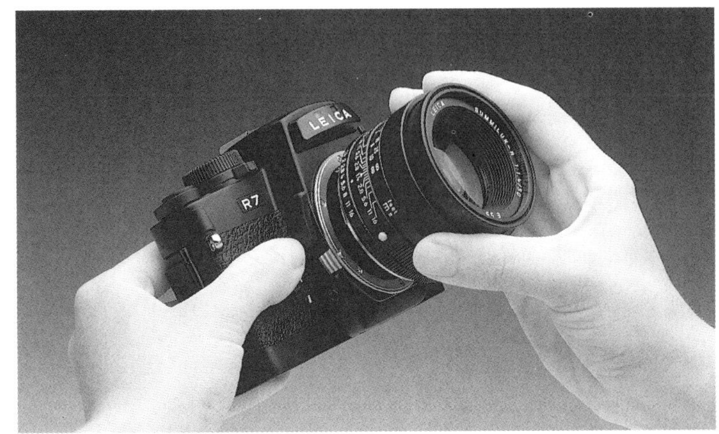

Lenses can be changed literally with your eyes closed.

not move. The upper red dot is raised and can easily be found by feel in the dark, a very useful facility in the theatre.

To remove the lens, press the bayonet lock and turn the lens to the left by the fixed ring. You should not change lenses in direct sunlight or in otherwise bright conditions: it's best to do so away from direct light, such as in the shadow cast by your own body.

Battery loading

The Leica R7 requires a battery of 6 volts to power its electronic functions and the exposure meter. This can be in the form of four silver

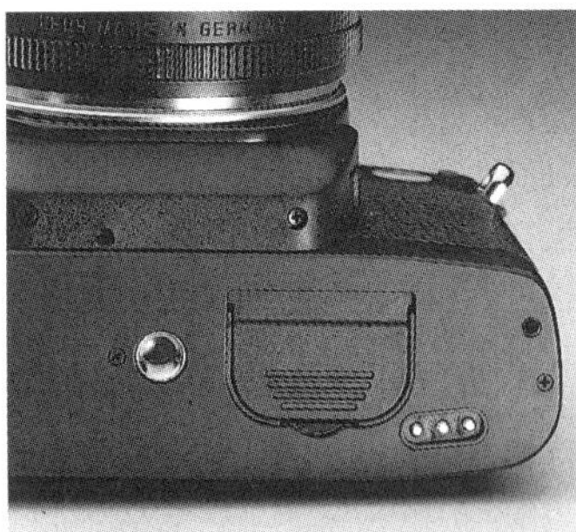

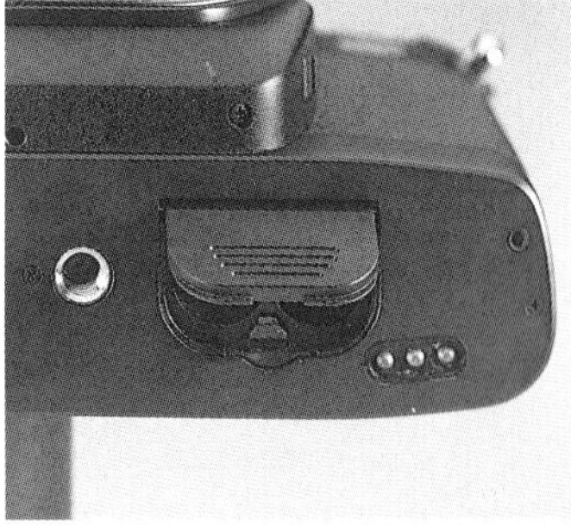

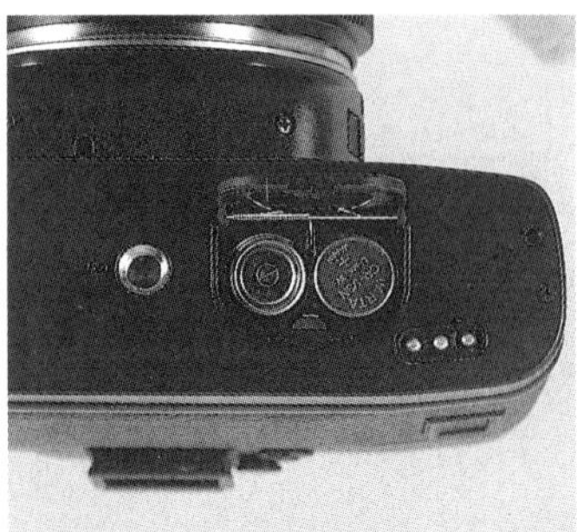

Battery replacement is child's play with the Leica R7 – no coins are required.

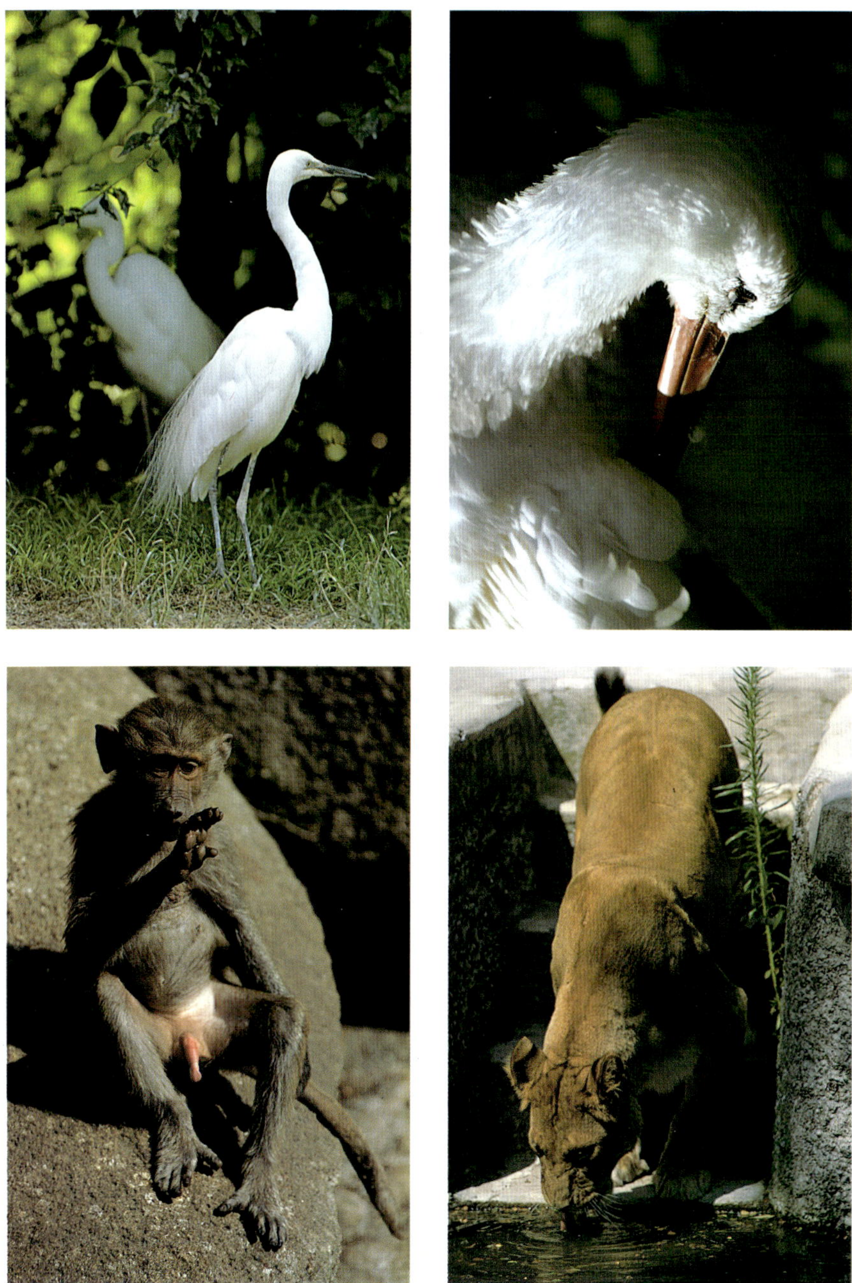

There are excellent Leica telephoto lenses and extenders which are ideal for animal photography.

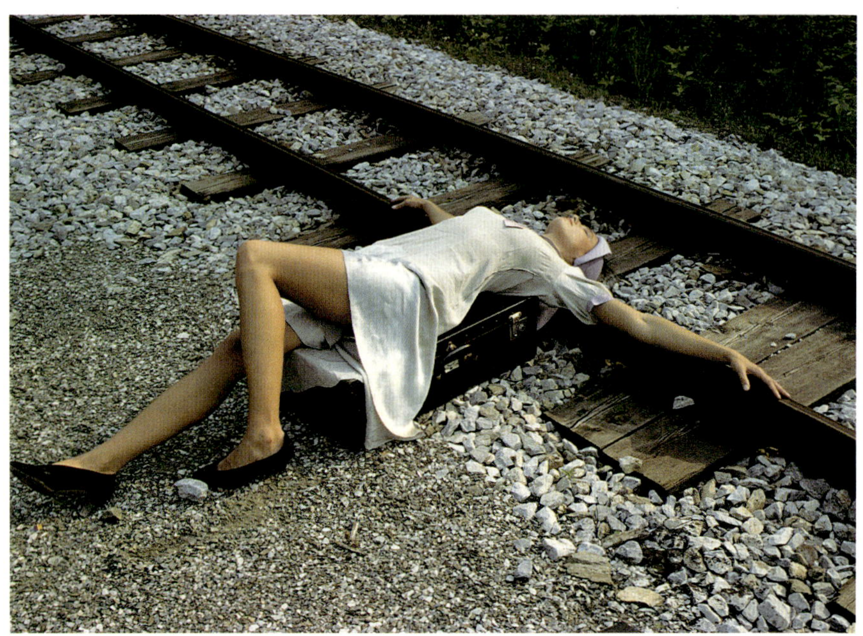

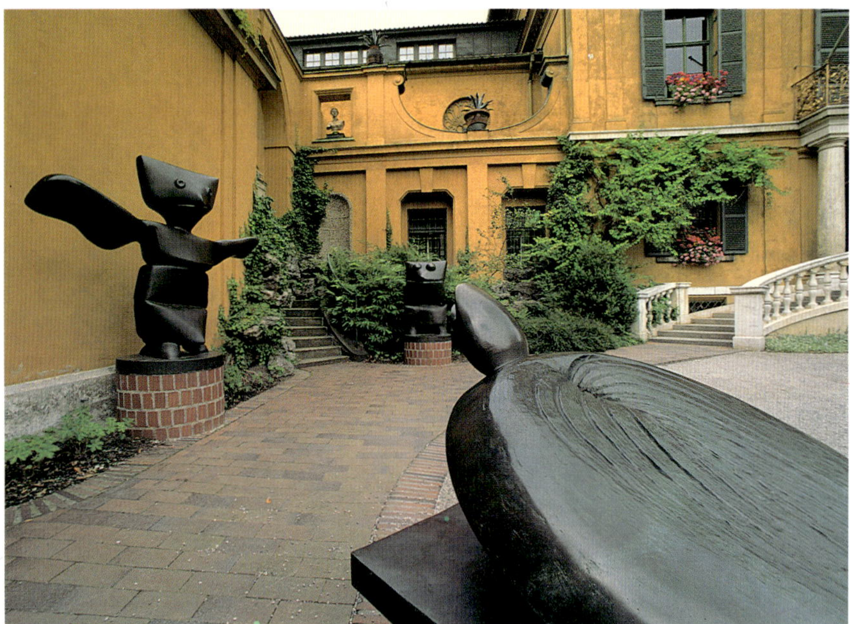

The difference in quality between fast films (top) and slow ones (bottom) is visible on the original transparencies: but every film has its own particular attractions.

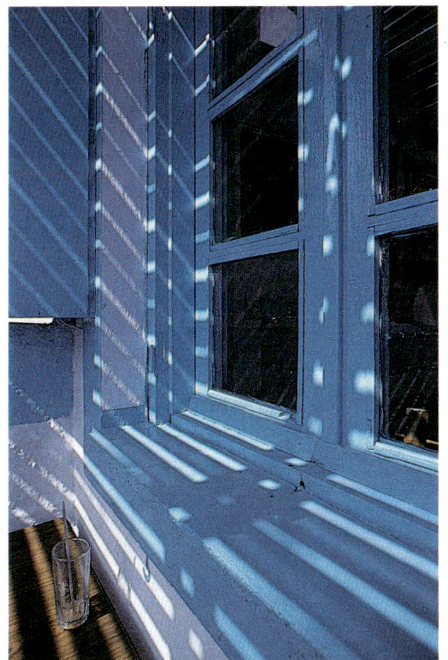
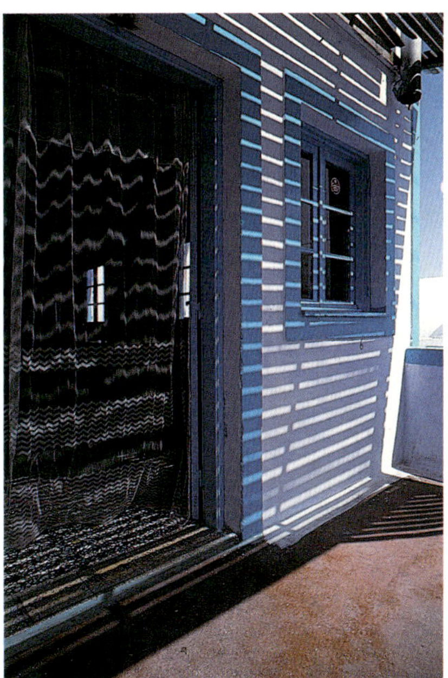
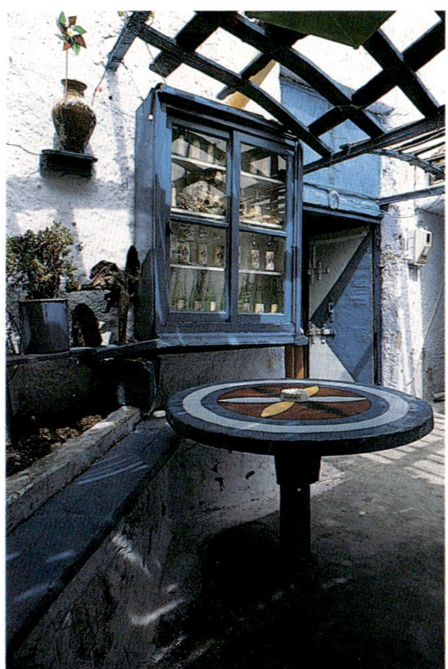
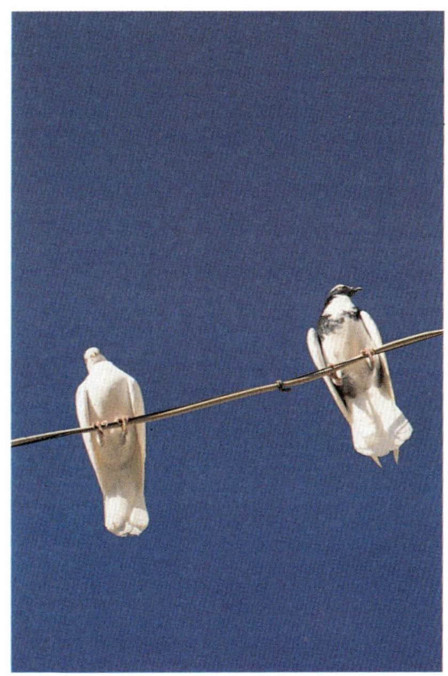

It's not the camera that makes for a good shot, but the photographer. A photographic idea, such as the creative use of the colour blue in these pictures, ought to come before pressing the shutter release.

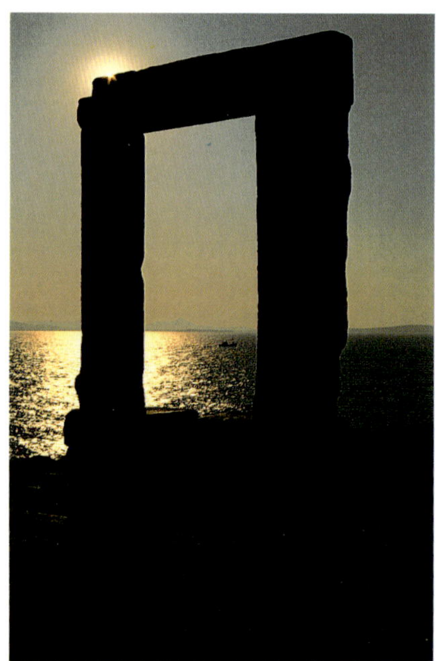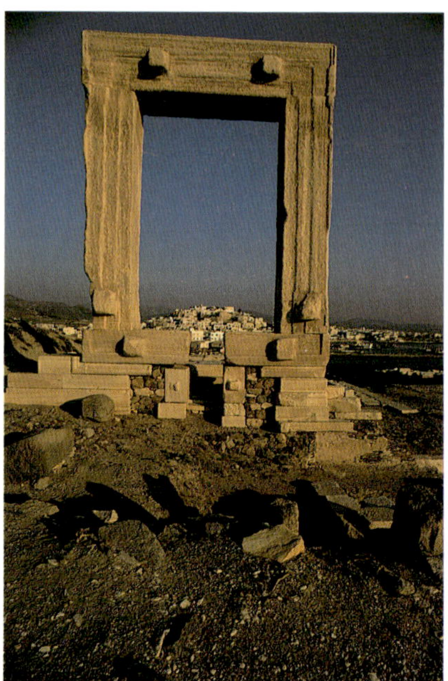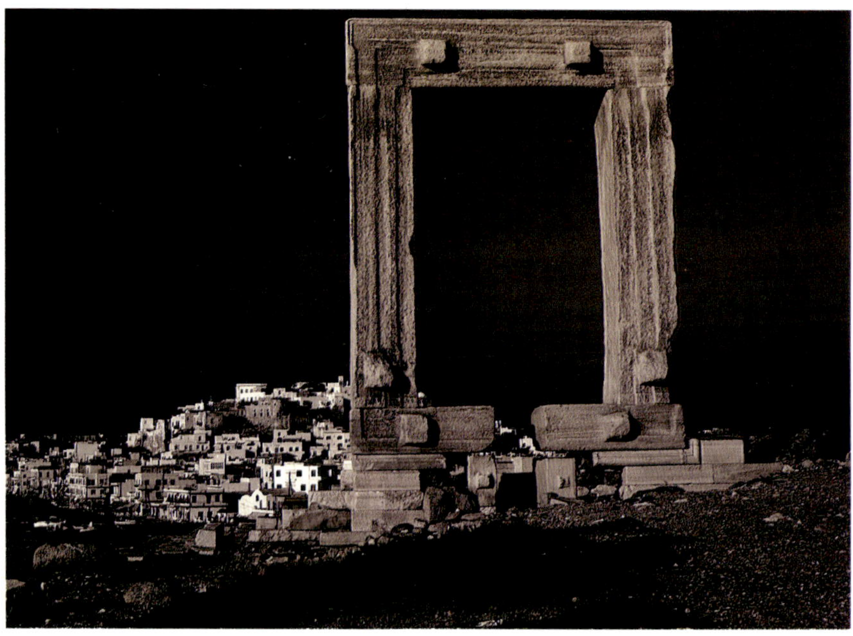

The decision whether to use colour or black-and-white film is one of the most difficult in photography and will always be subjective. The black-and-white print in this set has been tinted brown.

oxide button cells (1.5v each) or by two lithium cells (3v each). The battery compartment (37) in the camera base is opened by pressing the release button (36), ideally with your thumb, and at the same time pushing the cap towards the camera front. The batteries need to be inserted as shown in the diagram inside the battery compartment: always ensure they are the right way round, as indicated by the diagram. You should not use new and partially used batteries together, or combine different types or brands of battery. Disposing of used batteries in an environmentally friendly way should also be a matter of course.

At the time of going to press the following batteries can be used with the Leica R7:

1.5-volt silver oxide button cells

Duracell D 357 (10 L 14)	Philips 357
Everready EPX 76	Ray-o-vac 357
Kodak KS 76	Sony SR 44
Maxell SR 44	Ucar EPX 76
National SR 44	Varta V 76 PX
Panasonic SR 44	

3-volt lithium cells

Duracell DL 1/3 N	Ucar 2 L 76
Kodak K 58 L	Varta CR 1/3 N
Philips CR 1/3 N	

Automatic battery check

The Leica R7 is equipped with an automatic battery check function. If the battery voltage is falling off, the letters **BC** (battery charge) will light up in the bottom right of the viewfinder frame. You will still be able to expose several more films, but to be on the safe side you should change the batteries straight away. If the battery voltage drops even further, all viewfinder indicators, apart from **BC**, will disappear and the camera can no longer be released electronically. When the batteries are completely exhausted the letters **BC** also disappear. Never leave exhausted batteries in the camera.

Releasing without batteries (mechanical shutter speed)

If the batteries are exhausted and you don't have any spares with you (which shouldn't really allow to happen) you can set the shutter speed dial to **100** or **B** and release mechanically. But the mechanical shutter speed of 1/100 sec is only a stop-gap, and if you don't have a separate exposure meter with you, you will have to take a rough guess about what the exposure should be. The same goes for the **bulb** setting.

Adjusting the viewfinder eyepiece

The excellent optical quality of Leica R lenses will be wasted unless you focus precisely (always assuming accurate operation of all other functions). The viewfinder of the Leica R7 is equipped with a dioptric

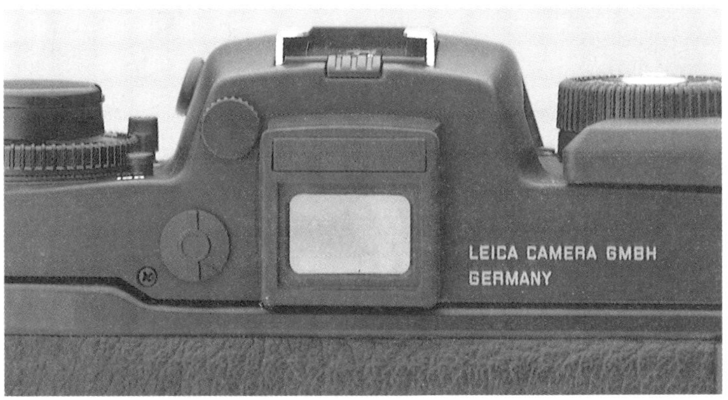

The small wheel at the top left of the eyepiece enables the viewfinder to be adjusted to suit the photographer's vision.

adjustment facility to enable photographers with defective vision to see the viewfinder image in focus. The viewfinder can be adjusted continuously within a range of +/–2 dioptres, allowing you to adjust it to your own visual acuity. If the +/–2 dioptre adjustment is insufficient, you can insert additional eyepiece correction lenses in the eyepiece mount. Correction lenses are available in half-step increments between +/–3 dioptres, but by combining the integral adjustment with the additional correction factors, the viewfinder can be adjusted within a range of +/–5 dioptres.

Adjusting the eyepiece is simplicity itself, although it's best to attach a lens in the medium telephoto range when doing this. Aim the lens at a bright, plain area at a great distance (e.g. the sky) and set it to its closest focusing distance (i.e. out of focus). Pull out the small wheel (31) top left next to the viewfinder eyepiece and turn it (you will notice it click through the different steps) until the circle enclosing the selective measuring field appears sharp and contrasty. Now push the wheel back in to fix the desired eyepiece setting: it can now be turned easily without clicking (in 'neutral'), but will not affect the eyepiece setting while in this position.

Focusing with the universal focusing screen

The camera is supplied with the universal focusing screen as standard. This provides a bright and high contrast viewfinder image that is suitable for most photographic applications. However, it is not particularly well suited for use with telephoto and slow lenses. The image is focused by turning the distance adjustment ring on the lens, as is usual with SLR cameras. The universal focusing screen is equipped with three focusing aids; these are:

1. The central split-image wedge is enclosed by a circle with a diameter of 3mm. If the edges and lines of the subject are displaced against each other, the subject is out of focus. To focus precisely, turn the focusing ring on the lens until the two partial images are no longer

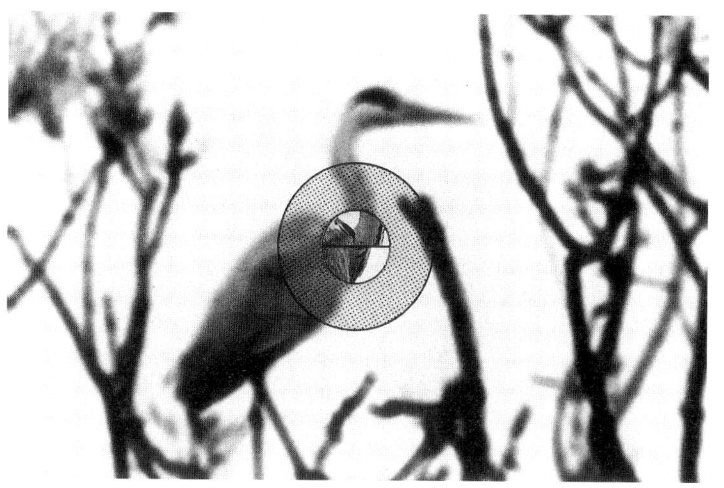

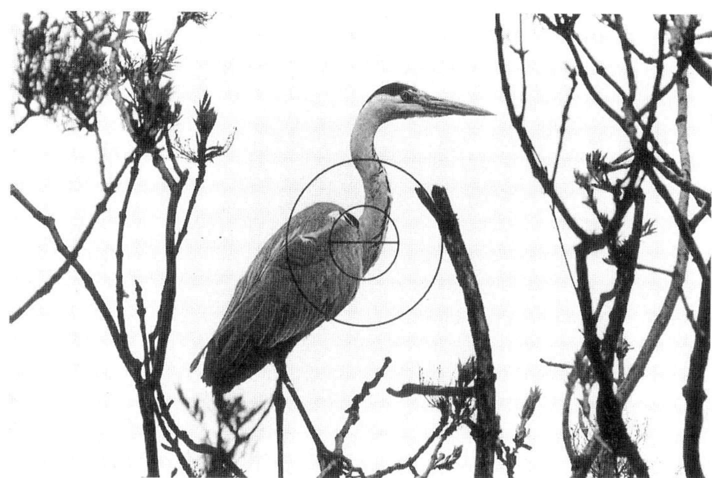

The Leica R7 is supplied with the universal focusing screen as standard, it has three focusing aids: split-image wedge, microprism ring and ground-glass surround.

displaced. The split-image wedge is positioned in such a way that, when holding the camera horizontally (landscape format), you can focus on vertical or slightly diagonal lines and edges. To focus on horizontal or near-horizontal lines, hold the camera portrait fashion to focus using the split-image wedge. Once focused, the camera can be turned back to landscape format. Simply proceed the other way around to focus on vertical lines and edges in portrait-format work.

2. The microprism pattern allows fast and precise focusing regardless of the orientation of lines and edges, and even with subjects lacking such structures altogether. The microprism pattern is positioned around the split-image wedge and consists of a ring of rectangular microprisms. It has an external diameter of 7mm, which also defines

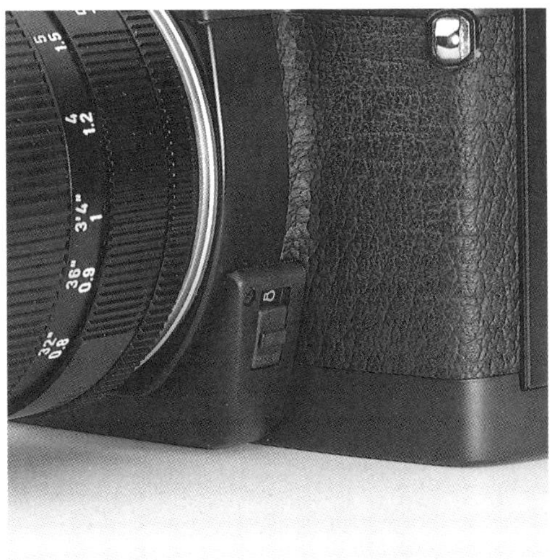

Ilumination for the aperture scale can be turned on by the small switch next to the camera bayonet.

the measuring field for selective metering. A noticeable flickering of the prism pattern indicates that the subject is out of focus. When focused precisely, you can see the image perfectly. However, in difficult light conditions the microprism ring may darken at apertures of f/4 and smaller, making focusing impossible. In such cases, as well as in the telephoto and close-up range, you will need to focus using the matte screen.

3. The area surrounding the microprism ring consists of very fine matte triangular prisms, which produce the groundglass screen effect. Here a degree of judgement is necessary, but with a little practice you will find the distinction between sharpness and unsharpness easy to identify.

Viewfinder displays

The viewfinder displays of the Leica R7 provide information about all important exposure data. The viewfinder field appears uncluttered, and the LED indicators are easy to see and clearly arranged. You will only see the data that is relevant at any one time, not the full range of displays shown in the illustration, and this proves very useful in practice. The brightness of the LED indicators, which are controlled by the 8-bit microprocessor, is always automatically adjusted to the subject brightness. This means that the LED indicators are always clearly visible.

The LED indicators are switched on by lightly touching the shutter-release button. If the shutter is cocked the indicators will be visible for about 12 seconds. If it isn't, the indicators will go out as soon as you take your finger off the shutter-release button, this indicates that the camera is not ready to make an exposure.

The aperture set on the lens is not indicated by an LED but is reflected into the viewfinder from the actual aperture scale on the lens. If the light is too dim to see the aperture setting easily, you can switch on a small viewfinder light by means of the switch near the bottom of the camera next to the bayonet mount. In program and shutter priority modes, the camera-controlled aperture is indicated by LEDs in the bottom right of the viewfinder frame.

The selective measuring area is engraved on all the interchangeable focusing screens. The viewfinder image shows 92% of the 24x36mm film format, which roughly corresponds to the image area of a framed slide.

All viewfinder indications are shown together on this diagram.

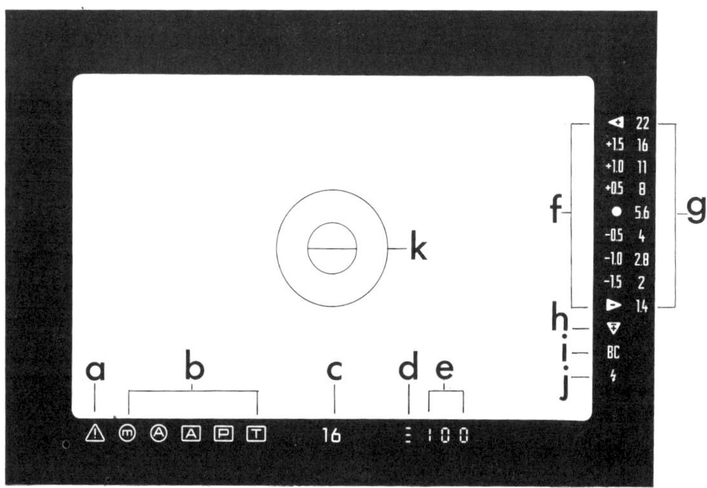

    a.   Low-light warning
    b.   Program mode symbols
    c.   Lens aperture (reflected off the aperture scale)
    d.   Fill-in flash symbol
    e.   Shutter speed (preset or camera-controlled)
    f.   Light balance for use in manual mode (M)
    g.   Computed aperture – in P and T modes
    h.   Warning signal for override (flashing) or warning signal if discrepancy between manually-set or DX-coded film speed (lit continuously)
    i.   Low battery warning
    j.   Flash ready and flash control indicator
    k.   Measuring area for selective metering

2. Some General Principles

The Leica R7 is ideal for advanced photography, but among today's cameras with their high degree of automation this unfortunately is not stating the obvious. The Leica R7 is literally built into the photographer's hand. Its layout makes no concessions to trendy design features. The arrangement of the operating controls could be described as classical, which makes their operation particularly easy because the controls are positioned where you expect to find them. The experienced photographer will have no problems working out the different functions straight away, and all features can be accessed without taking the camera from the eye. Less experienced photographers will have to start off by familiarizing themselves with the functions and handling of the camera.

Holding the camera

How you hold the camera is very important in photography. A good grip on the camera is crucial for shake-free operation and allows you to respond more quickly to a subject. It is also important for the manner in which you approach a subject: awkward situations where you are looking to achieve an unusual perspective, for example by selecting a very low shooting position, require a secure camera hold.

For landscape work, stand relaxed with your feet roughly the same distance apart as the width of your shoulders. Press the camera against your nose, which should be pointing slightly to the left, and against

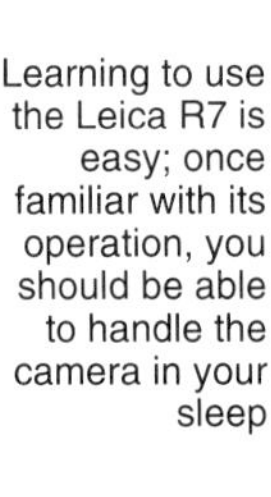

Learning to use the Leica R7 is easy; once familiar with its operation, you should be able to handle the camera in your sleep

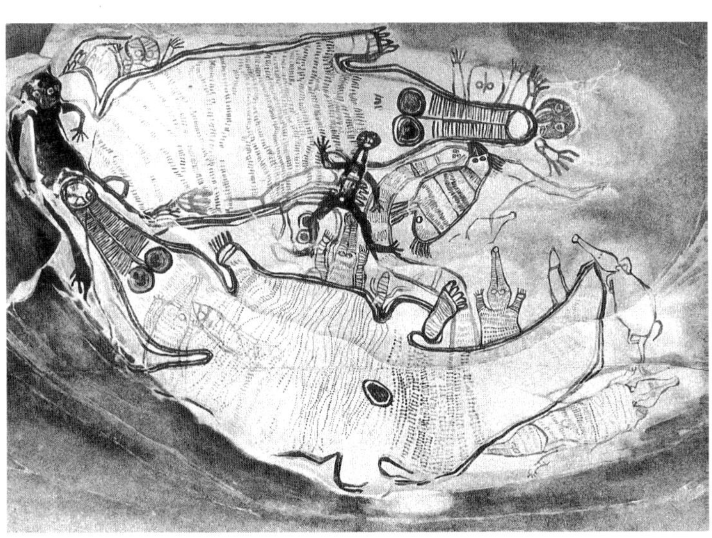

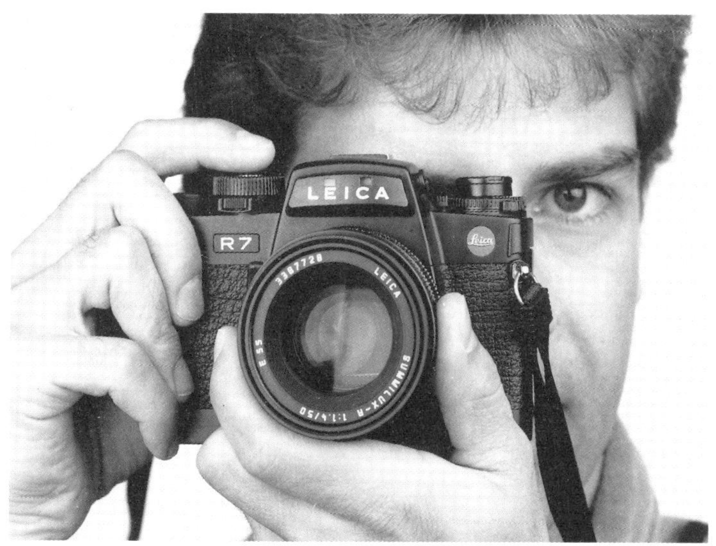

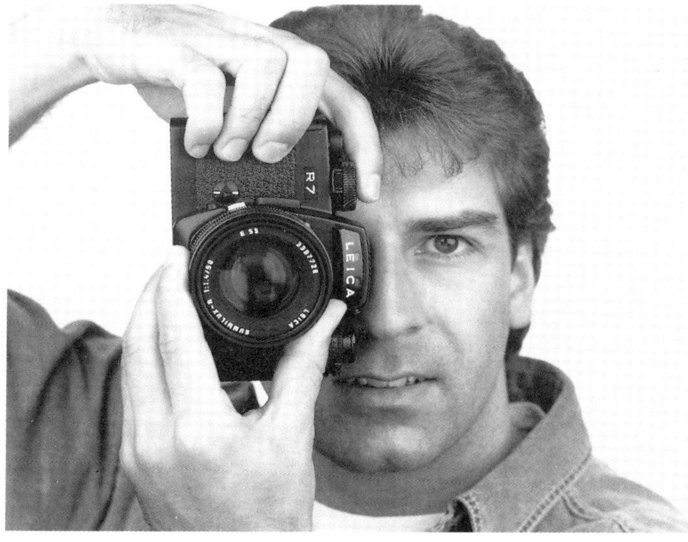

The camera holds for landscape- and portrait-format shots, as recommended by Leica.

your right eyebrow and cheekbone (if your right eye is your lead eye). Your thumb should be resting between the viewfinder eyepiece and the rapid transport lever, so your cheekbone will actually be pressing against the thumb rather than the camera back. In this way you bridge the gap between your cheekbone and the camera back, keeping stray light away from the eyepiece. The grip mould on the back of the camera body also helps with this grip. In this position you can reach all the controls without taking the camera from the eye. The right index finger operates the shutter-release button, the shutter speed dial, and the program selector. The middle finger of the right hand operates the depth of field button and the right thumb cocks the shutter. Support the base of the camera with the little and ring fingers of your left hand (both bent slightly). The middle finger of the left hand rests on the cable-release connection for independent mirror release, whilst thumb and index finger operate the aperture ring on the lens. Both elbows rest against the ribcage. Once all the settings have been made, all that remains is for you to breathe out, stop breathing, and gently press the shutter-release button.

The operating instructions recommend that for portrait format you simply need to turn the camera so that your right elbow is pointing upwards. This is certainly a suitable grip for 'snapshots', although it won't be as good for preventing camera shake as the grip described above. Therefore our recommended posture for portrait format work is as follows: middle and index fingers of the right hand clamp the fixed ring of the lens in scissor-fashion, whilst the little finger and ring finger rest on the camera base. The right thumb then operates the shutter-release button and the shutter speed dial whilst the remaining four fingers and the palm of your left hand grip your right hand. The left thumb can easily operate the aperture ring on the lens at the level of the camera base. The aperture display will darken slightly because of the shadow caused, but the supplementary viewfinder light can be switched on to deal with this small problem. The description of this camera grip may sound a little unusual, but once you've tried it you will soon find out how easy it is. Since both elbows can be rested against the upper body, it provides as good a safeguard against camera shake in the portrait format as the one described earlier does for landscape-format. Apart from the different ways of holding the camera, your feet should be positioned in the same way and you should employ the same breathing and shutter release technique.

The first 'dry-run'

Now you've familiarized yourself a little with the camera and prepared it for use, you can start to practise the use of the controls without a film in the camera. But first you will need to find out about the basic functions.

To start with we will work in program mode. To select program mode, press the locking button and turn the program selector (29) until the letter **P** appears in the viewing window (23). Set the aperture to the highest f/-number (= smallest aperture), and set the shutter speed dial to **30 P**. Then cock the shutter using the rapid transport lever. Pressing the shutter-release button lightly will cause the relevant exposure data to appear in the viewfinder frame. These data consist of the program

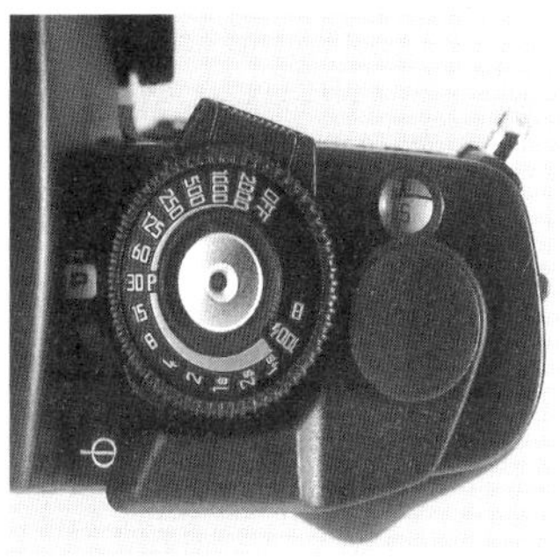

The Leica R7 in the automatic program, with normal program characteristics.

symbol (bottom left), the smallest aperture (projected into the bottom centre of the display from the actual aperture ring on the lens), the shutter speed calculated by the camera (to the right of the projected aperture), and on the right of the viewfinder the camera-controlled aperture. Now practise releasing the shutter several times in this basic program, focusing on different subjects in the landscape and portrait formats. You can, of course, select other programs, work out the differences between selective and integral metering, or input an exposure compensation – see the relevant chapters for details.

Loading and removing film

Once you've mastered the operation of the camera you can start taking real photographs. Open the back cover by pulling up the rewind crank (17). The back cover will click open and the frame counter will automatically be set to **S**. Now hold the camera by the lens with your left hand whilst holding the film cassette in your right hand. Push the film leader at an angle upwards into one of the slots of the take-up spool, so that it is gripped behind two of the silver lugs. Then insert the film

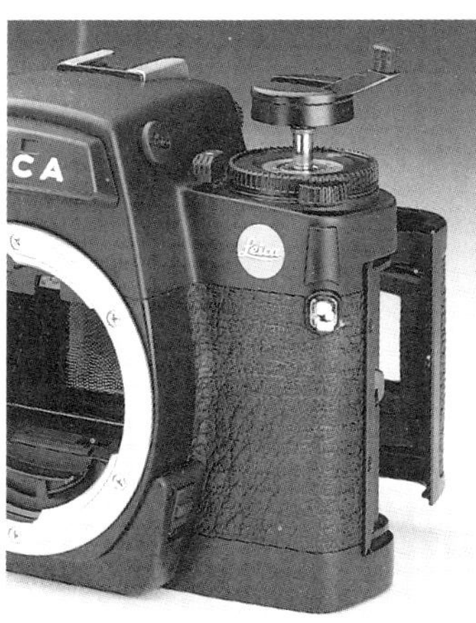

The camera back is opened by pulling up the rewind knob.

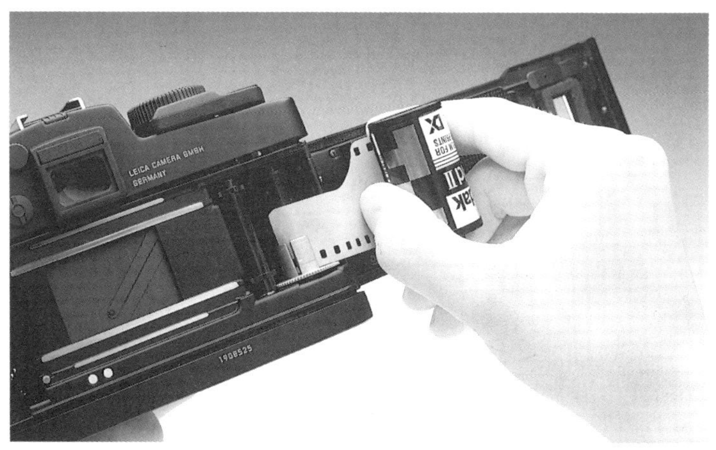

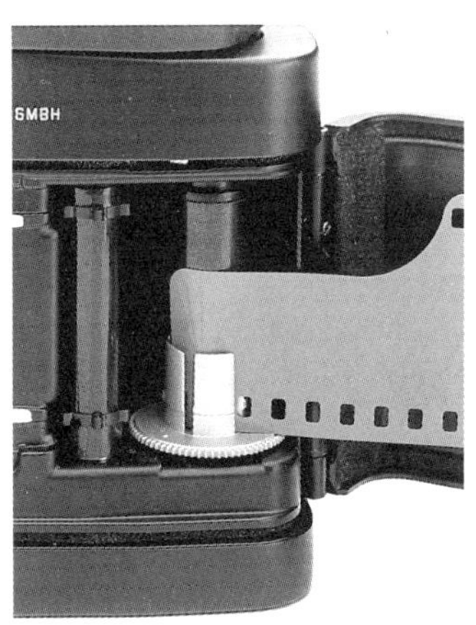

The film must be loaded so that the film leader is clamped tight behind two of the retaining clips.

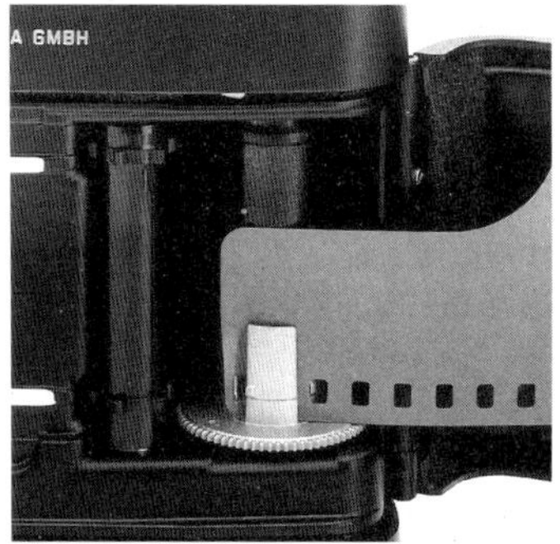

Not this way! The film leader should not protrude from behind the clip

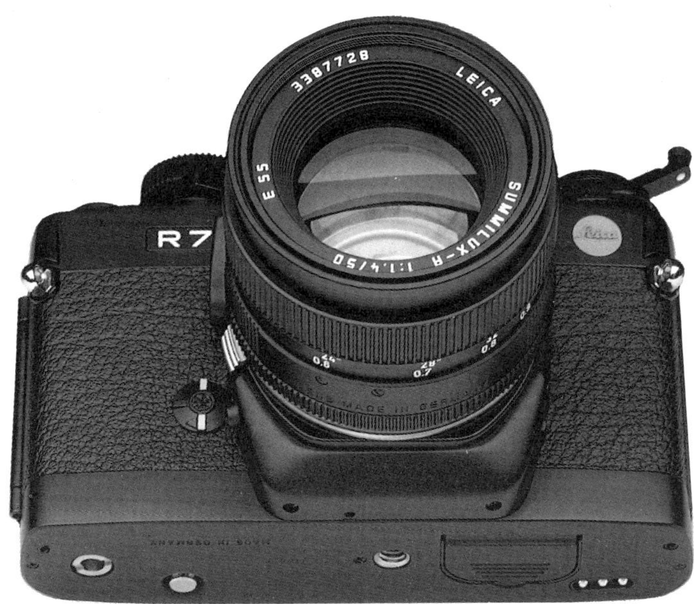

To rewind exposed films, press the rewind release button on the camera base, then unfold the rewind crank and turn it in a clockwise direction (as indicated by the arrow).

cassette into the empty cassette chamber (but make sure the rewind crank is pulled up fully first). With the cassette inserted push the rewind crank all the way down again. It is important to ensure that the edge of the film is parallel with the film guide. Now advance the film by one frame using the rapid transport lever. The sprockets of the transport drum need to grip the film perforations. Now press the back cover shut and advance the film by one more frame, release the shutter and finally advance the film again. The camera is now ready to shoot. At this point the frame counter shows 1 and counts forward to 37, with the figures 20, 24, and 36 indicating different film lengths and marked in red. You can advance the film beyond frame 37 but when the end of the film is reached you will feel a noticeable resistance.

When a film has been exposed, rewind it as follows. Press the rewind release button (39) on the camera base and fold out the rewind crank at the white spot (but don't pull it up, otherwise the back cover will open!). Turn the crank in the direction of the arrow (clockwise) until a slackening in resistance indicates that the film has been fully rewound into the cassette. Films that will be processed in a lab should be rewound completely to avoid confusion with unexposed films. If you process your own films you will find it easier to leave the film leader protruding from the cassette. This is most easily achieved by counting about 32 revolutions of the rewind crank and listening out for a click, which signals that the film leader has come off the take-up spool.

Always change films in the shade (or in the shadow cast by your body) as light can enter the film cassette if you work in direct sunlight.

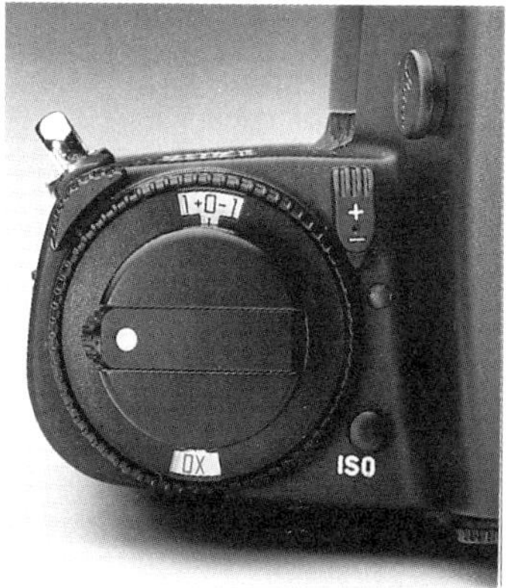

If DX film speed setting mode is selected, the relevant symbol will be visible in the viewing windows.

Setting the film speed and DX coding

On the Leica R7 the film speed can be set manually or automatically (DX) via the film speed dial (18). To set the speed manually, press the locking button (20, marked **ISO**) and turn the setting ring until the desired ISO value appears in the viewing window (19). Once you release the locking button the selected value is set and protected against accidental movement. The manual setting range lies between ISO 6/9° and ISO 12800/42°, but only the 'full' ASA values appear as figures (between 6 and 12800), the one-third increments are marked as dots.

Automatic DX-read-off is activated if the film speed setting ring is locked in the DX position beyond 12800 – **DX** appears in red in the viewing

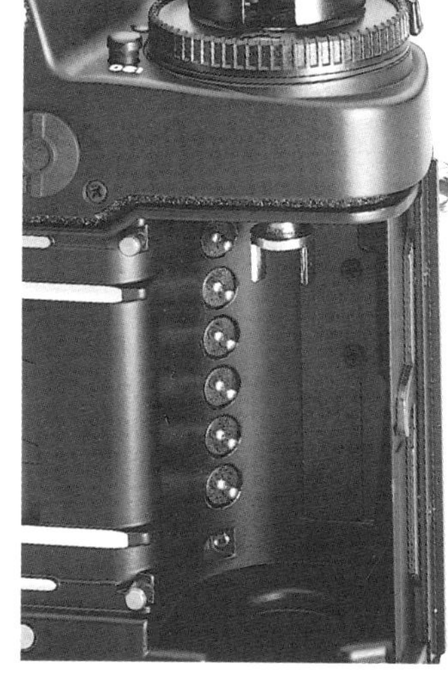

The DX contacts must be clean and grease-free, so they should never be touched.

window (19). The speed of DX-coded films is now set automatically in one-third increments between ISO 25/15° and ISO 5000/38°. If an uncoded film is loaded whilst the DX function is activated the letters **ASA** will flash in the viewfinder (instead of the shutter speed display). The external LED (21) next to the locking button will flash at the same time, and will also flash if no film is loaded in the DX setting. It is still possible to release the shutter with the selected aperture and shutter speed in any operating mode, but the warning indicators will continue to flash.

If a different film speed from the DX-coded speed of a film is selected manually, the manually selected value will override the DX coding. In this case the exposure compensation symbol on the right of the viewfinder frame will be lit continuously as a warning signal.

The optimum aperture

Lenses from other manufacturers normally need to be stopped down by two or three stops to achieve their best reproduction quality, but even at their maximum aperture Leica R lenses deliver excellent reproduction characteristics, which can be improved further by stopping down slightly, particularly in the close-up range. More on this in the chapters on lenses. If you want to make optimum use of the aperture, you need to know a few theoretical points about the relationship between aperture and reproduction quality.

The theoretical resolving power of a lens is greatest at its maximum aperture, but on the other hand, residual aberrations, which can never be entirely eliminated, are most noticeable at the maximum aperture.

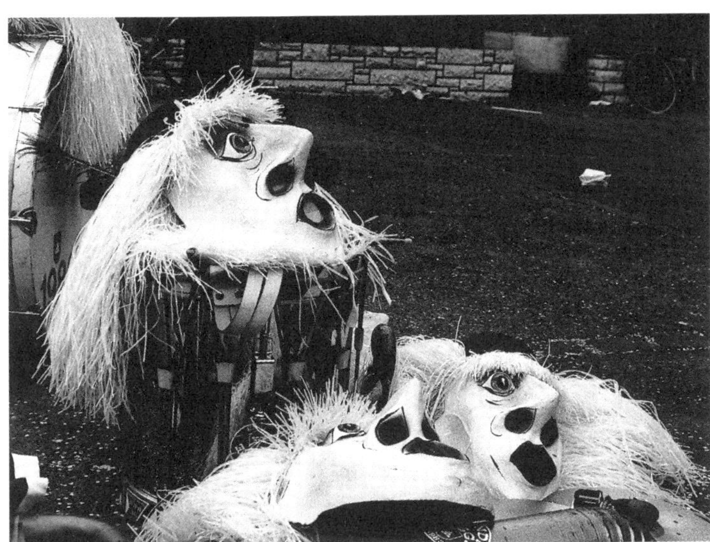

For sharp rendering of the masks a small aperture was required, which meant the wall in the background was also a little too sharp.

On Leica R lenses these aberrations are corrected to an unsurpassed degree and slight stopping down reduces their negative effects by literally deflecting intrusive marginal rays of light. On the other hand, stopping down also reduces the resolving capacity of a lens. This is due to the bending (diffraction) of the light waves which occurs whenever light passes through a small opening, such as the iris diaphragm. This means that a point is not reproduced as a point but as a small disc. The diameter of this disc increases as the aperture is stopped down. If you stop down so that this disc becomes larger than the permitted diameter for the circle of confusion, the overall sharpness of the photograph will be affected.

Apart from the aperture, the type of light (its wavelength) and the reproduction ratio also affect the diffraction. This diffraction is greatest in the close-up range where a smaller aperture is required to compensate for the more shallow depth of field at this range (Note, however, that macro lenses, together with enlarging and reproduction lenses, are computed to give their peak performance in the close-up range). So in practice the aim is to determine an aperture which balances the residual aberrations and the diffraction of the light. This aperture value is called the critical aperture and varies from lens to lens. On most Leica R lenses the critical aperture is reached by stopping down by one or two stops. However, in the close-up range in particular, greater stopping down is often required in order to achieve the desired depth of field. In this case professional photographers use a different formula: the aperture is determined depending on the permitted diameter of the circles of confusion and the reproduction ratio, so that the circles caused by the diffraction of the light and the circles of confusion have the same diameter.

Consequently Leica R lenses should be stopped down only as far as is required for the desired depth of field.

Aperture and depth of field

Every beginner knows that the depth of field depends on the aperture. Generally speaking, the depth of field is least at the maximum aperture and increases as the aperture is stopped down. You can see how this works by turning the aperture ring of the camera whilst pressing the depth of field lever. But in reality the depth of field is also affected by other parameters and so another brief theoretical detour is called for.

Apart from in reproduction work, photographic subjects are three-dimensional, whereas the image plane is two-dimensional. The laws of reproduction (Gaussian optics) mean that in these circumstances only one subject plane can be reproduced in focus on the image plane at any one time. But due to an optical illusion called depth of field, the areas in front of and behind the focused plane also appear more or less

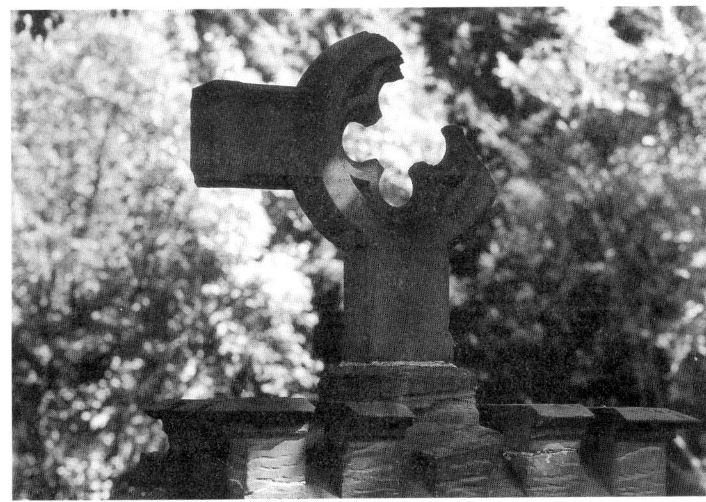

Careful control of the depth of field by means of the aperature setting.

in focus. The depth of field, which determines the three-dimensional, spatial impression of sharpness, depends on the diameter of the circles of confusion, the reproduction ratio, and the aperture.

In reality every point of the subject is reproduced as a disc rather than a point. These discs are termed 'circles of confusion'. Due to a sharpness tolerance of the human retina we perceive these discs as points, and therefore in focus, as long as they are smaller than the resolution capacity of the eye, which in theory lies at 40 (in practice at 50-90) seconds of arc. But the linear resolution of the eye changes with the distance from which a subject is viewed, which in turn is dependent on the image diagonal (not to be confused with the correct viewing distance in terms of perspective). Because of this the permitted diameter for the circles of confusion was set at $\frac{1}{1500}$ of the diagonal of the format, or of the standard focal length. This produces a diameter for the circles of confusion of 0.03mm in the 35mm format. For enlargements the permitted diameter of the circles of confusion changes at the same ratio as the magnification factor, which means that the depth of field is independent of the magnification ratio. Theoretically the depth of field extends $\frac{1}{3}$ in front and $\frac{2}{3}$ behind the focused plane. The greatest depth of field is achieved at the hyperfocal distance, more on this in a moment.

Apart from the diameter of the circles of confusion and the aperture, the focal length and the shooting distance (that is, the reproduction ratio) also determine the depth of field. Basically, at a constant reproduction ratio the depth of field increases the more the aperture is stopped down, and vice versa. At a constant shooting distance the depth of field is reduced as the focal length (more precisely, the focal length squared) is increased, and vice versa. At a constant focal length the depth of field

35

is reduced or increased proportionally with the shooting distance. But note that the effect of the focal length on the depth of field is the opposite of that of the shooting distance, so the two parameters compensate for each other. At the same reproduction ratio (from different shooting distances) all lenses, regardless of their focal length, have the same depth of field. So in practice, when determining the depth of field, you need to consider all the above factors.

The depth of field for any one photograph can be checked visually on the viewfinder screen at every aperture setting by pressing the depth of field lever. The depth of field scale engraved on the fixed ring of all Leica R lenses only gives an approximation of the depth of field. It shows the extension of the depth of field for all apertures at the shooting distance set at the time. The depth of field scale is also important for the hyperfocal setting, sometimes called close-up setting on infinity. In this setting the greatest possible depth of field is achieved each time. The hyperfocal distance is the distance between the camera and the beginning of the area of focus in the infinity setting and at a certain aperture. It can be calculated mathematically and is dependant on the focal length, the aperture, and the permitted diameter of the circles of confusion. At a focal length of 50mm and an aperture of f/16, the hyperfocal distance is 4.69m. This means that at the infinity setting and f/16 the depth of field of a 50mm lens extends from 4.69m to infinity. If the lens is set to 4.69m, ie the hyperfocal distance, the depth of field extends from 2.345m to infinity. But in reality you probably won't have the time to carry out these calculations, which can't be applied to lenses with this precision anyway. But in practice the Leica photographer can proceed as follows: taking the above example, simply align the infinity symbol ∞ with f/16 on the depth of field scale. You will see that the depth of field ranges from between 2 and 3 metres to infinity. If you do this on your camera you will see that the focus index will point to a little below 5m (4.69m exactly), that is exactly the value which corresponded to f/16 on the depth of field scale at the infinity setting. The hyperfocal distance is also useful for 'snapshots' as you can do without focusing altogether.

Choosing the shutter speed

The shutter speed can influence both the representation of subject movement and camera movement. Through conscious use of the shutter speed you can either 'freeze' movement or reproduce it blurred.

Moving subjects will cause unsharpness in the photograph if the shutter speed does not take account of the speed of the movement. Longer focal lengths and slower shutter speeds increase the movement blur. The required shutter speed can be determined by means of fairly complicated calculations or simple rules of thumb. But the direction of the movement, which can be taken into account as a further factor in the calculation, is as important as its speed. Here is an example: if you want

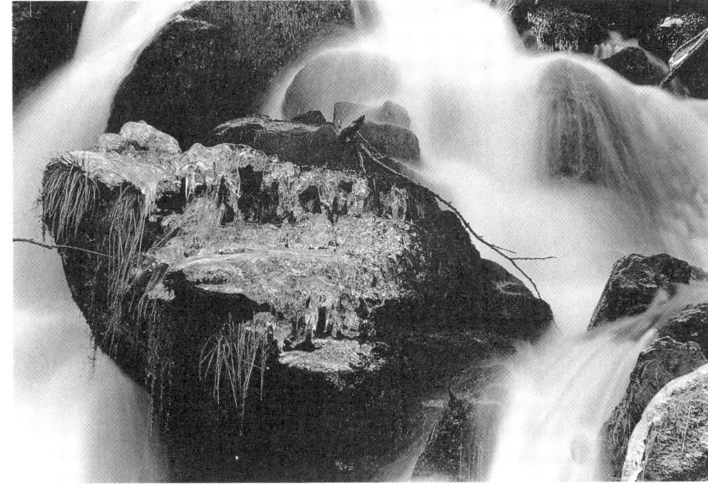

A shutter speed of 2 seconds shows the flow of the water, it even causes a 'velvety' rendering of the waterfall.

to take a photograph of a person walking at an average speed from a shooting distance of 5m and 'freeze' the movement, the slowest shutter speeds are roughly as follows:

– for movement across the camera:- $\frac{1}{500}$ sec

– for movement at an angle to the camera:- $\frac{1}{250}$ sec

– for movement parallel with the lens axis (towards the camera or away from it):- $\frac{1}{125}$ sec

If you want to show the movement speed-blurred, you need to select slower shutter speeds. In the case of the walker in our example these would be between $\frac{1}{15}$ sec and $\frac{1}{4}$ sec, and the blurred effect becomes more pronounced the slower the selected shutter speed.

A moving subject can be reproduced in sharp focus in front of a speed-blurred background by panning the camera; that is, following the movement of the subject. Once again, the shutter speed needs to take account of the speed of the subject.

For example, Ernst Haas created wonderful photographs with the conscious use of speed blur in the 1950s and 1970s. In the last few years deliberate unsharpness as a stylistic tool has become a great photographic fad. There's nothing wrong with this, but all types of unsharpness have been used and abused so many times in recent photographs that it should be used only consciously and sparingly.

Shutter speeds for hand-held exposures

It is not only beginners who find it difficult to hold the camera absolutely still during an exposure. Unsteady posture, jerky release of the shutter, and even the movement of the camera itself – due to vibra-

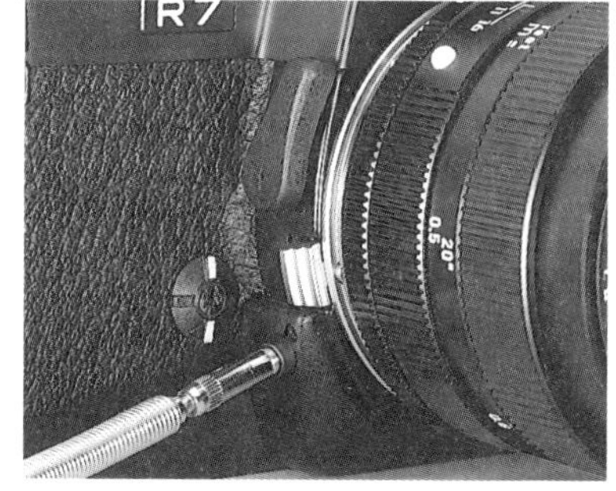

A separate cable release is used to raise the mirror independently of the shutter release.

tion of the mirror, the running of the shutter, and the spring-back diaphragm – can lead to camera shake. The factors relating to the camera's own vibration are reduced to a minimum on the Leica R7 and the Leica R lenses, and in practice are hardly noticeable. Unsteady body posture and jerky movements during shutter release, on the other hand, have ruined many a Leica photograph.

Movement blur caused through camera movement is generally recognizable by double or multiple images. The danger of camera shake increases with longer focal lengths and slower shutter speeds. One widely used rule of thumb for the slowest shutter speed for hand-held use is the reciprocal of the focal length, rounded up to the nearest value. According to this rule $\frac{1}{60}$ sec is the slowest shutter speed for hand-held photographs with a 50mm lens, and $\frac{1}{250}$ sec when using a 250mm telephoto. But this rule doesn't always guarantee shake-free hand-held photographs, even for experienced photographers. If you want to ensure that the excellent sharpness of the Leica R lenses isn't adversely affected by movement blur, it's best to double or quadruple the shutter speeds suggested above. At a focal length of 250mm, use a shutter speed of $\frac{1}{500}$ sec, better still $\frac{1}{1000}$ sec, for hand-held exposures.

Tripod exposures with independent mirror release

The best safeguard against movement blur is provided by a sturdy professional tripod and the independent mirror release function. On the Leica R7 the mirror can be flipped up and locked before the exposure by means of a cable release connected to the separate cable release thread (8) below the bayonet lock. This also closes the spring-back diaphragm to the selected value. The exposure itself is then made with a cable release connected to the thread of the shutter-release button. Starting the shutter release process without the cable release is not recommended. It is not possible to use a double cable release to flip up the mirror, nor would it be sensible as the camera needs a few seconds to stabilize after the mirror has flipped up before the exposure can be made free of the effects of mechanical vibration from the mirror.

The mirror automatically returns to its starting position after the exposure, moving it back to this position manually is not possible. You should not operate the depth of field lever when the mirror is flipped up as this is likely to cause an unwanted exposure. The independent mirror release function is carried out mechanically, which means that it is not possible to release the shutter electromagnetically by means of the self-timer, an electric cable release or the shutter-release button of a motor or winder.

In the independent mirror release function you need to work in manual exposure mode, as exposure metering and control are not possible after the mirror has flipped up.

Self-timer photographs

The self-timer function is selected by turning the self-timer knob (7), behind the bayonet lock, in the direction of the arrow (clockwise). Sensibly, this will only work if the shutter is cocked. The self-timer countdown starts if you lightly press the shutter-release button or press the locking button of the program selector. The countdown takes approximately 10 seconds and is indicated by a flashing LED (2) above the white Leica logo. The LED will be lit continuously for about 2 seconds directly before the exposure. The self-timer can be stopped before the countdown starts or during it by turning the self-timer knob.

The self-timer function is not only useful for self-portraits but also for shake-free exposures with slow shutter speeds without independent mirror release.

If the self-timer is to be used in the automatic programs it is advisable to protect the viewfinder eyepiece against stray light by means of the eyepiece cover. This is to ensure that the metering system is not adversely affected. The viewfinder eyepiece is blocked by a slight turn of the relevant button (30) in the direction of the arrow. When the cover is swung into place a white triangle will appear in the eyepiece; it can be swung back by turning the knob the other way.

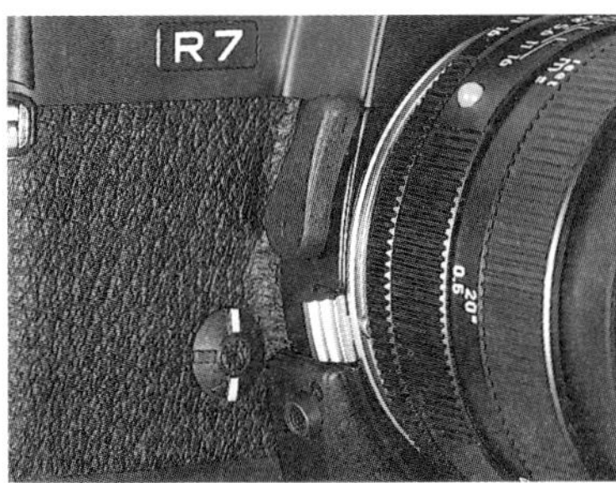

To operate the self-timer, turn the switch behind the bayonet release in the direction of the arrow.

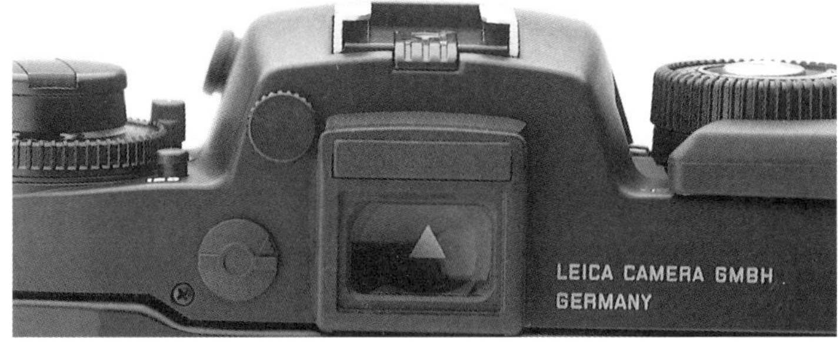

If the eyepiece is closed off, a white triangle will be visible.

Multiple exposures

The rewind release button (39) on the baseplate can be used to make multiple exposures because it uncouples the film transport mechanism. After the first exposure, press the rewind button and cock the shutter. The film will not be advanced. Cocking the shutter pushes the rewind release button out again, so to take several exposures on the same frame you need to press it once more after every exposure. Multiple exposures are also possible when a motor or winder is attached.

With multiple exposures details of the images overlap. The rule of thumb for exposure states that you need to divide the shutter speed determined for a normal exposure by the number of multiple exposures to be made (i.e., if the measured total exposure is $\frac{1}{500}$ sec. and you wish to make two exposures, say for a 'ghost picture', then each one should be $\frac{1}{1000}$ sec. However this can only be used as a guide, don't be afraid to experiment for yourself.

3. Exposure Metering in Practice

The exposure of conventional subjects in normal lighting conditions, which account for around 90 to 95% of all photographic situations, can be left to the automatic TTL exposure system, and in these cases the exposure will be correct. But adventurous photography is usually concerned with the remaining 5 to 10%. The aim then may be the correct exposure of high contrast subjects, the capture of a particular, and maybe fleeting, lighting mood or the placing of highlights. Left to its own devices even the most expensive and sophisticated TTL exposure system would fail in these circumstances. The reasons for this may become apparent in the next few pages.

The norm is medium grey

Every exposure metering system, whether manual or TTL, spot, selective or integral, whether for spot lighting, ambient light or flash light, meters the amount of light falling onto the metering area. The TTL metering system of the Leica R7 meters the light reflected from the subject in the direction of the camera through the lens (TTL). The TTL

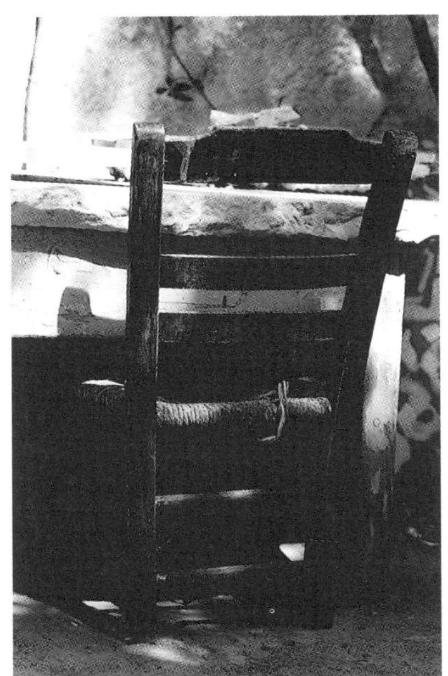

There are certain lighting moods, as in this picture and the one overleaf, which can only be captured by deviating from the metered exposure value. This is where the true art of exposure metering begins.

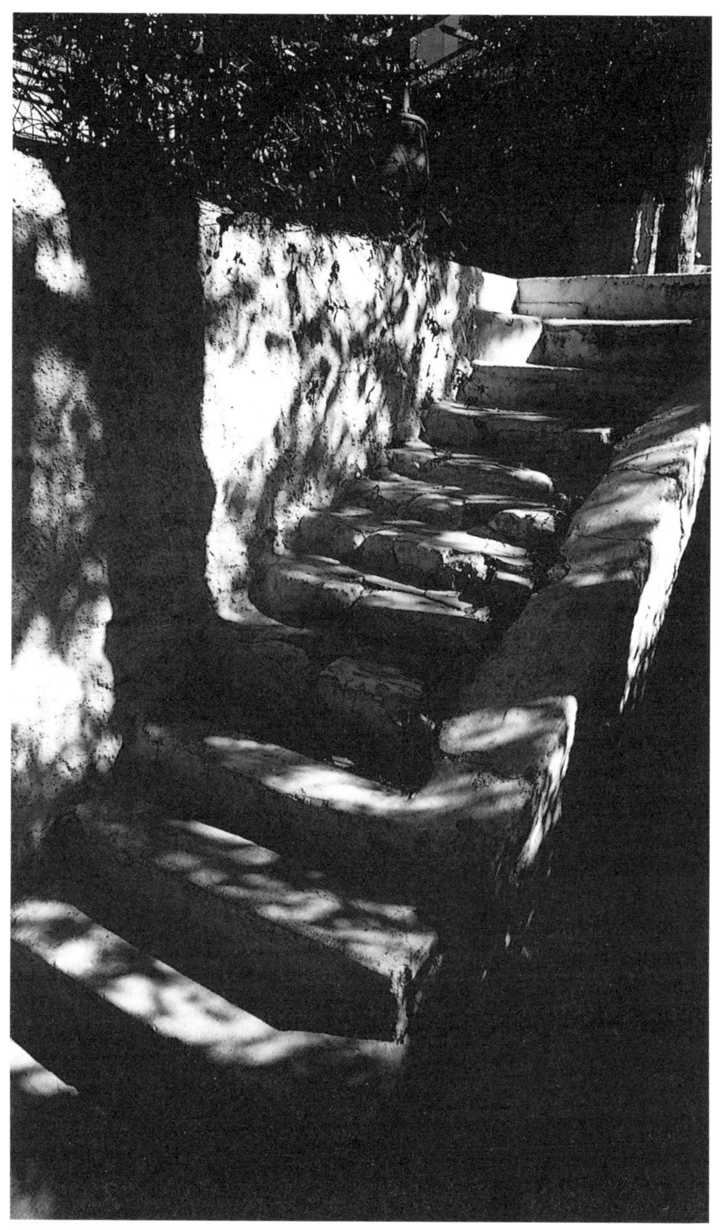

metering system can't tell whether the same amount of light is reflected by a dark subject lit brightly or a bright subject in low light. Every photographer has taken photographs in which a predominant area supposed to be white, like a wedding dress, is reproduced grey, or on other occasions when a black subject has come out as grey. This is due to the fact that all exposure meters are calibrated to a medium grey. This medium grey corresponds to a subject brightness caused by an 18% remission (diffuse reflection). A remission of 18% (17.68%, to be exact) is equal to the logarithmic mean value between white and black. So all exposure meters are calibrated to reproduce every metered area as standard grey in the photographic positive. Knowing this is vital in photography, and explains why bright subjects are underexposed, and dark ones overexposed, if you use the value determined by the exposure meter without any correction.

Centre-weighted full-field integral metering

The full-field integral metering system of the Leica R7 has a centre-weighted characteristic. The metering area of this system roughly corresponds to the entire viewfinder field, but the metering sensitivity is not distributed evenly. Starting from the image centre, the metering area is divided into four oval and almost concentric zones, with the metering sensitivity reduced by one light value towards the image edge in each case. The central zone is fully taken into account in the exposure measurement. Put simply, one light value is automatically deducted from the measurement taken in the second zone (going outward from the centre), two light values are deducted from the measurement in the third zone and three in the marginal zone. In practice, the metering sensitivity is not reduced abruptly by one light value from one zone to

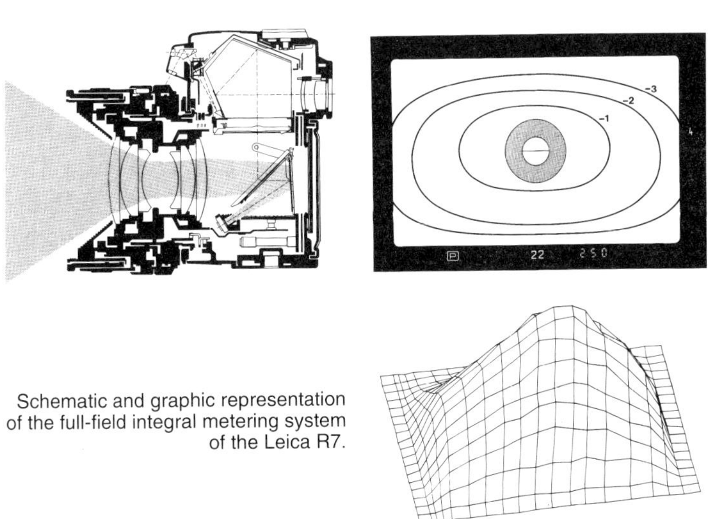

Schematic and graphic representation of the full-field integral metering system of the Leica R7.

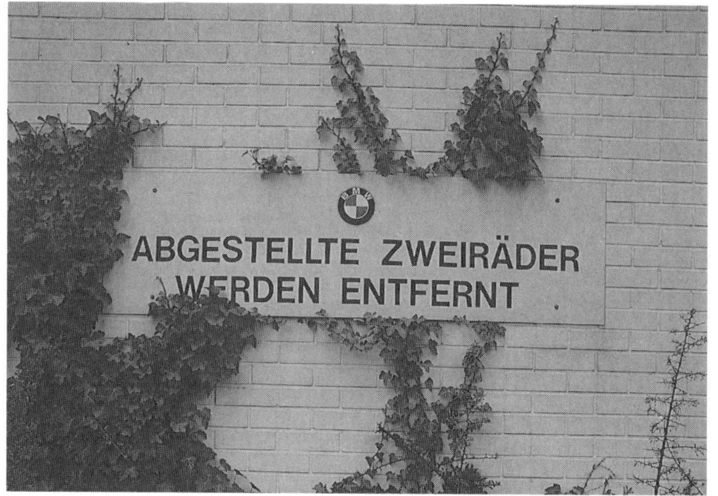

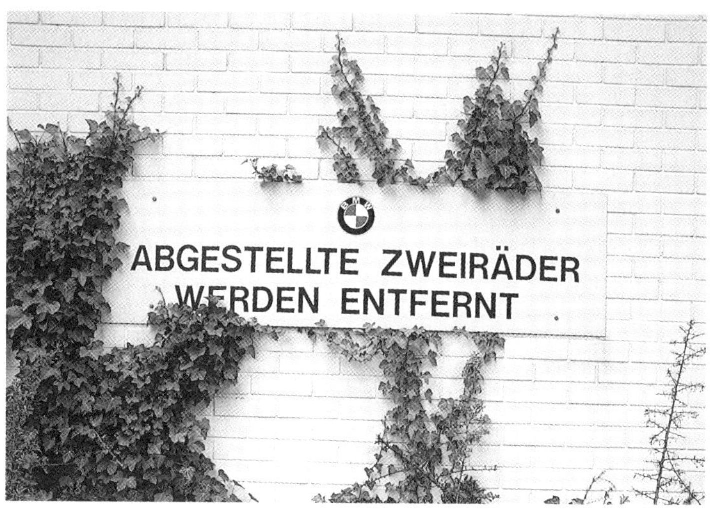

the next, but continuously. Moreover, the metering zones, apart from the central zone, are slightly displaced in a downwards direction so that, for the exposure measurement, the lower half of the image is taken into account slightly more than the upper half. This makes sense for photographs in the landscape format but can cause slight underexposure in the portrait format if large portions of sky are positioned in the upper half of the image. In such cases an exposure compensation (override) can be useful.

The full-field integral metering system is combined with the program, aperture priority and shutter priority modes and indicated as a rectangle in the viewfinder and in the program control window. The silicon photo cell is located in the base, behind the swing mirror. Integral metering is well-suited for subjects with a normal contrast range, without great colour contrasts and with an even distribution of bright and dark portions.

Selective metering

The metering area for selective metering is largely identical to the central circle of the full-field metering system, with its diameter of 7mm clearly marked on every focusing screen. This metering area roughly corresponds to 4.5% of the 24x36mm film format. Selective metering is combined with manual exposure mode and shutter priority and is indicated in the viewfinder and in the program control window by the letters **m** and **A** enclosed by a circle. In selective metering a converging lens, which takes into account only the light reflected from the selective metering area, is moved in front of the silicon photo cell used for integral metering. The diameter of the metering area (7mm) and the ratio between the metering area and the image area (4.5%) remain constant with every lens. However, the metering angle of selective metering is reduced in proportion to the angle of view of the current lens, ie the metering angle becomes tighter as the focal length increases.

Selective metering allows deliberate metering of details that are important for an exposure and is therefore very useful for subjects with a wide contrast range, i.e. backlit situations, subjects in front of very bright or very dark backgrounds, and other difficult lighting situations.

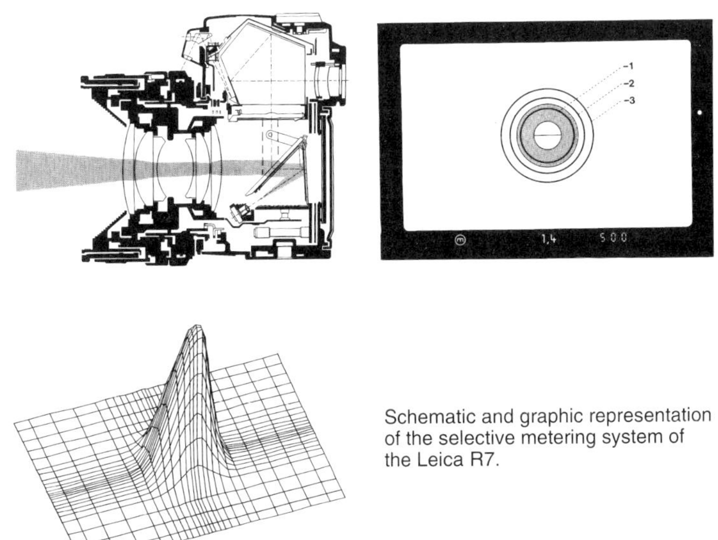

Schematic and graphic representation of the selective metering system of the Leica R7.

Exposure lock

In aperture priority mode with selective metering the exposure value can be locked by pressing the shutter-release button as far as the second pressure point. If the exposure value is locked the aperture priority symbol (letter **A** in a circle) in the viewfinder disappears. The value remains in the camera's computer memory for as long as you hold the shutter-release button, facilitating exposure sequences with a winder or motor with the exposure value locked.

Thanks to the exposure lock function you can meter a subject detail on the edge of the photograph and make the exposure with the exposure value determined in this way. If the aperture is changed while an exposure value is locked the camera's computer will adjust the shutter speed to correspond to the exposure value stored in its memory.

The exposure value cannot be locked if the shutter is not cocked. This protective mechanism ensures that you won't miss a picture because the camera wasn't ready to shoot.

Exposure compensation (override)

The Leica R7 allows exposure compensation (override) within a range of +/−3 light values in half-stop increments. The operating controls for exposure compensation are located next to the rewind crank. The locking button (14) on the side is pressed in and remains locked in this position. With the button in this position the desired compensation factor can be selected with the override lever (16). The compensation factor can then be locked by pressing in the locking button and turning it to the left. The selected value can be read off the exposure compensation scale (15), and the relevant symbol will flash bottom right in the viewfinder frame.

Exposure compensation can be selected in every operating mode and with every metering method, but is more appropriate with strong subject contrast, in backlit situations, or for capturing a certain lighting mood with integral metering.

With integral metering and seaside subjects, very bright subjects, snowy landscapes, backlit situations, and subjects lacking in contrast, as in overcast weather conditions, an exposure compensation of between +½

This example shows an exposure compensation of +2EV.

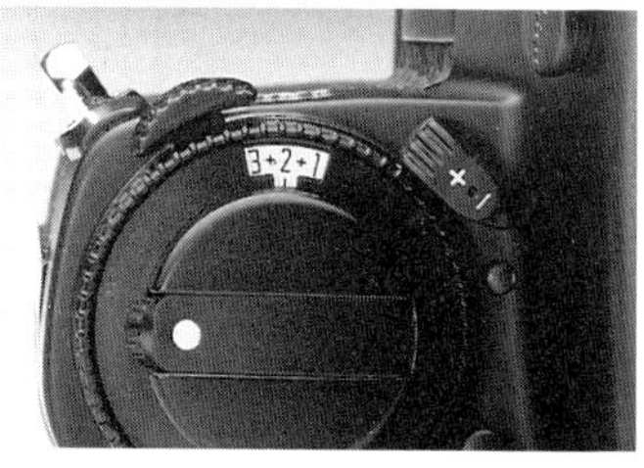

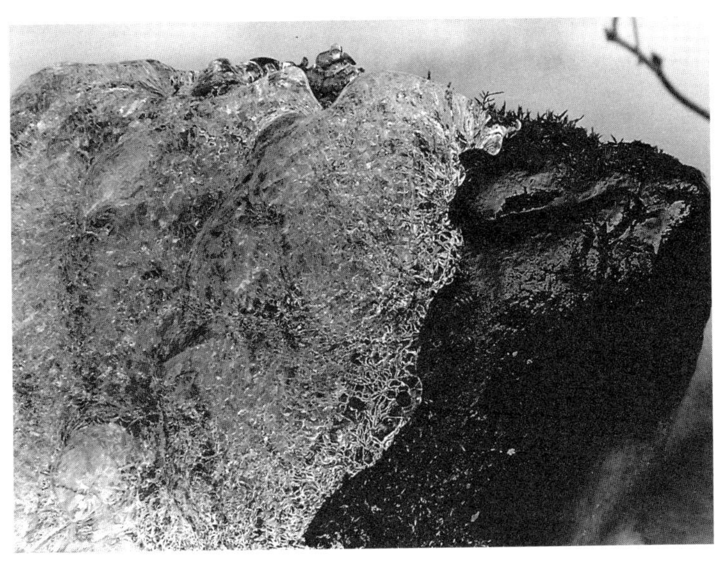

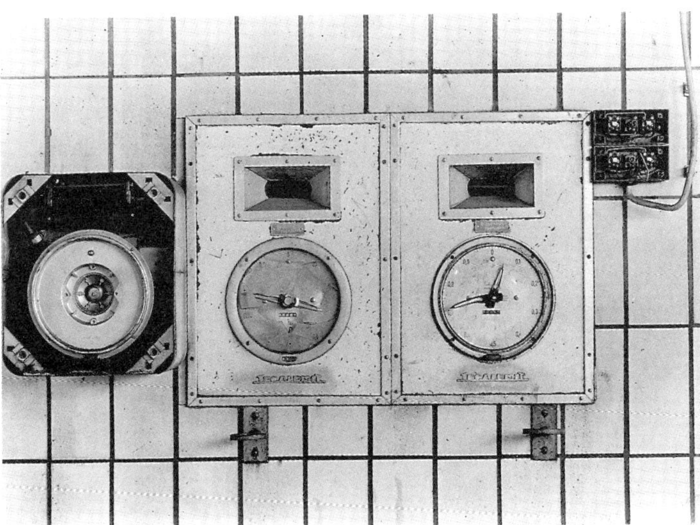

Subjects with this amount of brightness difference can only be mastered with exposure compensation. Without exposure compensation both subjects would be rendered grey.

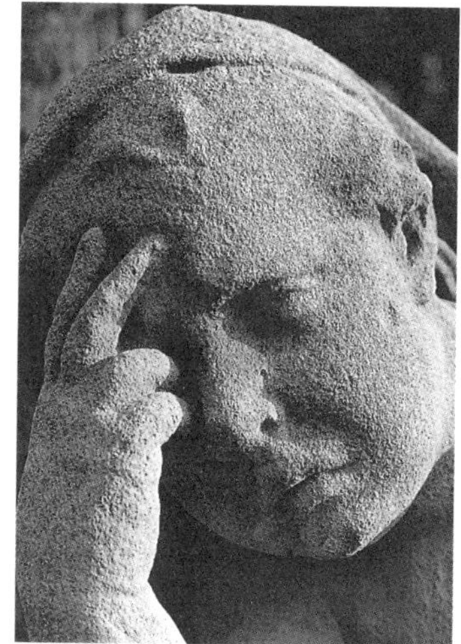
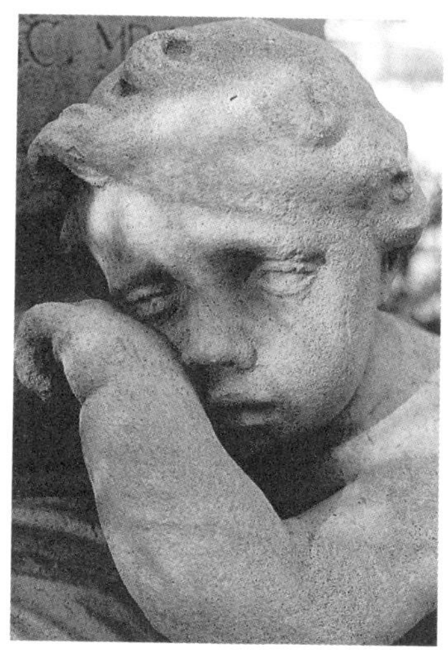

and +2 EV is required, depending on the lighting conditions. Very dark subjects on the other hand require a negative compensation. But be careful with photographs at night or at dawn or dusk: theoretically these would require a negative exposure compensation, but if shutter speeds slower than 1 second are metered, the reciprocity effect becomes noticeable, so that an exposure compensation of +3 will be needed.

Open aperture metering and working aperture metering

Open aperture metering is the usual method of operation with the Leica R7. It works with all Leica R lenses with automatic spring-back diaphragms. Open aperture metering provides convenient working because the viewfinder image remains bright both before and after the exposure (the diaphragm is fully open). The lens can always be stopped down with the depth of field lever to check the depth of field.

Because of their construction the following lenses do not have an automatic spring-back diaphragm, which means that working aperture metering needs to be used: PC-Super-Angulon 28mm,f/2.8, PA-Curtagon 35mm,f/4, Telyt-R 400m,f/6.8, Telyt-R 560mm,f/6.8, Telyt-S 800mm,f/6.3 and MR-Telyt-R 500mm,f/8. The same applies to some accessories, such as the older bellows unit and extension tube combinations. With working aperture metering the exposure has to be metered at the selected aperture for the exposure, which leads to a darkening of the viewfinder image. However, this process is made easier on some lenses and accessories where the iris diaphragm can be opened and closed again to a preset aperture by means of a stop-down lever.

Lenses and accessories without spring-back diaphragms can only be used with manual mode and aperture priority mode (but with both integral and selective metering).

Subject-specific, professional exposure metering

Thanks to the two metering methods, you can master even difficult lighting situations without additional manual exposure meters for spot and light metering. Moreover, the metering methods allow 'manipulated' exposures, where the photographer deliberately exposes the film differently from the actual measured exposure, for example to convey a certain lighting mood or even to create these on the film (moonlight effect, high and low key). A knowledge of the working method of TTL

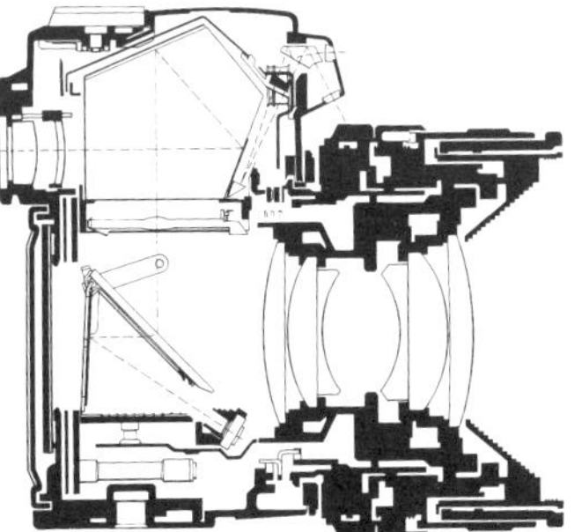

Part of the incident light is directed into the viewfinder, the rest to the metering sensor.

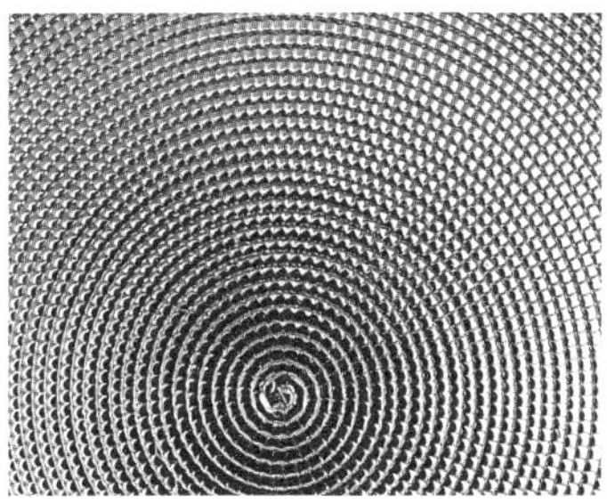

A Fresnel reflector with 1345 round micro-reflectors concentrates the light and directs it towards the metering sensor.

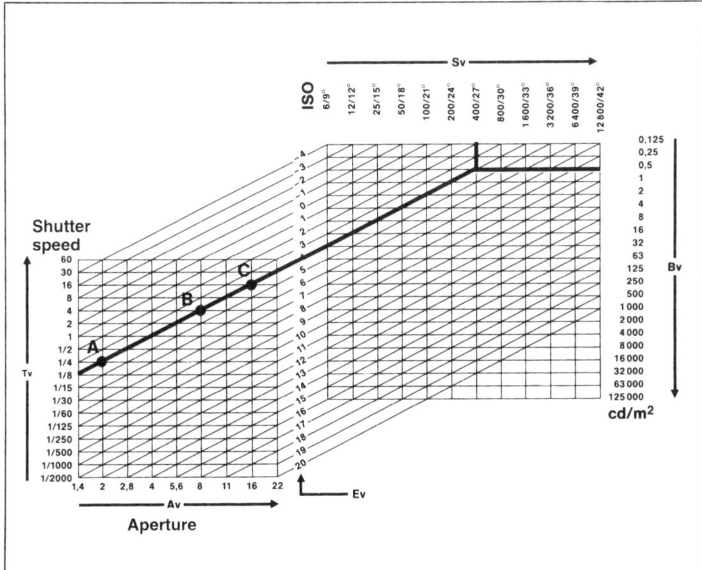

Working diagram of an exposure meter, showing an example (at ISO 400/27° and a light intensity of 0.5cd/m²).

exposure metering and the ability to analyse a subject from all subject-specific points of view are pre-requisites for the achievement of interesting effects. Let's start by looking at a seemingly simple standard situation.

With most average subjects with a normal contrast range, without great colour contrasts, and with an even distribution of bright and dark portions, the exposure value determined through TTL metering (regardless of the metering method) corresponds to the medium grey with 18% reflectance. These subjects are usually exposed correctly by the full-field integral metering system. But if the bright and dark portions in a subject are distributed unevenly, or take up varying amounts of the overall image area, integral metering can produce incorrect results. In addition, the integral metering system can fail even with a normal contrast range if the various contrast values are not grouped around the medium values. For example, a landscape with a field in the foreground and roughly the same amount of sky with a few small clouds has a contrast range of 5 light values. At a constant aperture of f/11 selective metering will produce ⅟₁₅ sec for the darkest portion of the field and ⅟₅₀₀ sec for the brightest portion of the clouds. Theoretically, both integral metering and a colour slide film can cope with a contrast range of 5 light values if the contrasting portions are evenly distributed. But this example scene exposed at ⅟₁₈₀ sec after integral metering is underexposed by about one stop. Why? Because the brightness values for the field fall in the medium range of tones, those of the sky within the bright range, and the medium value determined by integral metering consequently falls between the medium and bright tones. This inevitably leads to underexposure. To avoid this you need to adjust the integrally metered value by +½ to +1 EV. You could also tilt the camera further down, so that more of the foreground is taken into account for the measurement, and then reframe after locking the exposure and expose at this value. But tilting the camera will result in a fairly inaccurate measurement which will rarely produce a balanced exposure. So for an accurate exposure measurement you need to use a different metering method, even in this simple example.

One possibility is a substitute measurement on part of the field. Experienced photographers know that green grass reflects about half as much light as the standard grey card with 18% reflectance, so that the exposure would need to be one stop tighter than the value determined with the substitute measurement. But an exposure at this value, in this case ⅟₃₀ sec, will cause the sky to be reproduced too bright, even causing burn-out of the clouds. In such cases metering two different points is the right method to use. Using the selective metering method to meter the brightest and darkest parts in the subject and using a mean exposure value from these will lead to a balanced exposure. In our case you would first meter the clouds (⅟₅₀₀ sec), then the darkest part of the field (⅟₁₅ sec). The mean value would be ⅟₉₀ sec. This is the only

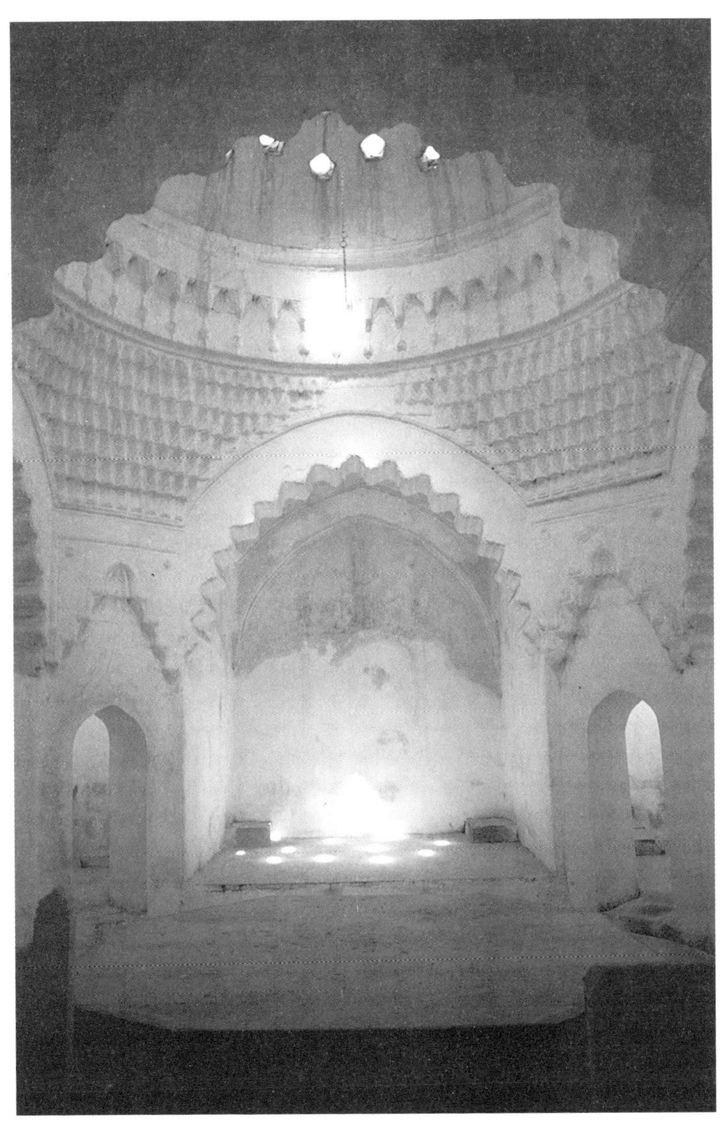

Deliberate overexposure in order to render the white room white.

exposure value that would lead to a balanced exposure on slide film, with both the shadows (darkest parts of the field) and the highlights (brightest parts of the clouds) still showing contrast.

Even if the subject and lighting situations are analysed correctly, making exposures either side of the determined value is an important safeguard. Start with the metered value and make a series of exposures, varying the exposure in even increments towards both under and over-exposure. You can make as many of these bracketed exposures as you like at increments of your choosing, but in practice the following method has proved best. For negative films, make two additional exposures with a compensation of +1 and −1 EV. For slide films your exposure sequence can consist of five exposures varying by +½ EV increments: −1, −½, 0, +½, and +1 EV. If you are shooting important subjects or are working professionally you can extend your exposure sequences to between +3 and −2 EV. Such sequences are most easily achieved with the exposure compensation function. For exposure sequences where all the photographs need to be taken with the same aperture or the same shutter speed, you can use the manual exposure mode.

The exposure sequences described above bear no relation to the so-called 'overkill' method, whereby you take several photographs in the hope that one of them will succeed. Exposure sequences are used by experienced photographers, and not only in difficult lighting conditions, as they are often the only way of achieving photographs exposed correctly down to half or one-third of an exposure value. The method is widely used by professional photographers, as film is the cheapest item in the production chain. Finely graded exposure sequences are indispensable for photographers who make the highest demands on the photographic results. This is particularly important when working with slide film and can be illustrated with a number of everyday photographic examples. A slide projected with a projector with a 150-watt bulb should be a shade brighter than a slide intended for a 120-watt projector. A slide that is to be scanned by a repro house for inclusion in a publication needs to be around half a stop brighter than one intended for a slide show. Moreover, the correctly exposed photograph is not always the most expressive.

So it is important to know both the possibilities and the limitations of each of the different exposure metering methods. Don't let automatic exposure systems lull you into a false sense of security, even in seemingly simple lighting conditions. Always stay on your toes, analyse the subject and take account of the exposure tolerance of the film.

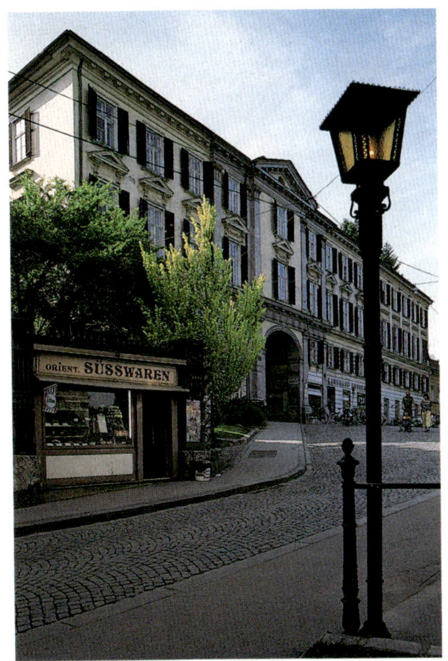
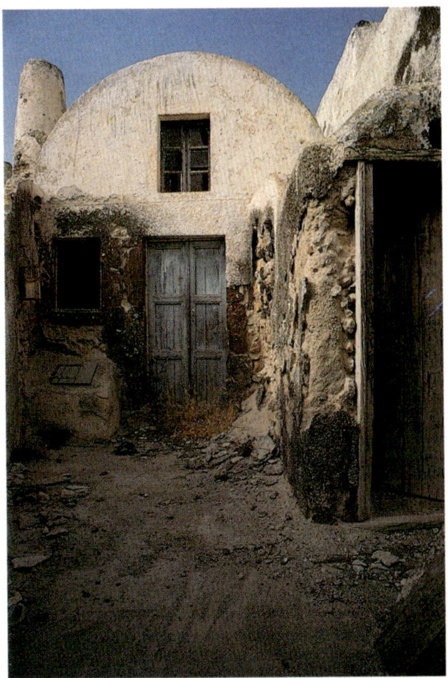
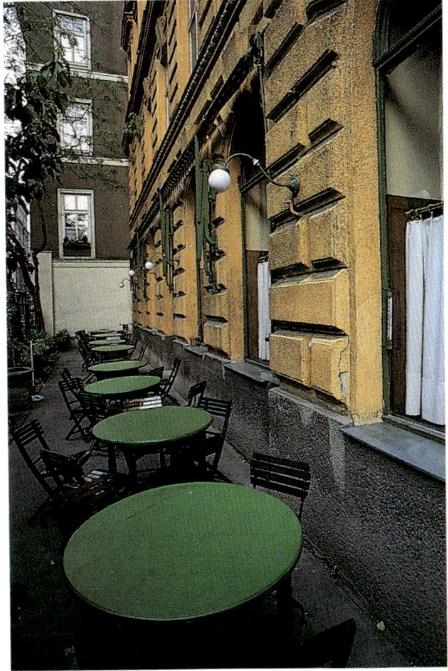
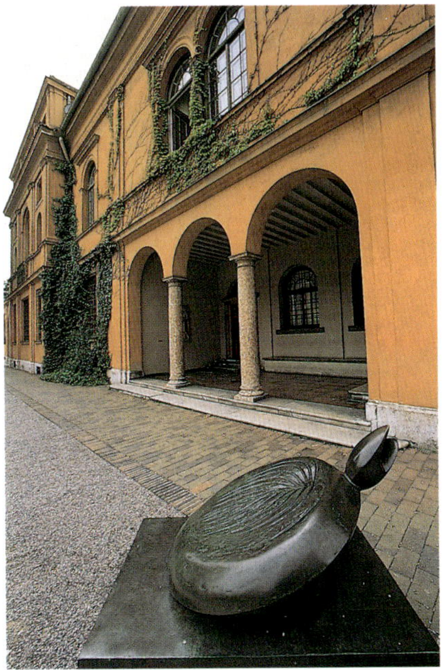

Towns have many faces – providing inexhaustible scope for ambitious urban photography.

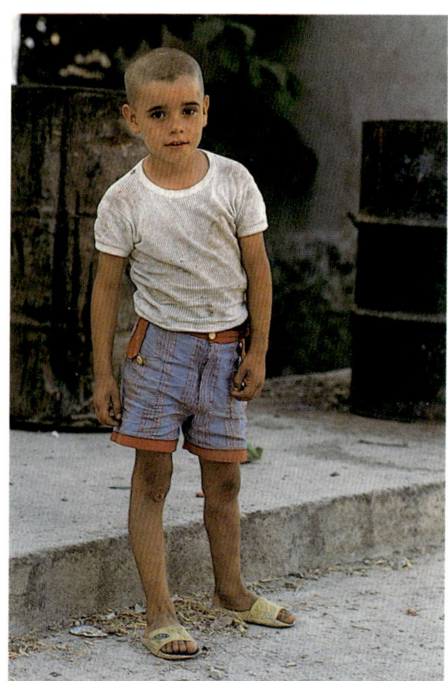
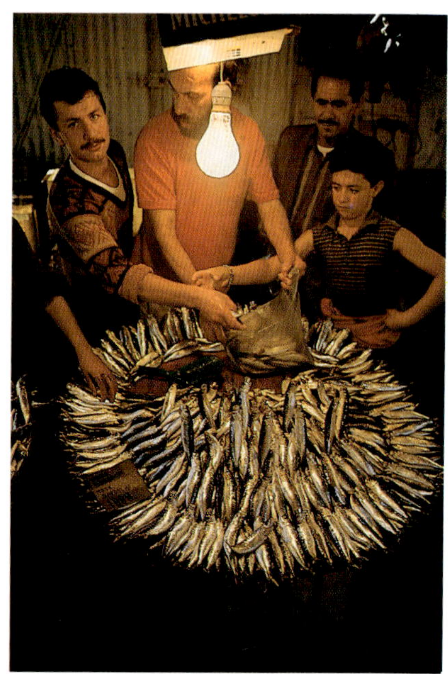
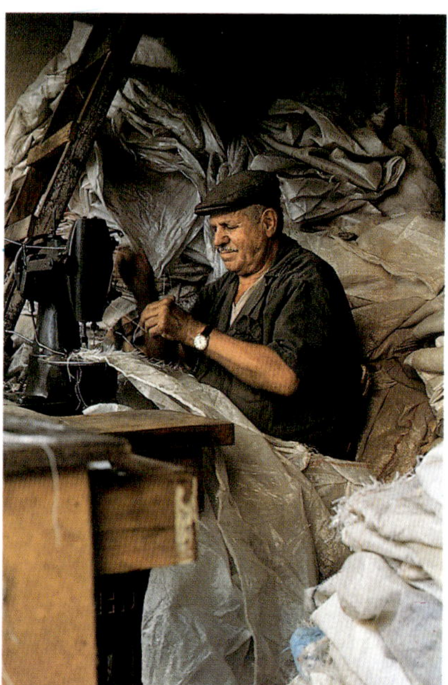
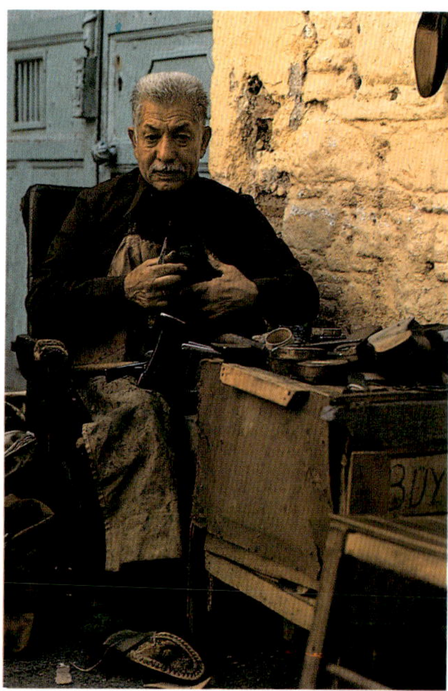

Showing people in their surroundings demands sympathy and sensitivity and the ability to master the camera effortlessly.

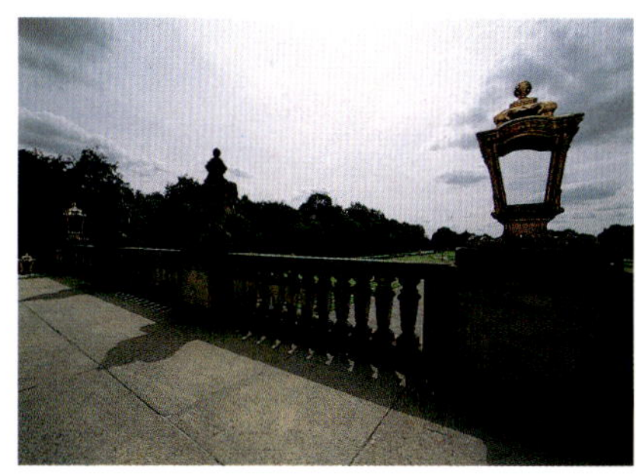 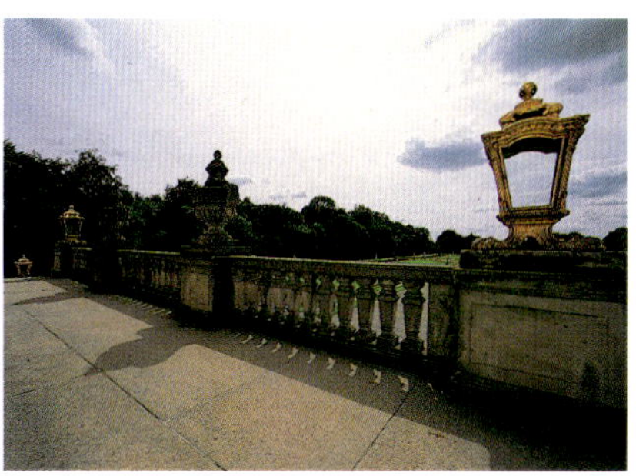

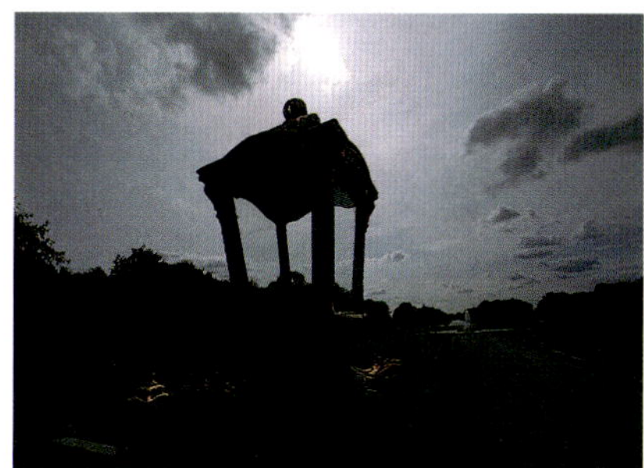 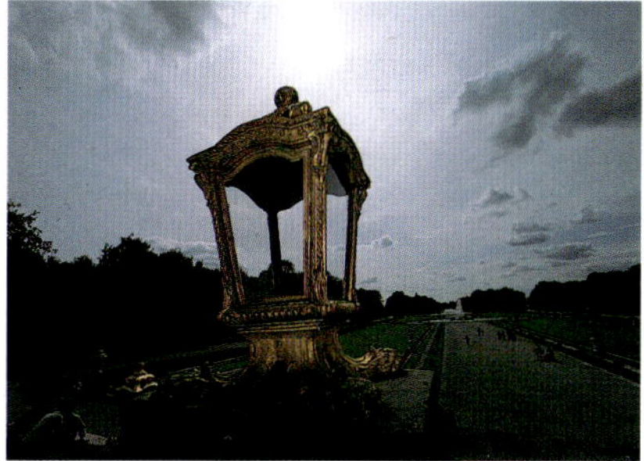

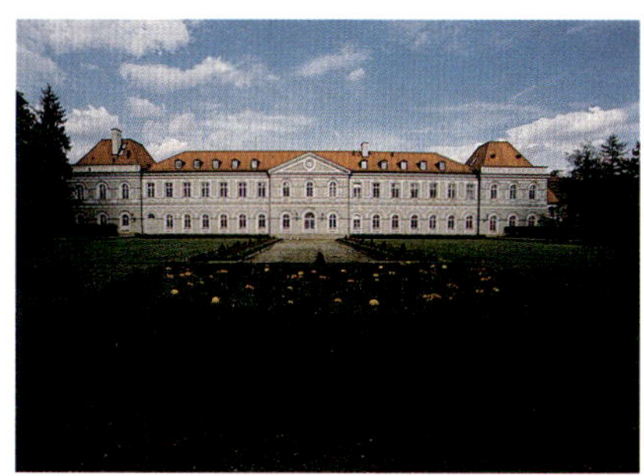 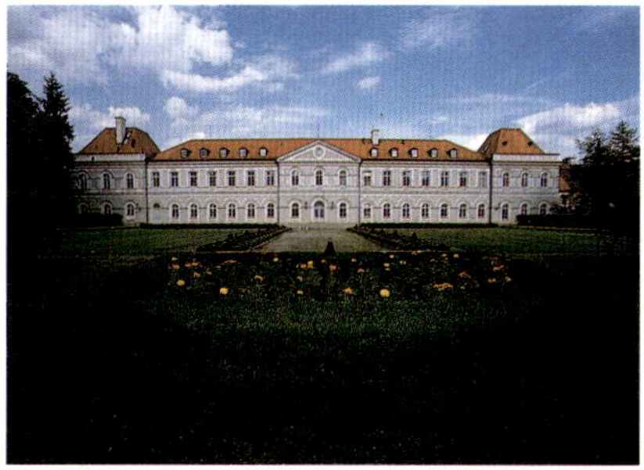

The shots on the left were taken without flash. Those on the right demonstrate the strengths of the sophisticated TTL fill-in flash control system of the Leica R7.

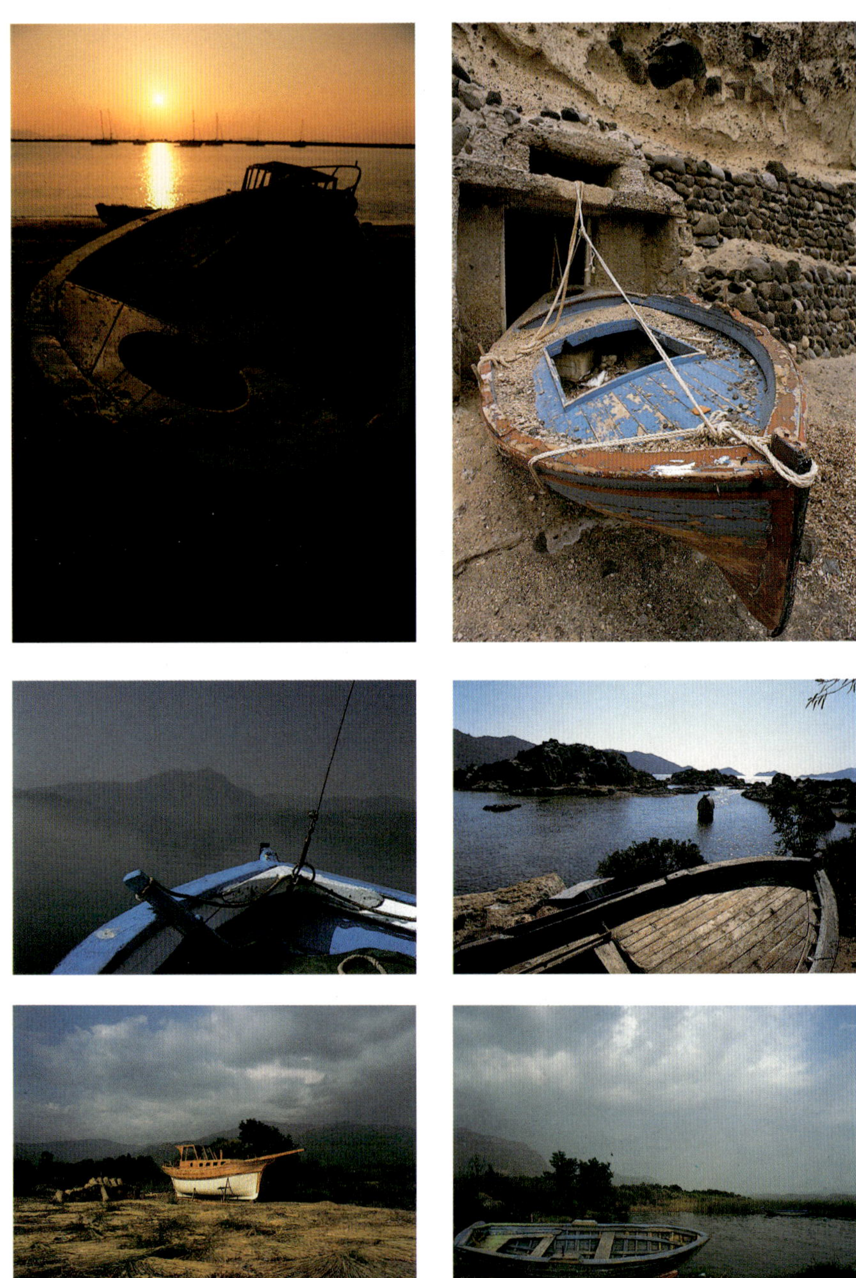

In good travel photography, too, its the photographic idea which makes the picture.

4. The Operating Modes in Practice

The five operating modes of the Leica R7 are combined with the two metering methods. Thanks to the computer-controlled automatic exposure programs the photographer can master every subject situation conveniently and easily. The desired mode is selected with the program selector and indicated in the viewfinder as well as in the window adjacent to the program selector knob.

Variable automatic program mode with integral metering

The letter **P**, enclosed by a rectangle, appears in the viewing window and in the viewfinder when this mode is selected. The smallest aperture must be selected on the Leica R lens to ensure that the whole aperture range is available for automatic control. If the smallest aperture has not been selected the program symbol, bottom left in the viewfinder, will flash, and no aperture will be indicated on the right of the viewfinder frame. The aperture set on the lens is projected onto the bottom of the viewfinder, whilst the automatically controlled aperture is shown by LEDs on the right of the viewfinder.

The variable automatic program mode with full-field integral metering is useful if you want to be ready to shoot quickly without giving much thought to the selection of aperture and shutter speed. Shutter speed and aperture are selected automatically, although you can influence the program characteristics by adjusting the shutter speed dial.

To ensure faster shutter speeds the shutter speed dial should be set to speeds between ¹⁄₆₀ and ¹⁄₂₀₀₀ sec. The automatic program will now work

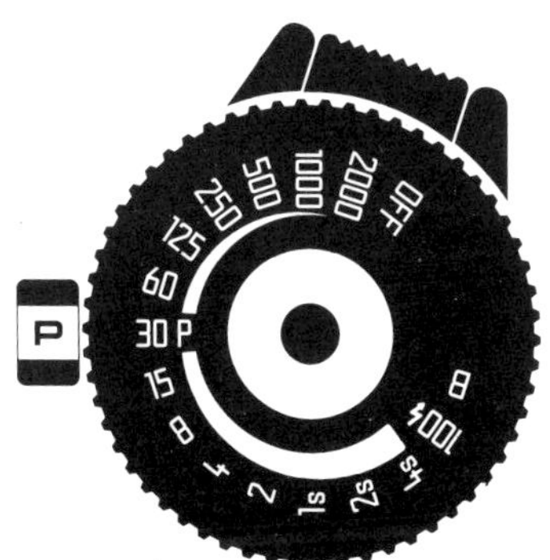

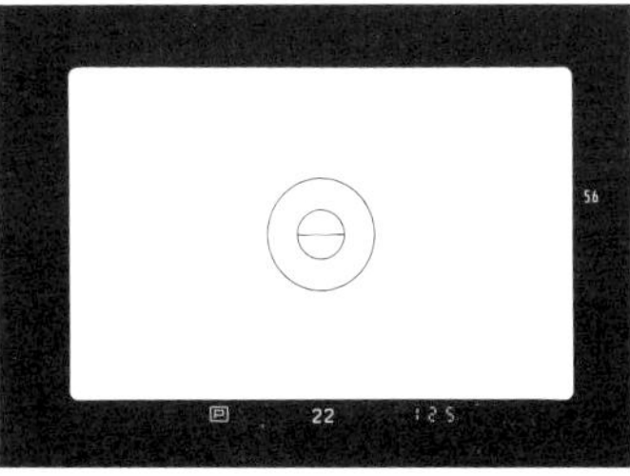

The variable automatic program with whole field integral metering.

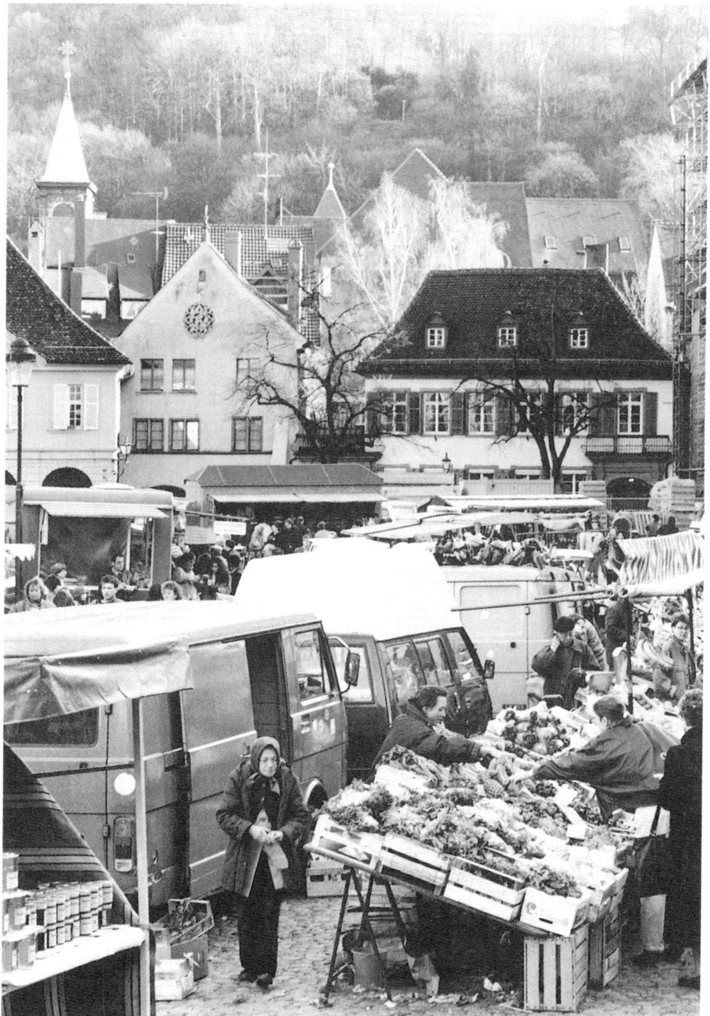

with a tendency towards faster shutter speeds, which is more pronounced the faster the selected shutter speeds are. This program characteristic is ideal for sports and action photography, for snapshots with medium telephoto lenses, or for portraits because the fast shutter speeds lead to wider apertures and therefore to a shallower depth of field. It is also important, particularly when working with telephoto lenses, that a shutter speed setting that is faster than the reciprocal of the focal length is used. At a focal length of 250mm the shutter speed dial should be set to 1/500 sec. or faster.

The standard program is activated if the shutter speed dial is set to 1/30 sec. On the shutter speed dial the letter **P** behind the shutter speed

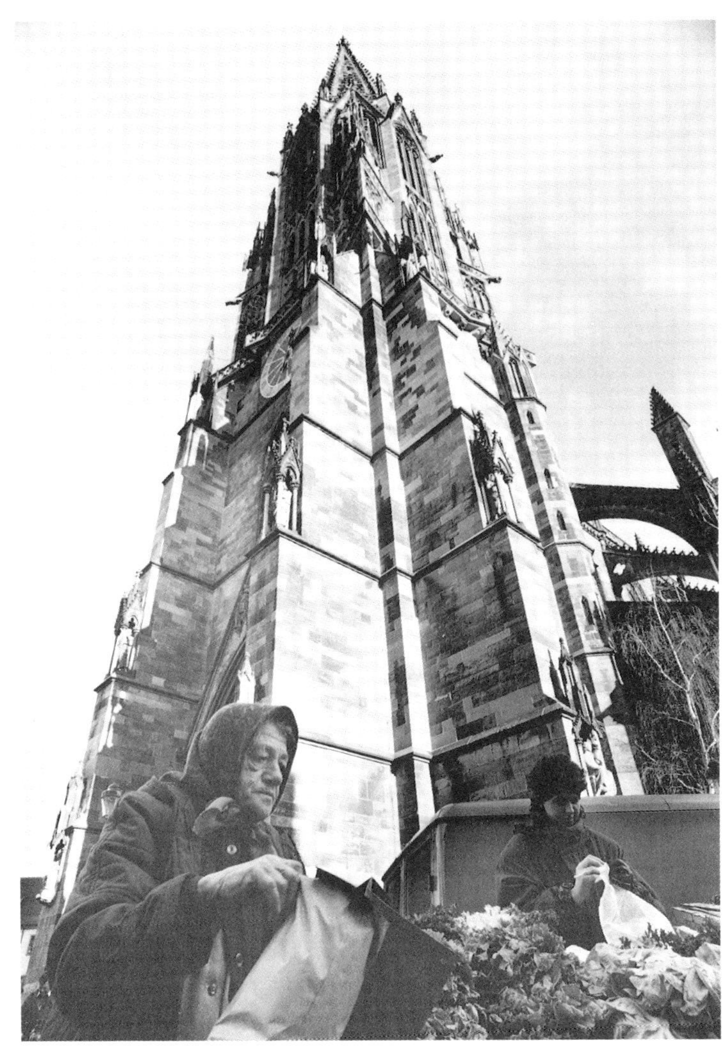

marking for ⅓₀ sec. provides an additional indication of the standard program setting. This program characteristic is well-suited for snapshots and standard subjects which can be photographed with focal lengths between 28 and 90mm. In this setting the program will normally automatically set the fastest possible shutter speed at the smallest possible aperture. This results in an aperture/shutter speed combination for shake-free photographs with the greatest possible depth of field, which is suitable for many normal situations.

If the shutter speed dial is set to a value between ⅛₅ sec. and 4 seconds, the automatic program will work with slower shutter speeds and smaller apertures. This program characteristic is good for subjects

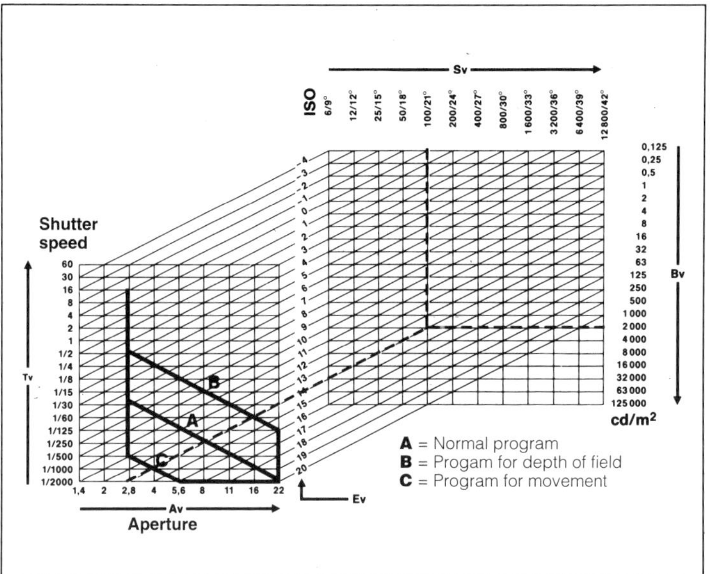

requiring great depth of field, such as landscape or architectural photography. On the one hand the slower shutter speeds increase the danger of camera shake, on the other they lead to a blurred reproduction of movement (panning effect, running water, unsharpness as a stylistic feature).

Note, however, that the camera will not normally select the shutter speed set on the shutter speed dial, but one corresponding to the more or less pronounced tendency of the selected program characteristic. The program tendency can be seen in the relevant graphic illustrations. The increasing or decreasing marking behind the shutter speeds on the shutter speed dial will give an approximate idea.

The shutter speed and corresponding aperture controlled by the camera are indicated in the viewfinder. The automatic program works with all Leica R lenses with fully automatic spring-back diaphragms.

Changing the program characteristics by means of the position of the shutter speed dial is the same as a program shift function. It allows the photographer to adapt the aperture/shutter speed combination to individual creative ideas simply by turning the shutter speed dial.

Aperture priority with integral metering

The letter **A** within a **rectangle** appears in the viewing window and in the viewfinder on selection of this mode. In aperture priority mode with full-field integral metering the desired aperture is selected on the lens while the camera automatically and continuously selects a suitable

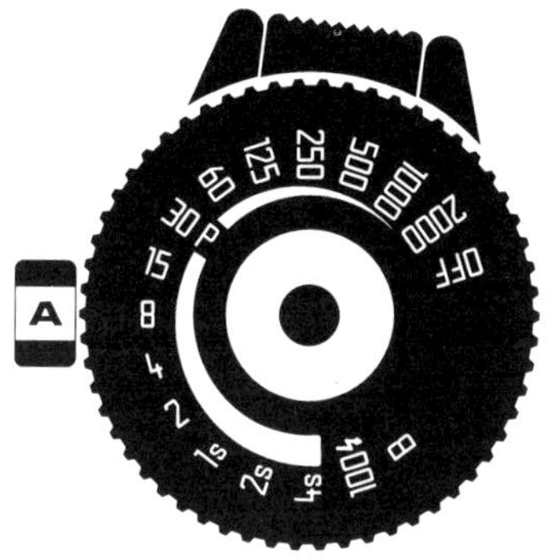

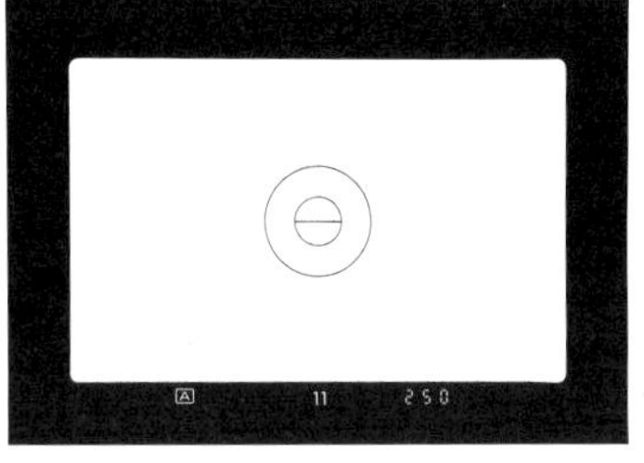

Aperture priority with full-field integral metering.

shutter speed between ½₂₀₀₀ sec. and 16 seconds. The shutter speed is indicated in half-step increments in the viewfinder, next to the aperture projected in from the aperture ring. If the subject is too bright the ½₂₀₀₀ sec. shutter speed display will flash, while if the light is too low the indication **16"** will appear. However, the over or underexposure can still be made. In such cases you should select a smaller or wider aperture if possible. If the values fall below the metering range, the relevant symbol on the left of the viewfinder will flash (! enclosed by a triangle).

Aperture priority with integral metering allows conscious control of the depth of field and is well suited for landscape and architectural work. Remember that here, too, integral metering is suitable for normal lighting conditions, although exposure compensation may be needed to cope with great subject contrasts.

Aperture priority with selective metering

The letter **A** in a **circle** indicates this mode in the viewing window and in the viewfinder. The desired aperture is selected on the lens while

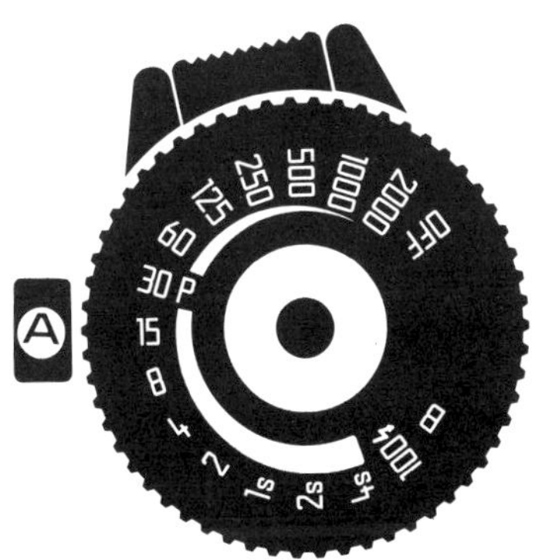

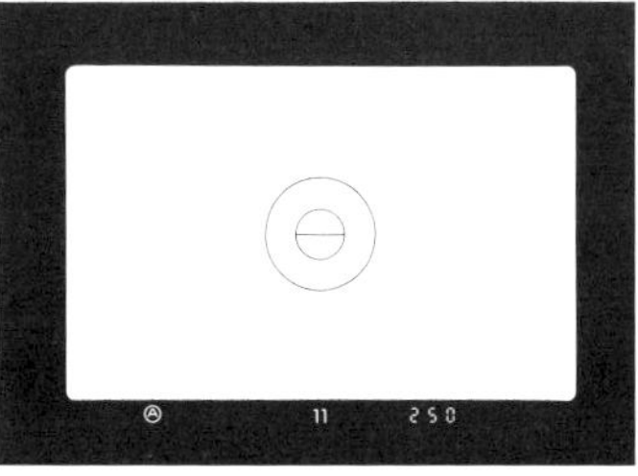

Aperture priority with selective metering.

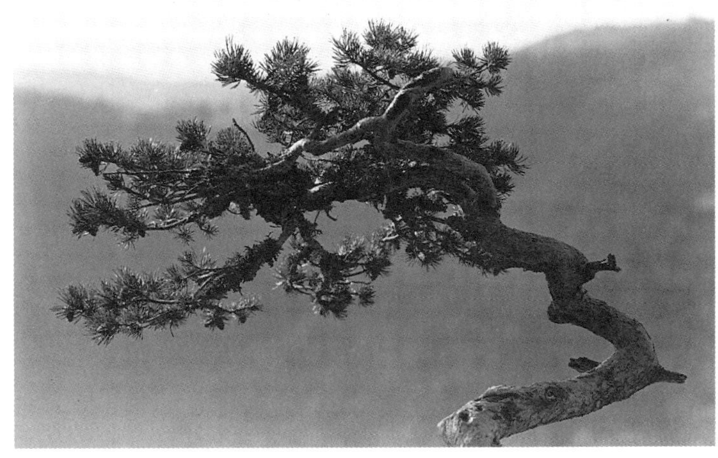

the camera automatically and continuously controls the corresponding shutter speed between ½₂₀₀₀ sec. and 16 seconds. The shutter speed (rounded up or down to the nearest half-step increment) is indicated next to the aperture on the right of the viewfinder. If the subject is too bright, the shutter speed indication ½₂₀₀₀ will flash to warn of over-exposure, while if it is too dark the indication **16"** will warn of under-exposure. However, the over or underexposure can still be made. To avoid this incorrect exposure, select a larger or smaller aperture if possible. If the resulting light values fall below the metering range the relevant symbol (! in a triangle) will flash in the bottom left of the viewfinder.

Aperture priority allows creative use of the depth of field, while the selective metering helps you cope with high-contrast subjects and backlit situations. This operating mode is ideal for portrait work.

The measurement determined with selective metering can be locked by pressing the shutter-release button to the second pressure point. Once the value is locked the aperture priority symbol in the viewfinder (letter **A** in a circle) disappears. The exposure value is maintained for as long as your finger stays on the shutter-release button, this allows for exposure sequences with a winder or motor in combination with the exposure lock function.

The exposure lock facility allows precise metering of a subject outside the centre of the frame so that the exposure can be made using this value. If the aperture is changed while the exposure is locked, the camera's computer will set a new shutter speed to correspond to the stored light value.

If the shutter is not cocked the exposure value cannot be locked. This protective mechanism ensures that you don't miss a shooting situation because the camera wasn't ready to shoot.

Shutter priority with integral metering

The letter **T** in a rectangle appears in the viewfinder and in the viewing window with this mode. In shutter priority the desired shutter speed is selected while the camera automatically selects the correct aperture, depending on the lighting conditions. Shutter speeds between ½₂₀₀₀ sec. and 4 seconds can be selected in half-step increments. Shutter priority works with all Leica R lenses with fully automatic spring-back diaphragms. Always select the smallest aperture on the lens to ensure the whole aperture range is available. If the smallest aperture is not selected the **T**-symbol in the viewfinder will flash, and no aperture will be indicated on the right of the viewfinder frame. When the Fisheye-Elmarit 16mm,f/2.8 is used, however, the T-symbol will flash even if f/16 is selected. This is due to the construction of the lens and in this case does not affect the correct functioning of shutter priority mode.

The smallest (or manually selected) aperture is projected into the aperture window at the bottom centre of the viewfinder screen. The automatically controlled aperture is indicated by LEDs on the right of the viewfinder. The smallest or largest aperture indication will flash if the automatically controlled aperture range is not sufficient for a correct exposure with the pre-selected shutter speed. In this case the camera's computer will select a different shutter speed from the pre-selected speed to ensure a correct exposure. The viewfinder will then show the computed rather than the pre-selected shutter speed. If the aperture and shutter speed indications flash simultaneously, the correct values fall above or below the working range of the camera. If the light values are below the metering range, the relevant symbol (**!** in a triangle) bottom right of the viewfinder will also flash.

Shutter priority with integral metering is well-suited for photographs of moving subjects. Sports, action and snapshot photography are ideal applications for the shutter priority mode. Depending on the pre-selected aperture, movement can either be frozen or reproduced as speed-blurred effects. Shutter priority can also be used to ensure shake-

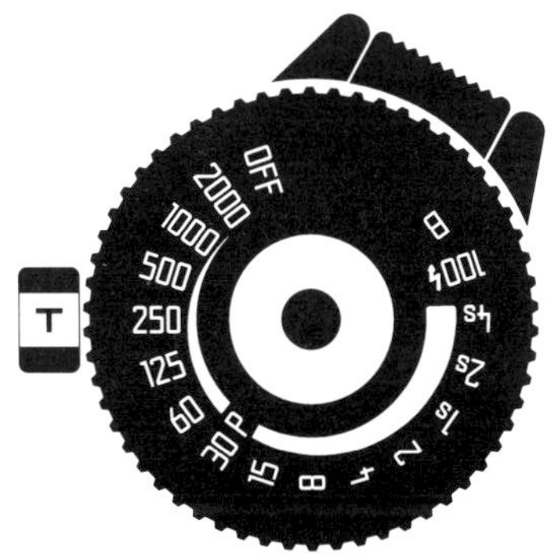

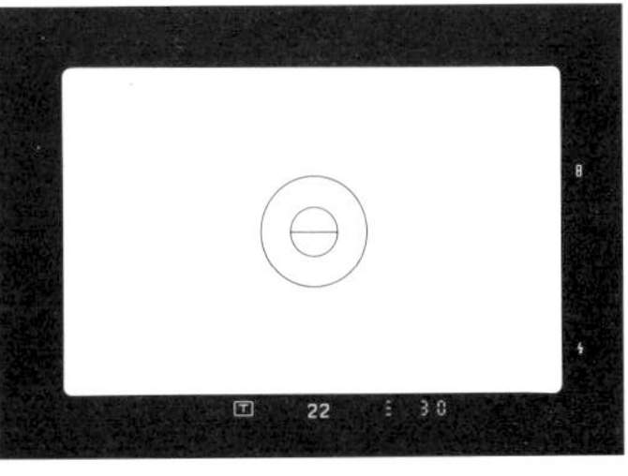

Shutter priority with full-field integral metering.

free telephoto work. Integral metering is suitable for subjects with normal contrast and even brightness distribution, although exposure compensation may be necessary for subjects in difficult light conditions.

Manual exposure mode with selective metering

The letter **m** inside a circle indicates selection of manual mode in the viewfinder and in the viewing window. In manual mode both aperture and shutter speed are selected by the photographer, in half-stop/step

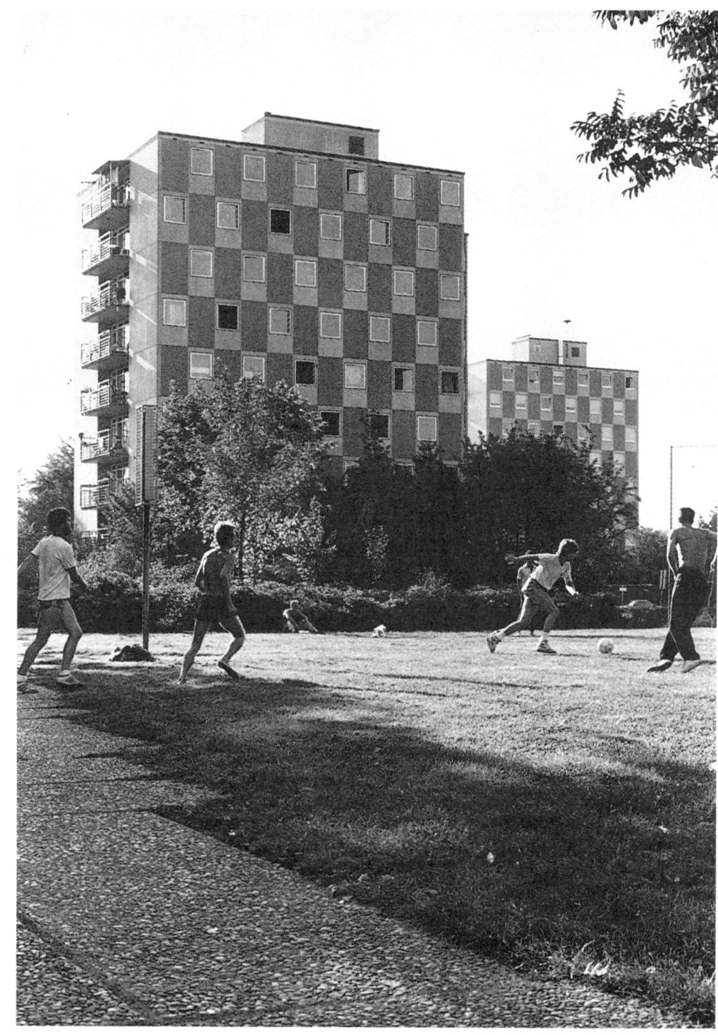

Left and right: Shutter priority is the right program for 'freezing' movement, or if you need to be ready to shoot quickly whilst minimizing the danger of camera shake.

increments. The exposure is adjusted via an exposure index, shown by LEDs on the right of the viewfinder frame in this operating mode. This indicates the deviation from the metered exposure value, which corresponds to the zero-value (shown by a round LED). The deviation is shown in half-stop increments in the range between −1.5 and +1.5 EV. If the deviation is greater than 2 EV the relevant + or − symbol will light up. Aperture and shutter speed need to be adjusted until the symbol at the centre of the scale lights up. If the resulting light value falls below the metering range of the camera, the ! in a triangle bottom left of the viewfinder will flash.

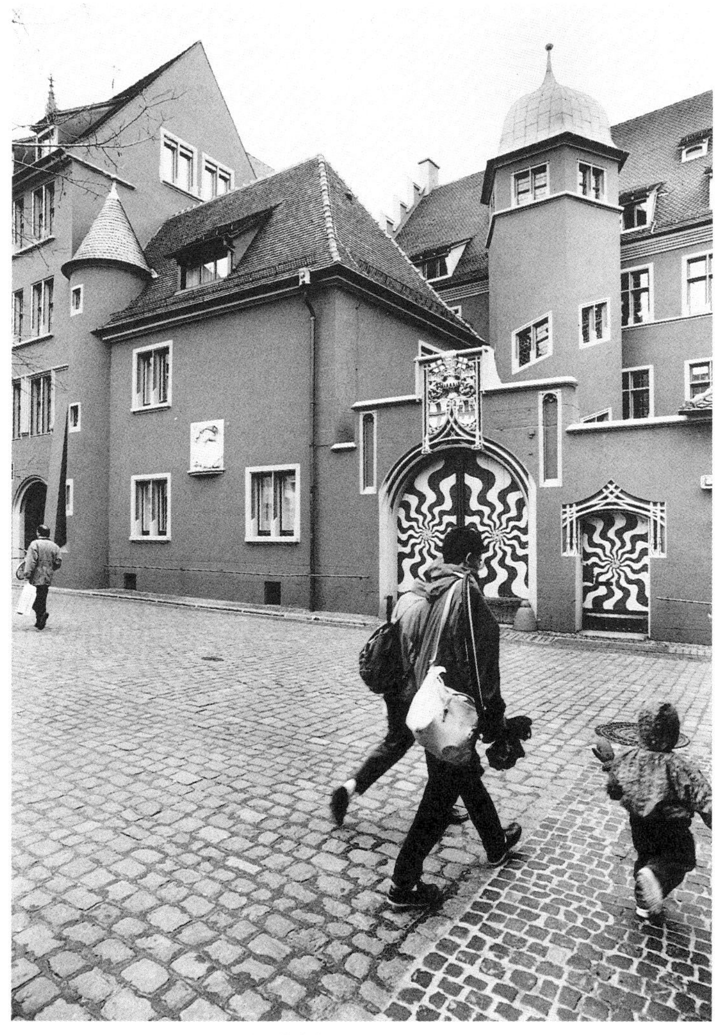

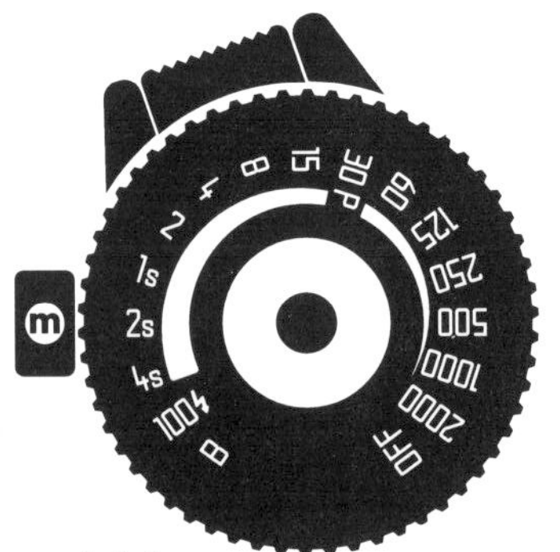 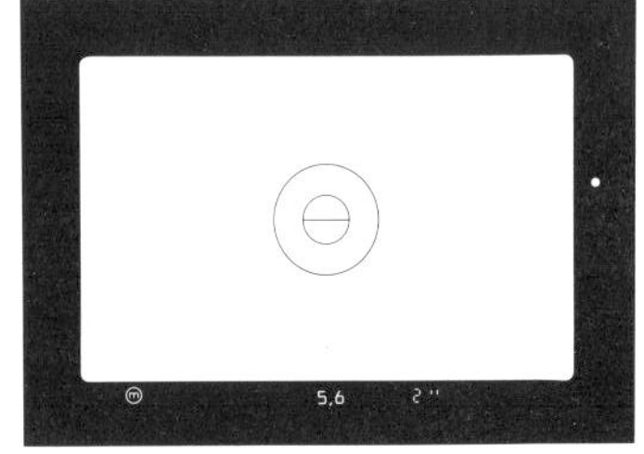

Manual exposure mode with
selective metering.

In this operating mode all Leica R lenses and all accessories such as
extension tube combinations or the Bellows R can be used. Manual
exposure mode is ideal for tackling difficult shooting situations, such
as backlight, deliberate over or underexposure, low- or high-key effects,
exposure sequences, experimental photography, work with very dark
filters or trick filters, infra-red photography, multiple exposures, and
flash exposure sequences.

5. Practical Flash Photography

In conjunction with system-compatible flash units, flash photography with the Leica R7 is as easy and reliable as daylight photography. Thanks to a sophisticated TTL flash control system, which can be combined with the operating modes, SCA 300- and SCA 500-system flash units can be used to provide primary or fill-in light. All other flash units or studio flash banks can, of course, be connected via the central contact or the flash socket, but TTL control and TTL flash exposure metering are not available in this case.

A separate silicon photo cell for TTL flash exposure metering is located next to the photo cell for integral and selective metering. Regardless of the operating mode, this cell has an integral metering characteristic, and it works with flash units that can be connected via one of the adapters SCA 351 or SCA 551. Flash-ready, flash control after the exposure and, if appropriate, fill-in flash are indicated in the viewfinder. If the flash is ready to shoot, the SCA 351 or SCA 551 will also automatically set the flash sync. speed of ¹⁄₁₀₀ sec., regardless of the position of the shutter speed dial.

With the SCA 351 or SCA 551 adapters the flash light is controlled depending on the ambient light. In this case the ISO setting on the flash unit is ignored as the film speed selected on the camera determines the TTL flash exposure measurement. Depending on the operating mode, faster shutter speeds can be selected, or the aperture controlled automatically. This does not apply if older adapters of the SCA 350 or SCA

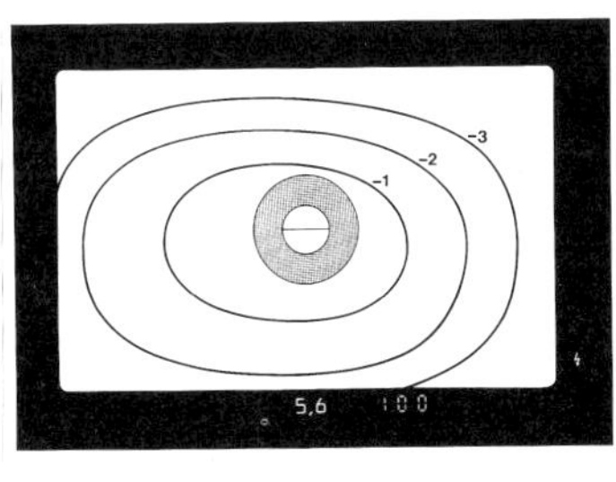

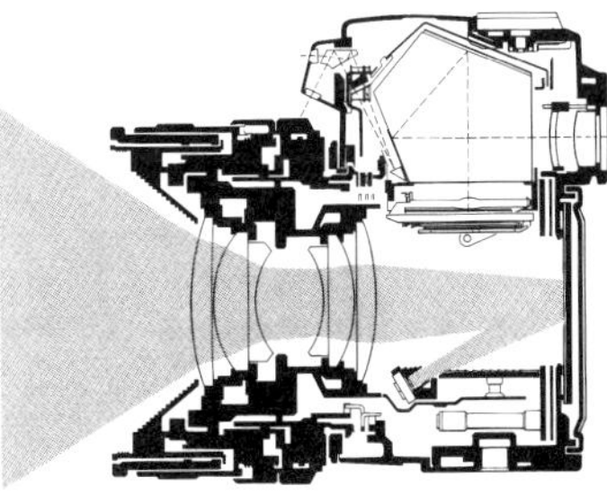

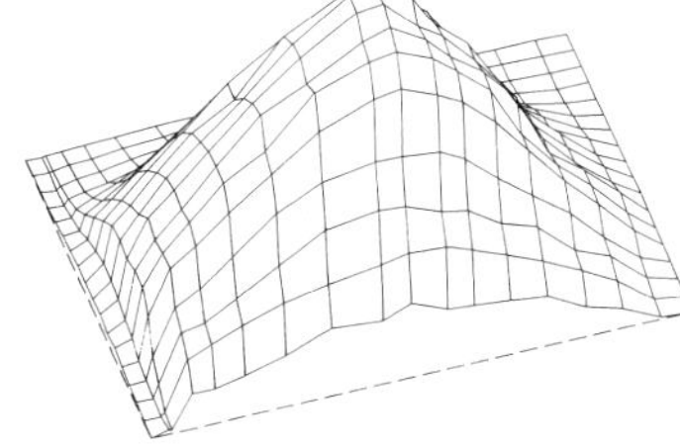

Schematic and graphic representation of the TTL flash exposure metering system of the Leica R7.

The TTL flash exposure metering system of the Leica R7 only works in conjunction with flash units in the SCA 300 or SCA 500 series and the adapters SCA 351 or SCA 551.

550 type are used, which do not allow TTL flash control. Moreover, if these adapters are used, the flash light is controlled by the metering cell of the computer flash unit which means that the film speed set on the flash unit determines the exposure.

To prevent interference, the two flash contacts should not be used at the same time. But several flash units can be connected to the **x** contact by means of a suitable adapter plug.

Flash-ready indication

With the SCA 351 or SCA 551 adapters full flash charge is indicated in all operating modes as well as the **100** and **B** settings. A flash symbol bottom right in the viewfinder will flash at a frequency of about two times per second to indicate full flash charge.

Flash control indicator

With the Leica R7 you can check easily whether or not the flash light was sufficient for a correct exposure. If you are using the SCA 351 or SCA 551 adapters and leave your finger on the shutter-release button after the exposure, the flash symbol bottom right in the viewfinder will indicate the following:-

- The symbol is flashing twice a second: the flash illumination was sufficient, the condenser was discharged only slightly and the flash unit is ready for the next exposure.

- The symbol is flashing about eight times a second: the flash illumination was sufficient, but the condenser discharge was greater and the flash is not ready to shoot again. After a short period of recharging the symbol will revert to flashing twice a second to signal that the flash is ready.

- The flash symbol disappears: the flash illumination was not sufficient. Wait for the flash ready symbol to reappear and repeat the exposure with a wider aperture.

Flash synchronization

The flash sync. speed is $\frac{1}{100}$ sec. In shutter priority and manual exposure modes all speeds between $\frac{1}{100}$ sec. and 4 seconds are flash synchronized (and can be selected in half-step increments). In addition there is a separate sync. speed of $\frac{1}{100}$ sec, which is marked **x** on the shutter speed dial. The bulb setting **B** is also flash synchronized.

If the camera is used with system-compatible flash units (SCA 300, SCA 500) and adapters (SCA 351, SCA 551), the flash sync speed of $\frac{1}{100}$ sec. is automatically selected in all operating modes. With non-system-compatible flash units the flash sync speed has to be selected manually.

TTL flash with manual exposure mode

In manual exposure mode all apertures, as well as shutter speeds between $\frac{1}{90}$ sec. and 4 seconds, can be selected. If faster shutter speeds are selected the SCA adapter automatically switches the camera to $\frac{1}{100}$ sec. The flash unit is used as the primary source of light, and the ambient light is taken into account in the measurement. If the ambient light is too bright, the shutter speed indicator 100 will flash. In this case a smaller aperture should be selected if possible. Used in conjunction with slow shutter speeds, flash illumination offers a number of creative possibilities such as panning effects with blurred background and the main subject reproduced sharply and in focus.

In the **B** and **100** settings the flash unit is used as the primary source of light and TTL-controlled regardless of the operating mode. But in this case the ambient light is not taken into account. Flash synchronization in the bulb setting allows effective long exposures, such as bright backgrounds (illuminated buildings, fireworks, street lights) and dark foreground (person or object), which are then illuminated by the flash light.

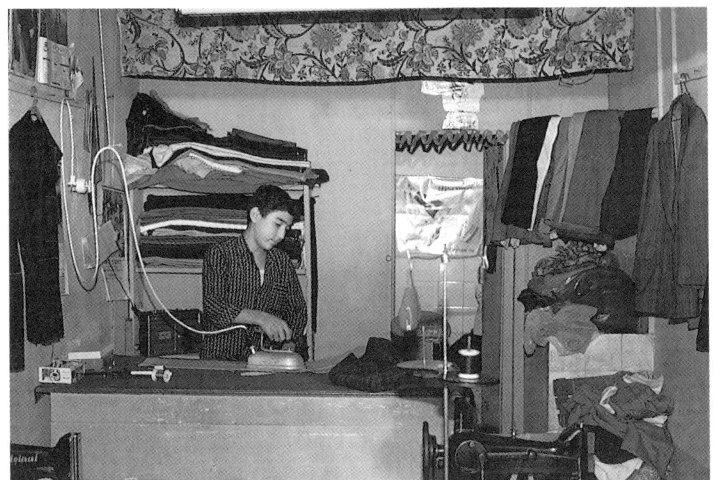

Balanced exposure thanks to TTL flash exposure metering in manual exposure mode.

TTL flash in aperture priority mode

TTL flash with aperture priority mode applies to both integral and selective metering. In aperture priority mode all apertures can be selected in half-stop increments. When the flash is ready to shoot the SCA adapter automatically switches the camera to the $\frac{1}{100}$ sec. sync speed. The flash unit acts as the primary source of light, and its output is controlled depending on the TTL flash measurements. With overexposure, the indicated flash sync. speed flashes, but the incorrect exposure can still be made. In such cases, to avoid overexposure, it's best to select a smaller aperture.

TTL fill-in flash control in shutter priority mode

One of the most important features of the Leica R7 is the fill-in flash control function in shutter priority mode. All shutter speeds between $\frac{1}{90}$ sec. and 4 seconds can be pre-selected in half-step increments. If the shutter speed dial is set to a faster shutter speed, the camera automatically switches over to $\frac{1}{100}$ sec. In shutter priority the aperture is selected automatically and is dependant on the ambient light. The flash unit is TTL-controlled by the camera with a reduced output in such a way that shadows or backlit parts of the subject close to the camera are illuminated without affecting the background illumination to any great extent.

In this operating mode the fill-in symbol of three short parallel lines appears at the bottom of the viewfinder. If the ambient light is too dark for the fill-in flash at the sync. speed of $\frac{1}{100}$ sec., the camera automatically selects a slower shutter speed to compensate. If, on the other hand,

Flash control possibilities with Leica R7 in combination with SCA351 and SCA551 adaptors

Mode	Shutter speed setting	Automatic shutter speed	Aperture setting	Automatic aperture setting	Flash control
(m)	4 s - 1/90s	1/100 [1]	any [2]	—	Primary light
(A) A	any	1/100s	any [2]	—	Primary light
T	4 s - 1/90s	1/100s [1]	smallest	Corresponding to ambient light	Fill-in flash
P 3)	any	1/100s	smallest	5,6	Primary light
P 4)	any	1/100s	smallest	Corresponding to ambient light	Fill-in flash
P 5)	any	1/2000s	smallest	Corresponding to ambient light	No flash
any	»100 ⚡ «, »B«	—	any [2]	—	Primary light

1) Automatic switchover to 1/100s when shutter speed is set to 1/124s and shorter.
2) Fill-in flash, provided that ambient light is sufficient for correct exposure at 1/100s and automatic aperture setting.
3) When the aperture range is under limit (underexposure), the flash is automatically switched to primary light (full intensity).
4) When the aperture range is over limit (overexposure), shutter speed is set to 1/2000s and the corresponding aperture (depending on ambient light) is set automatically.
5) The flash remains inactive.

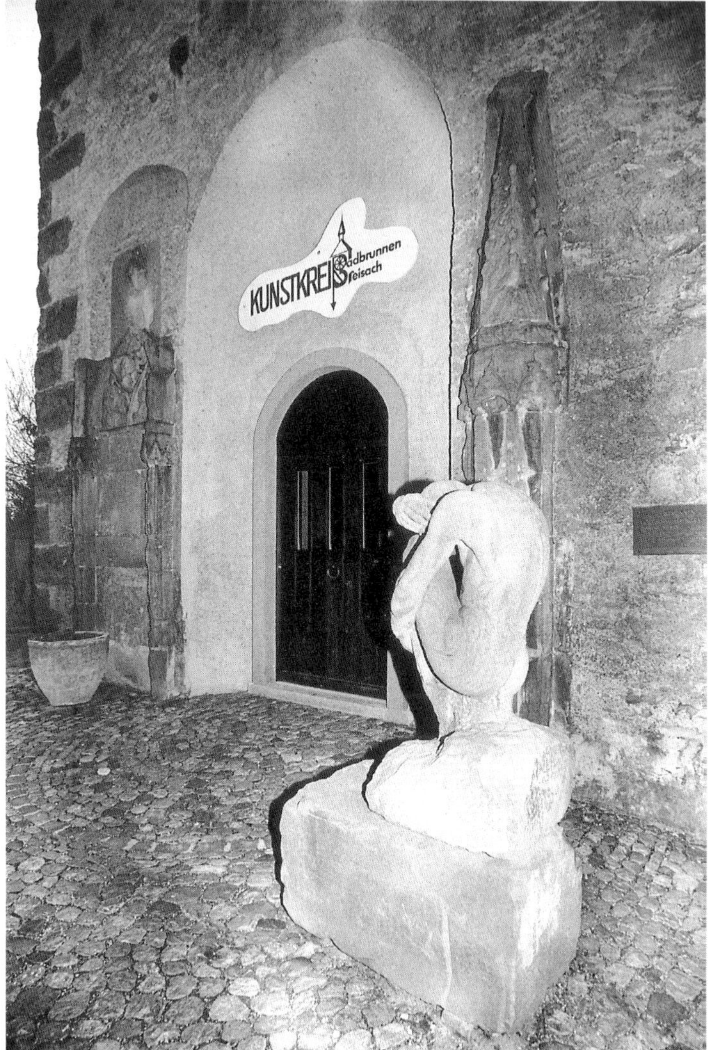

As it was fairly dark when this shot was taken, the variable flash control system in the automatic program decided on full flash illumination and produced a correct exposure. However, the more 'atmospheric' shot on the right was achieved with TTL fill-in flash control in shutter priority mode.

the ambient light is too bright for the fastest flash sync. speed, the indication **100** will flash, but the overexposure can still be made.

Variable TTL flash control in the automatic program

The variable flash control in the automatic program allows trouble-free flash photography in all photographic situations. In this function the

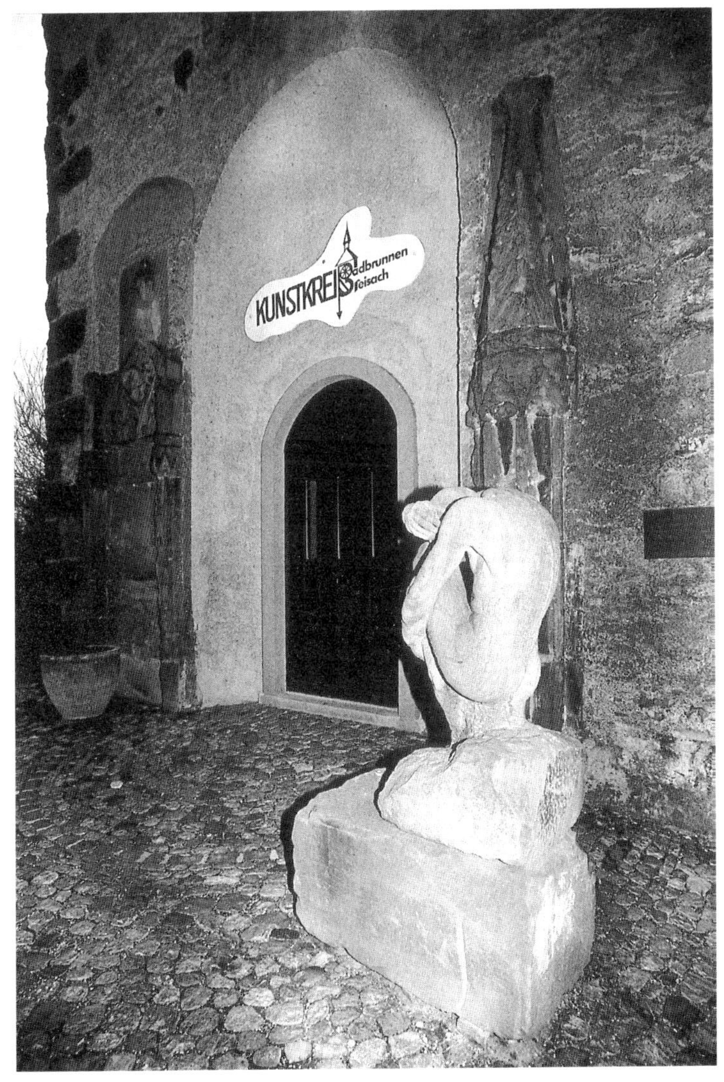

ambient and flash light are automatically balanced, and the flash unit is used as either the primary or the secondary source of light accordingly.

In normal lighting conditions the flash unit will take on a fill-in function. The flash sync. speed of $\frac{1}{100}$ sec. is automatically selected and the aperture is also controlled automatically, depending on the ambient light. This causes the background to be correctly lit, whilst fill-in light illuminates the foreground. The fill-in symbol appears in the viewfinder.

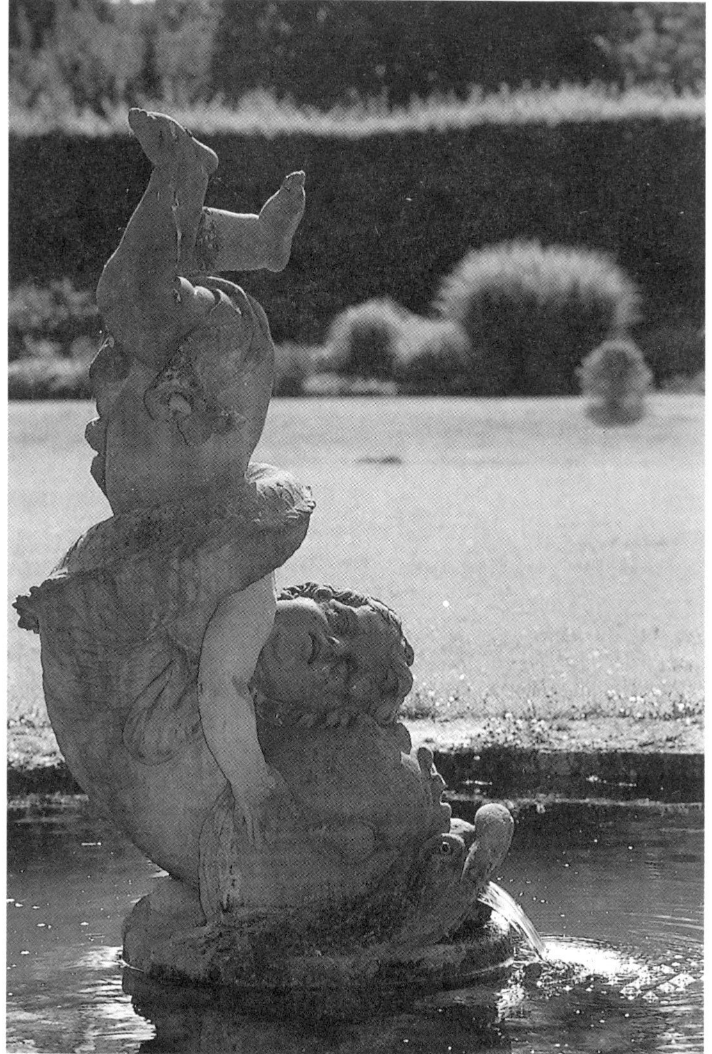

In this back-lit situation (left) the variable TTL flash control system in the automatic program rightly decided on fill-in flash (right).

In low lighting conditions the flash unit takes on the role of primary light source. The flash sync. speed of ¹⁄₁₀₀ sec. and an aperture of f/5.6 are selected automatically. The flash illumination is controlled precisely by the TTL flash control system.

If the ambient light is too bright for the flash sync. speed of ¹⁄₁₀₀ sec. and for the smallest aperture, the camera automatically switches to ¹⁄₂₀₀₀ sec. The aperture is now controlled according to the new shutter speed, so

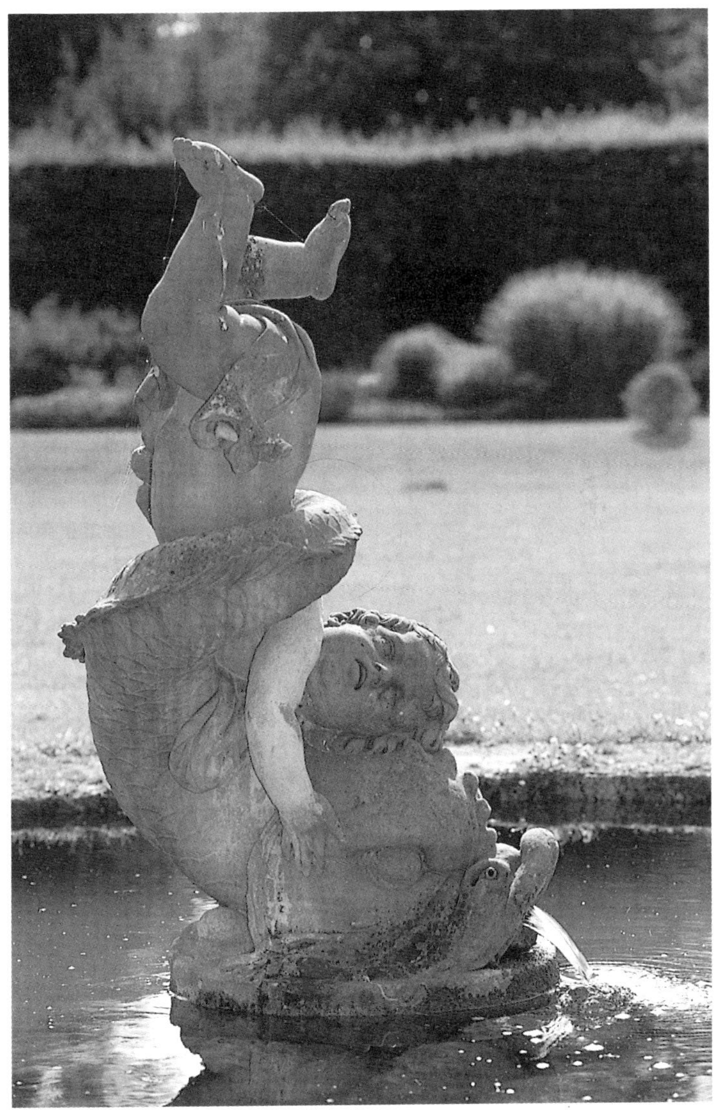

that the film will be exposed correctly. The new exposure data are displayed in the viewfinder. The flash unit will fire, but because of the fast shutter speed it does not affect the exposure.

6. The Leica R Lenses

Real progress makes no concessions to fashion but is distinguished by decades of hard work. This principle has benefitted not only the new lenses from the Leica stable, such as the Apo-Telyt 400mm,f/2.8 and the Apo-Extender 2X, but the older lenses also. Leica lenses designed some years ago can still compete with modern lens designs, indeed, some of these older lenses are still ahead of their time. This is demonstrated in their outstanding ability to produce a photographic image, unparalleled in the world of photographic lenses. The uncompromising quality of Leica lenses, down to the last detail, applies as much to their mechanics as to their optics. They have been computed to yield the finest *possible* photographic image, to be completely neutral in their colour rendering, to filter out UV light so that additional UV filters are unnecessary, to give long trouble-free service in all climatic conditions and to function perfectly in a temperature range between −25° and +60°. The automatic diaphragms are free of bounce and vibration, so that exposures are consistently accurate; the pupils are located in almost the same position in every lens, so that the viewfinder image is evenly illuminated with all focusing screens; no control elements protrude from the back of the mount, so Leica lenses can be stood on their bayonet mounts without damage. The choice of high-quality materials and the

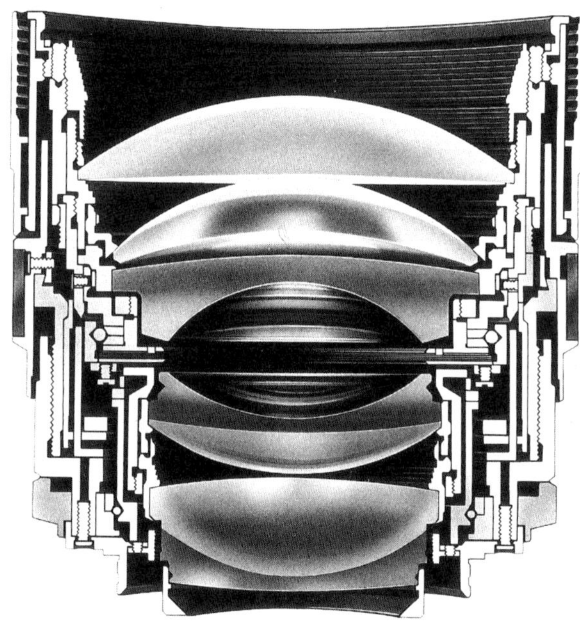

Special glasses and a brass and aluminium mount form the basis for highest optical quality and precision.

Lens	Maximum aperture focal length in mm	Angle of view	Number of elements/ components	Smallest aperture	Focusing range in m	Smallest object area in mm	Recommended filter size series	Length in mm	Diameter in mm	Weight in g	Order No.
SUPER-ELMAR-R	f / 3.5/15	110°	13/12[1]	22	∞ – 0.16	70 x 106	built in[2]	92.5	83.5	910	11213
FISHEYE-ELMARIT-R	f / 2.8/16	180°	11/ 8	16	∞ – 0.30	401 x 601	built in[2]	60	71	460	11222
ELMARIT®-R	f / 2.8/19	96°	12/10	22	∞ – 0.30	264 x 396	built in[3]	60	71	560	11258
SUPER-ANGULON®-R	f / 4/21	92°	10/ 8	22	∞ – 0.20	148 x 221	series 8.5	43.5	78	420	11813
ELMARIT-R	f / 2.8/24	84°	9/ 7[1]	22	∞ – 0.30	250 x 374	series 8	48.5	67	400	11257
ELMARIT-R	f / 2.8/28	76°	8/ 8	22	∞ – 0.30	188 x 282	series 7	40	63	310	11247
PC-SUPER-ANGULON®-R	f / 2.8/28	73/93° [4]	12/10[1]	22	∞ – 0.28	146 x 219	special filter 67 EW[5]	84	75	600	11812
SUMMILUX®-R	f / 1.4/35	64°	10/ 9[1]	16	∞ – 0.50	266 x 399	E 67	76	75	690	11144
SUMMICRON®-R	f / 2/35	64°	6/ 6	16	∞ – 0.30	140 x 210	E 55	54	66	430	11115
ELMARIT-R	f / 2.8/35	64°	7/ 6	22	∞ – 0.30	140 x 210	E 55	41.5	66	310	11251
PA-CURTAGON®-R	f / 4/35	67/78° [6]	7/ 6	22	∞ – 0.30	140 x 210	series 8	51	70	330	11202
SUMMILUX-R	f / 1.4/50	45°	7/ 6	16	∞ – 0.50	180 x 270	E 55	50.6	66.5	400	11777
SUMMICRON-R	f / 2/50	45°	6/ 4	16	∞ – 0.50	180 x 270	E 55	41	66	290	11216
MACRO-ELMARIT-R	f / 2.8/60	39°	6/ 5	22	∞ – 0.27 (with adapter to 1 : 1)	48 x 72 (24 x 36)	E 55	62.3 (92.3)	67.5	400 (530)	11253
SUMMILUX-R	f / 1.4/80	30°	7/ 5	16	∞ – 0.80	192 x 288	E 67	69	75	700	11881
SUMMICRON-R	f / 2/90	27°	5/ 4	16	∞ – 0.70	140 x 210	E 55	61	69	520	11254
ELMARIT-R	f / 2.8/90	27°	4/ 4	22	∞ – 0.70	140 x 210	E 55	57	67	450	11154
APO-MACRO-ELMARIT-R	f / 2.8/100	25°	8/ 6	22	∞ – 0.45 (with ELPRO 1 : 2 – 1.1 : 1)	48 x 72 (22 x 33)	E 60	104.5 (140)	73	760 (950)	11210
MACRO-ELMAR	f / 4/100	25°	4/ 3	22	to 1 : 1.6 (with adapter to 1 : 1.6)	72 x 108 (38 x 57)	E 55	90 (120)	67.5	530 (660)	11232
MACRO-ELMAR-R	f / 4/100	25°	4/ 3	22	Bellows only ∞ – 1.1 : 1)	24 x 36	E 55	62.5	68	290	11270
ELMARIT-R	f / 2.8/135	18°	5/ 4	22	∞ – 1.50	220 x 330	E 55	93	67	730	11211
ELMARIT-R	f / 2.8/180	14°	5/ 4	22	∞ – 1.80	193 x 290	E 67	121	75	810	11923
APO-TELYT-R	f / 3.4/180	14°	7/ 4	22	∞ – 2.50	276 x 414	E 60	135	68	750	11242
ELMAR®-R	f / 4/180	14°	5/ 4	22	∞ – 1.80	175 x 262	E 55	100	65.5	540	11922
TELYT®-R	f / 4/250	10°	7/ 6	22	∞ – 1.70	124 x 186	E 67	195	75	1280	11925
APO-TELYT-R	f / 2.8/280	8,5°	8/ 7	22	∞ – 2,50 [7]	195 x 293	E 112 series 5,5	261	125	2800	11263
TELYT-R	f / 4,8/350	7°	7/ 5	22	∞ – 3,00	171 x 257	E 77	286	83,5	1820	11915
APO-TELYT-R	f / 2.8/400	6°	11/ 9	22	∞ – 4,70 [7]	280 x 420	series 5,5	365	166	5500	11260
TELYT-R	f / 6,8/400	6°	2/ 1	32	∞ – 3,60 [8]	158 x 236	series 7	384	89	1830	11953
TELYT-R (System Novoflex)	f / 6,8/400	6°	2/ 1	32	∞ – 2,40 [8]	90 x 135	filter drawer	406	89	2930	11926
MR-TELYT-R	f / 8/500	5°	5/ 5	8	∞ – 4,00	180 x 270	5 filters in delivery [9]	121	87	750	11243
TELYT-R (System Novoflex)	f / 6,8/560	4,3°	2/ 1	32	∞ – 4,15 [8]	124 x 187	filter drawer	534	98	3200	11927
TELYT-S	f / 6.3/800	3°	3/ 1	32	∞ – 12.50	320 x 480	series 7	790	152	6860	11921
VARIO-ELMAR-R	f / 3.5–4.5/ 28–70	76 – 34°	11/ 8	22	∞ – 0.50	336 x 504 114 x 216	E 60	84	74.8	465	11265
VARIO-ELMAR-R	f / 3.5/35 – 70	64 – 34°	8/ 7	22	∞ – 1.00	632 x 947 338 x 507	E 67	66.5	76.5	450	11248
VARIO-ELMAR-R	f / 4/70 – 210	35 – 12°	12/ 9	22	∞ – 1.10	264 x 396 96 x 144	E 60	157	73.5	720	11246

[1] with floating elements

[2] filter turret with UV-yellow-orange and blue conversion filter for artificial light exposures on daylight film

[3] filter turret with neutral coating filter (ND x 1) yellow-green-orange and blue conversion filter for artificial light on daylight film

[4] horizontal or vertical offset up to 11 mm, diagonal offset up to 9.5 mm

[5] filter for special wide-angle holder with aperture, from B & W Filterfabrik, D-6550, Bad Kreuznach

[6] offset up to 7 mm

[7] inner focusing

[8] fast-focusing attachment by adjustable lens front component

[9] special screw-in filter M 32 x 0.5: UV neutral gray 4 x, yellow, orange

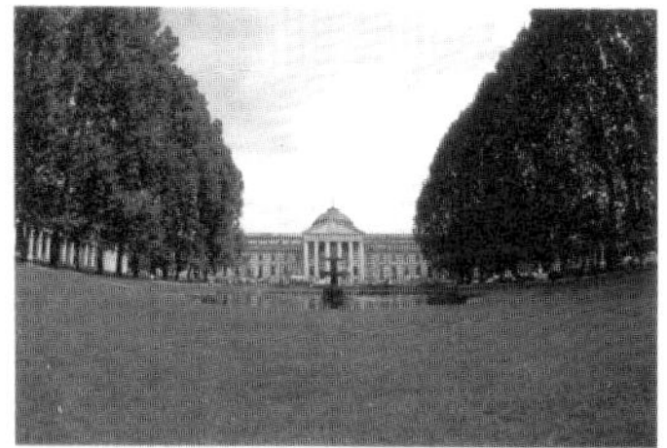

16 mm Fisheye

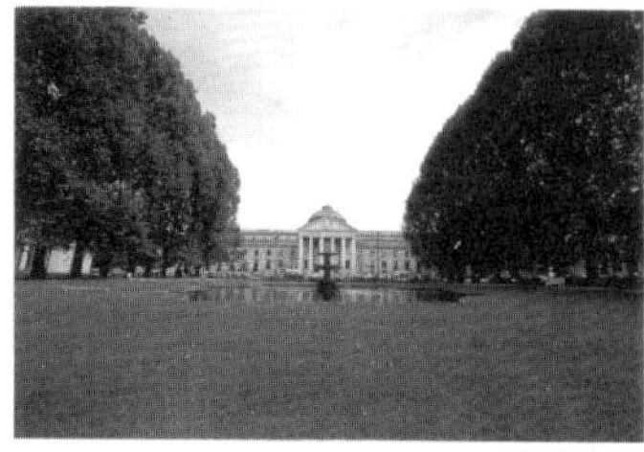

15mm lens

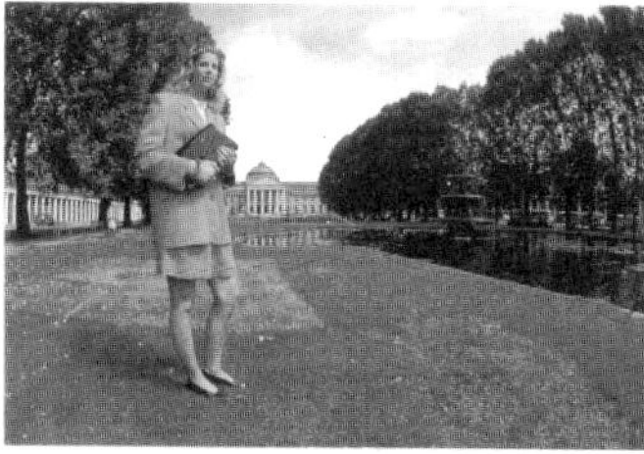

16mm Fisheye, distance 1.40m

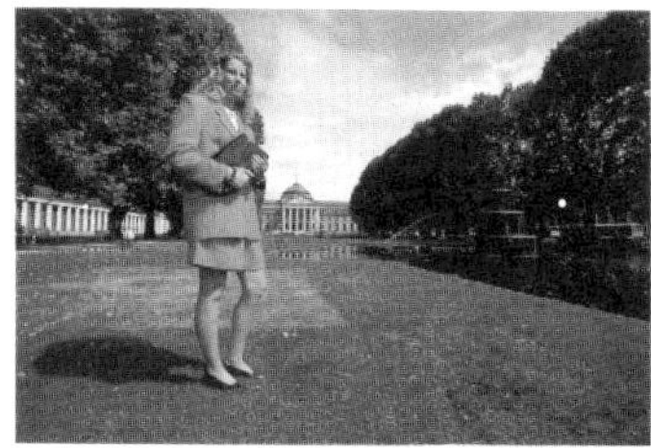

15mm lens, distance 1.35m

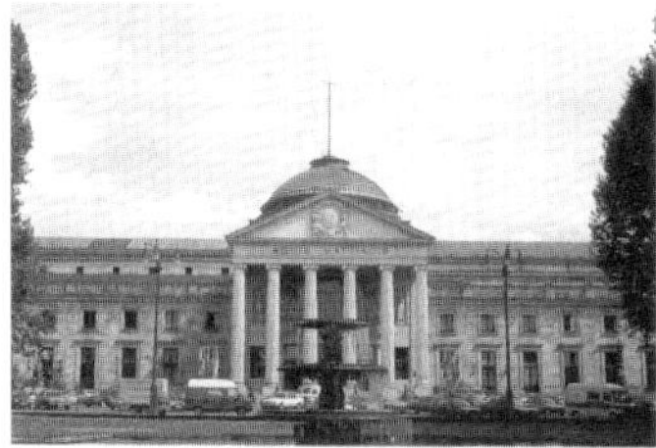

50mm lens

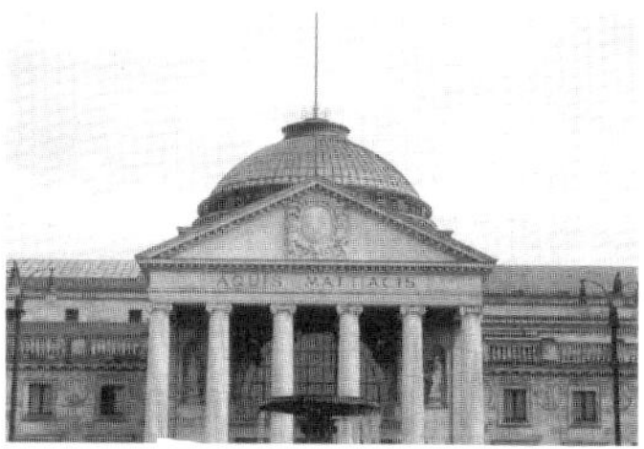

90mm lens

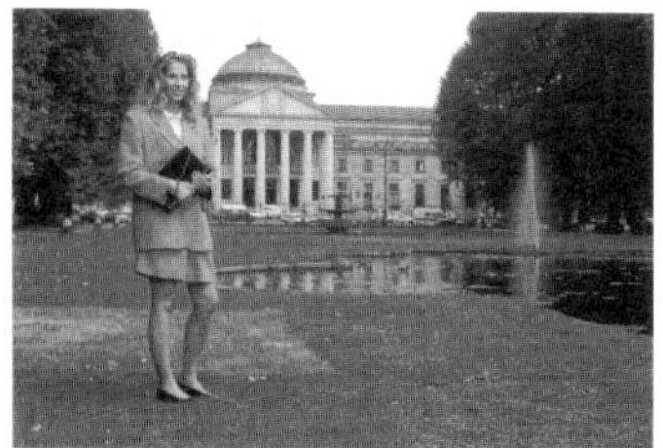

50mm lens, distance 4.50m

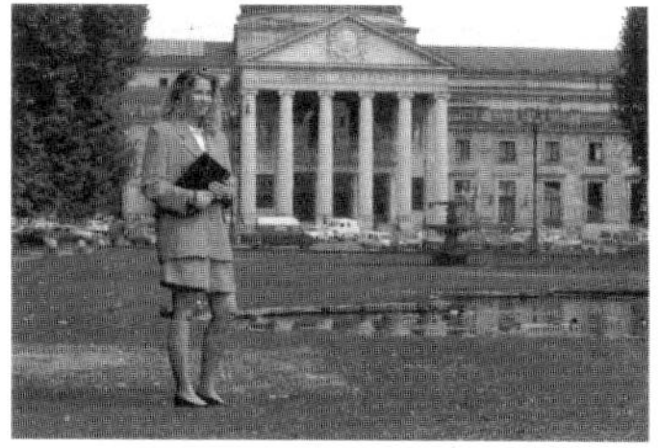

90mm lens, distance 8.10m

Focal length and perspective comparisons with Leica R lenses.
The choice of shooting distance as well as the camera position – not the focal length –
determine the perspective. The focal length only determines the angle of view, as can be
seen in the top sequence in each case. The shots in this sequence were taken from the
same shooting position with different focal lengths. The focal length comparison has the

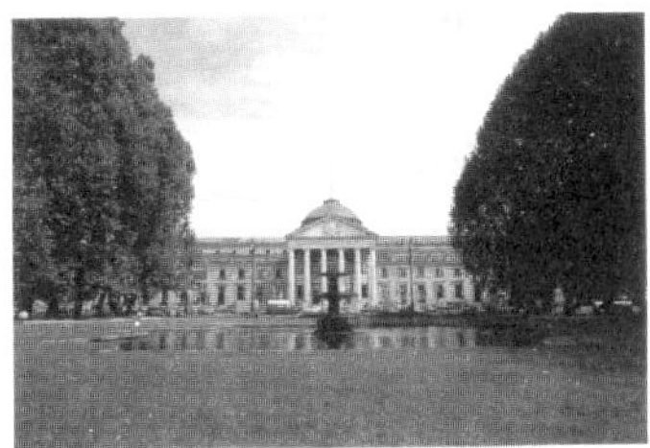

24mm lens

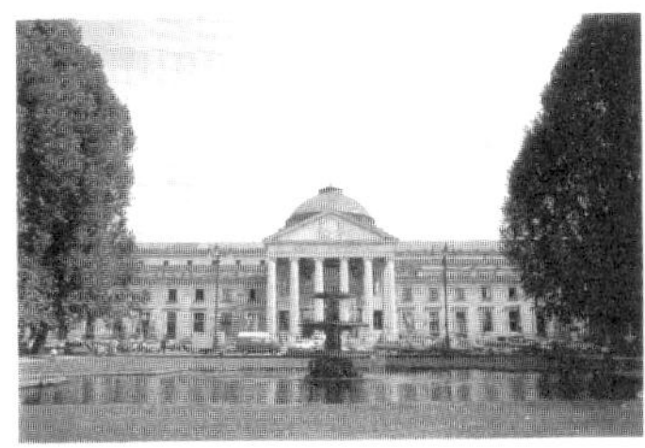

35mm lens

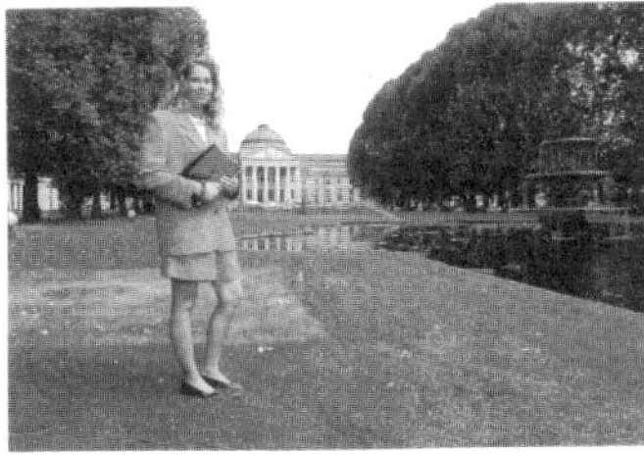

24mm lens, distance 2.16m

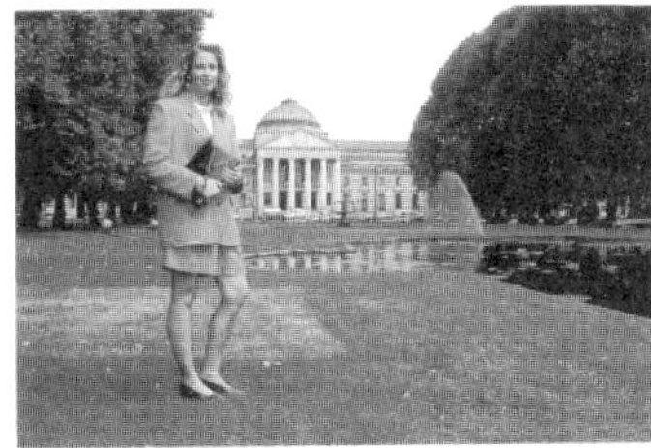

35mm lens, distance 3.15m

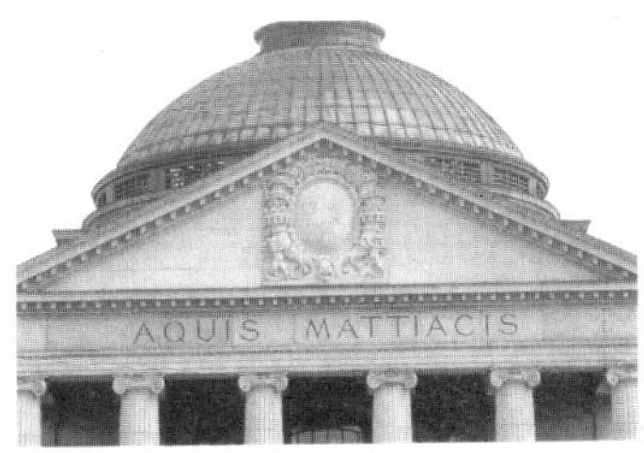

180mm lens

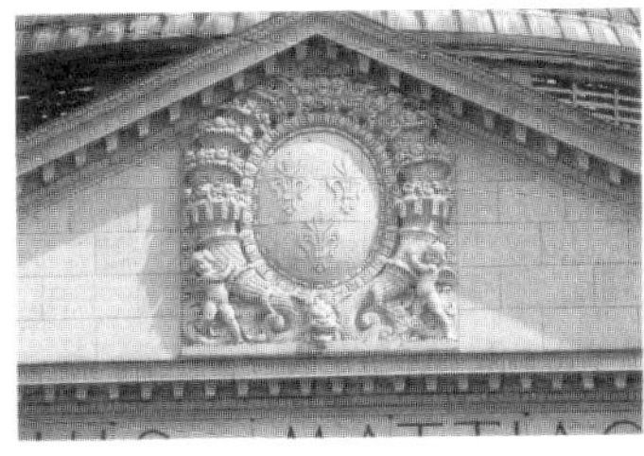

400mm lens

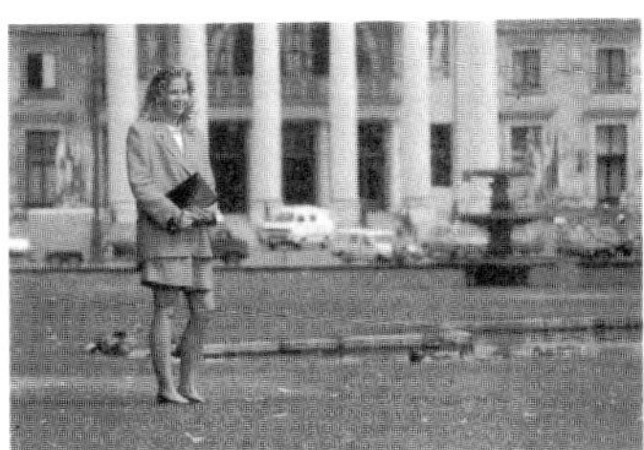

180mm lens, distance 16.20m

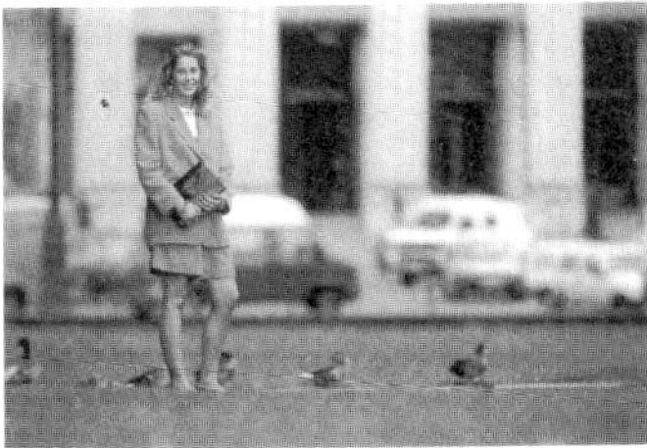

400mm lens, distance 36.00m

same effect as gradually increasing sectional enlargements from an extreme wide-angle shot. In a perspective comparison the reproduction ratio of the main subject (the young woman) is maintained at the different focal lengths through changes in the shooting position. The change in focal length and shooting position creates different spatial impressions, which also affect the overall message of the picture

meticulous quality control and testing of each individual lens guarantee it will have a consistently high optical and mechanical performance for decades.

Over the years Leica have developed many special glasses with unique properties for their lenses. This has enabled them to produce high speed lenses, very long focus lenses with near-apochromatic properties, and their apochromatic lenses without resorting to plastic elements, crystalline elements or aspherical surfaces. All but the cheapest photographic lenses for a hundred years or more have been corrected achromatically, which means they bring two different wavelengths of light to focus at the same point. This generally meant at the blue-yellow end of the spectrum. Apochromatic lenses are corrected to bring three different wavelengths to focus at the same point, including the red end of the spectrum. The consequent improvement in sharpness can be very noticeable with long focal lengths. With Leica apochromatic lenses there is no need to apply a focus correction for infra-red film so they are not provided with an infra-red index mark.

The range of Leica R lenses is such that you will find a suitable lens for every photographic task in a focal length range from 15mm to 800mm. Special lenses such as shift, macro, or magnifying lenses further extend the possible applications of the Leica R7. The pages which follow contain a brief description of every Leica R lens along with its practical applications.

Interchangeable lenses

Interchangeable lenses greatly increase the range of applications of a camera, and they also extend our scope for turning photographic ideas into pictures. But firstly it i necessary to understand the role of lenses in the creation of pictorial images. The obligatory focal length comparison, where a subject is photographed from the same distance with different lenses – from extreme wide-angle to extreme telephoto – is quite irrelevant for picture composition as such. The focal length comparison has the same effect as increasing enlargements from smaller and smaller portions of an extreme wide-angle photograph (although in practice the grain of the film would impose a limit). The focal length comparison, however, does demonstrate that the focal length does not affect the perspective. Perspective is only affected by the distance of the camera from the subject. So a perspective comparison will tell us more about picture composition and focal length.

In our picture sequence the reproduction ratio of the main subject (the young woman) is maintained throughout the changes in the focal length and camera position. The perspective comparison shows the different spatial effects that are caused by changing the focal length and camera position.

Even for experienced photographers, it is worth while taking time out to experiment with the different focal lengths you have available. Become fully familiar with all the possibilities of each lens. A little photographic excursion, taking along just one lens, is the best way to familiarize yourself with the way a lens 'sees' its surroundings. Select just one subject, trying different shooting positions and distances: keep checking the depth of field by pressing the depth of field lever, and take it into account for picture composition. Don't be afraid to use the portrait format too. Our comparison photographs of the Munich Propylaea on page 82, taken with the Fisheye-Elmarit-R 16mm,f/2.8, show how much image effects and messages can differ. In this way you will discover two or three 'favourite' focal lengths, which you will probably use for more than 80 per cent of your photographs.

An important point to take into account is the fact that lenses 'see' differently to the human eye. We see things three-dimensionally, and our 'optical' perception really takes place in our brains. But a lens reproduces images in two dimensions, and the spatial impression of a photograph mostly derives from its lighting and the careful use of the depth of field. Furthermore, the image perceived by the eye is, in a sense, permanently 'corrected', so that, for example, we do not perceive converging verticals with the eye because the brain knows they do not converge in reality. Photographic lenses, on the other hand, record what they see. Moreover, our perception is selective, we see only what seems important to us, but the lens registers everything that is captured within its angle of view. How often have you failed to notice the overhead wires in a picturesque village when you took the picture, only to be disappointed when they unexpectedly appeared on the enlargement?

The art of photography means conscious, focal length-specific, picture composition. These notes can only cover some of the basic principles; they can never be a substitute for your own experiments and experience.

The extreme wide-angle range (15mm to 21mm)

Extreme wide-angle lenses with focal lengths between 15mm and 21mm have important technical applications for recording large areas of a subject, usually in confined spaces. But photographers in the past two decades have thoroughly explored their use in pictorial composition. Because of their wide angle of view (between 110° and 92° in the diagonal) extreme wide-angle lenses offer a different, rather unusual view of things. An unusual view because it is so much wider than our own angle of vision, and therefore our way of seeing the world. This opens up new creative possibilities for picture composition, but it also makes the use of these lenses more difficult (not only for beginners): there can be problems with the exposure, with aiming the camera, as well as with the picture composition.

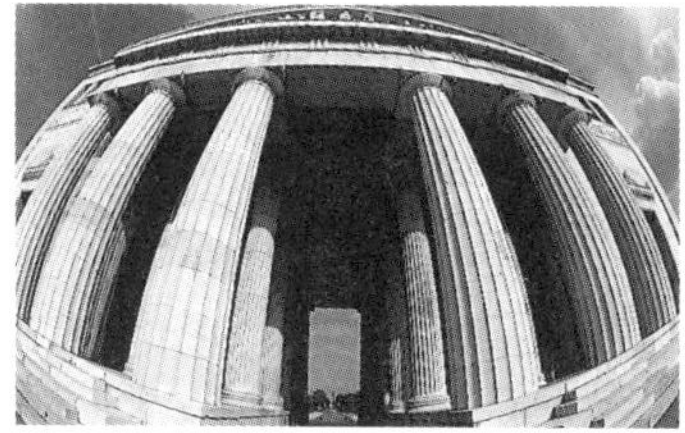
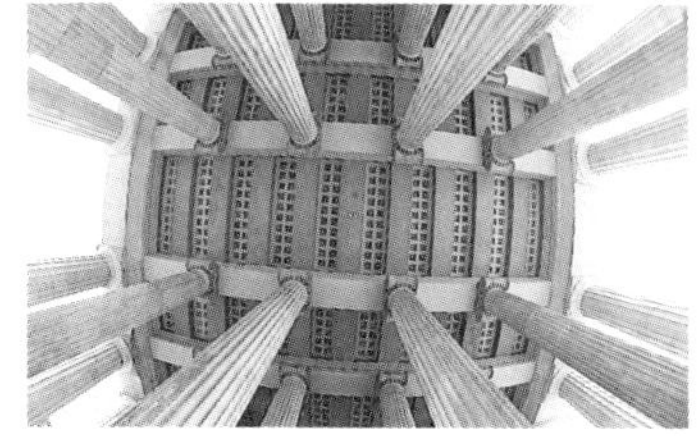
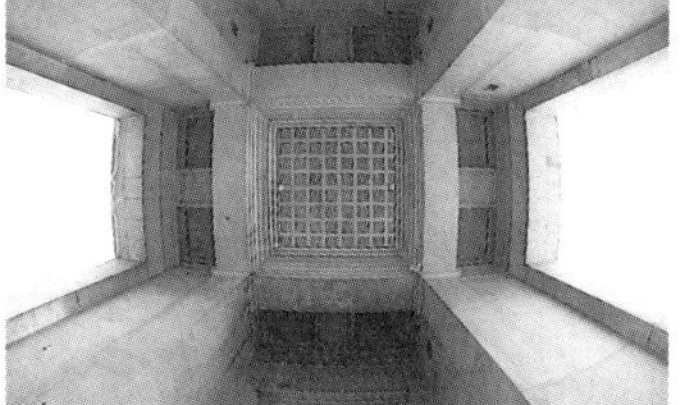
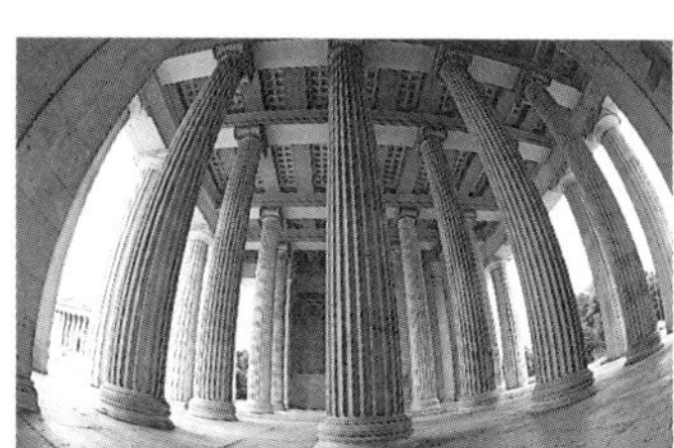
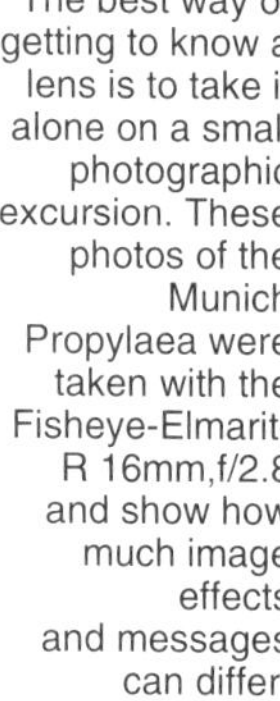

The best way of getting to know a lens is to take it alone on a small photographic excursion. These photos of the Munich Propylaea were taken with the Fisheye-Elmarit-R 16mm,f/2.8 and show how much image effects and messages can differ.

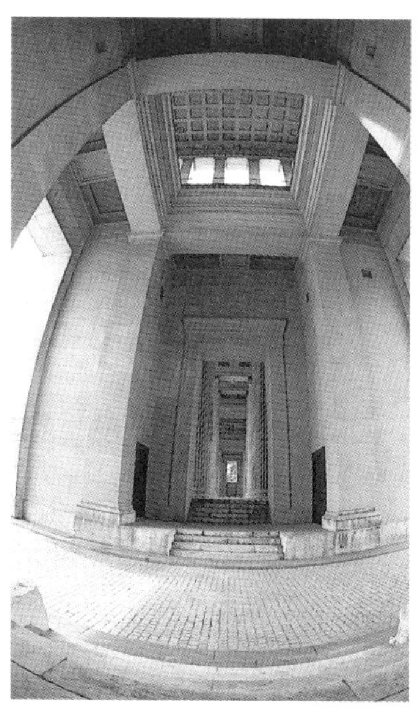
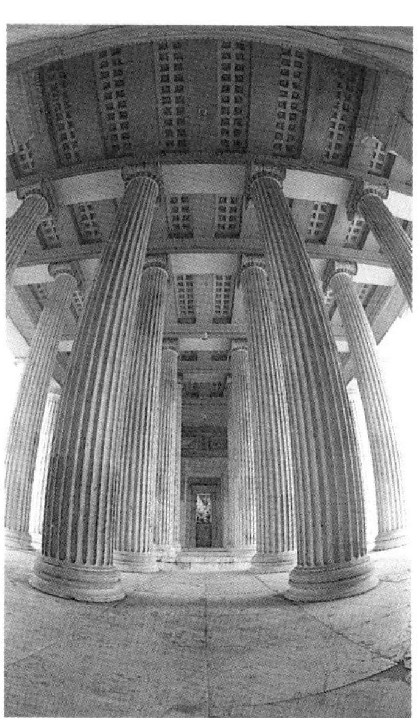

Extreme wide-angle lenses produce a dramatic spatial effect. The foreground dominates the picture, whilst the background recedes. At their a closest focusing distances, 16cm in the case of the Super-Elmar-R 15mm,f/3.5, even small subjects can be made to dominate their surroundings. Picture composition becomes very critical in photographs with a huge foreground, strongly receding background, and wide horizon.

Extreme wide-angle lenses offer a very great depth of field, even at maximum aperture, which can be increased still further by stopping down. This means that you can reproduce both foreground and back-

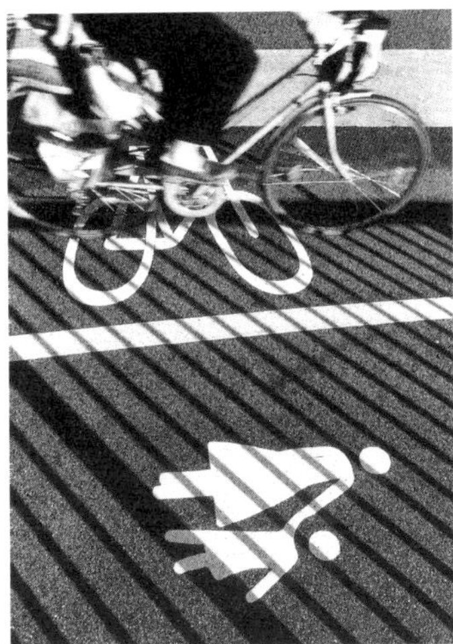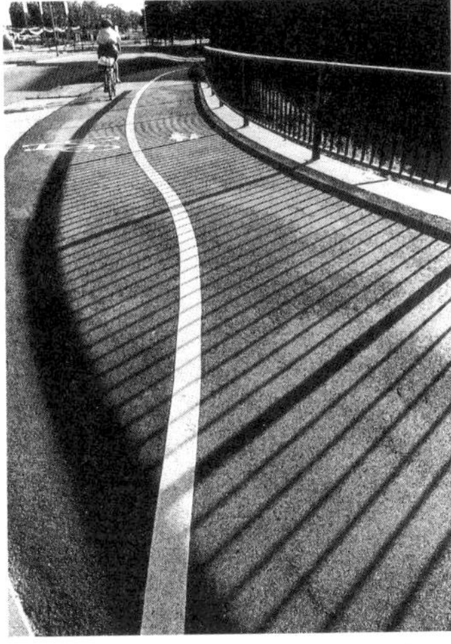

This sequence is part of a report on cycling paths in Freiburg in Germany. It was taken with extreme wide-angle lenses to convey an impression to the viewer of being right in the midst of events.

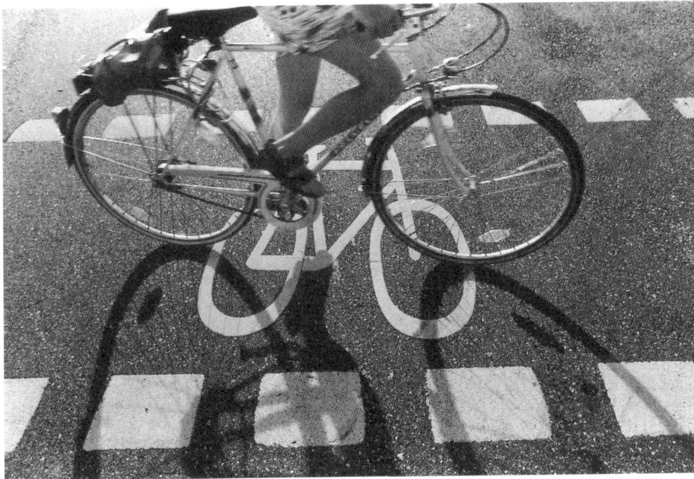

ground in focus simultaneously. The enormous depth of field and the strongly emphasized receding perspective increase the impression of space and lend the image great depth and width. Photojournalists make particular use of this when the proximity of the camera to the main subject and the simultaneous sharp reproduction of its wide surroundings give the impression to the viewer of being in the midst of an event: the enormous depth of field also means they do not have to worry about focusing.

Vignetting can be a problem with extreme wide-angle lenses, partly the result of the laws of optics and partly due to physical obstruction by the lens mount or attachments. The second form has been largely eliminated from Leica lenses by careful design. The 'natural' vignetting is

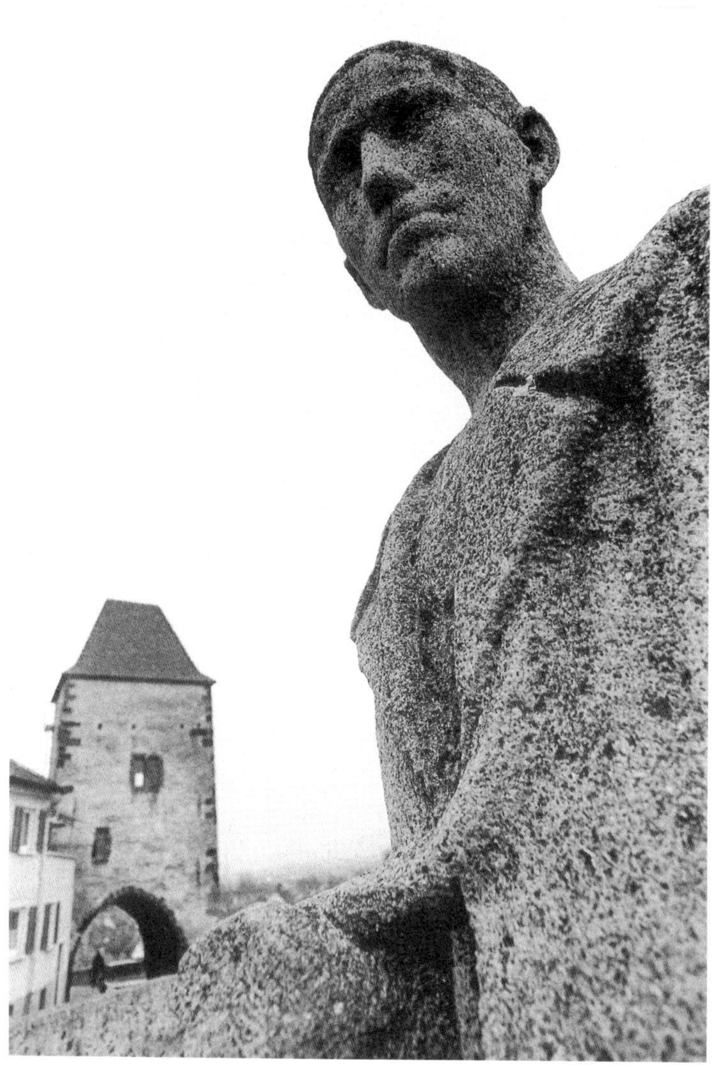

Don't be afraid of extreme wide-angle lenses and unconventional shooting positions.

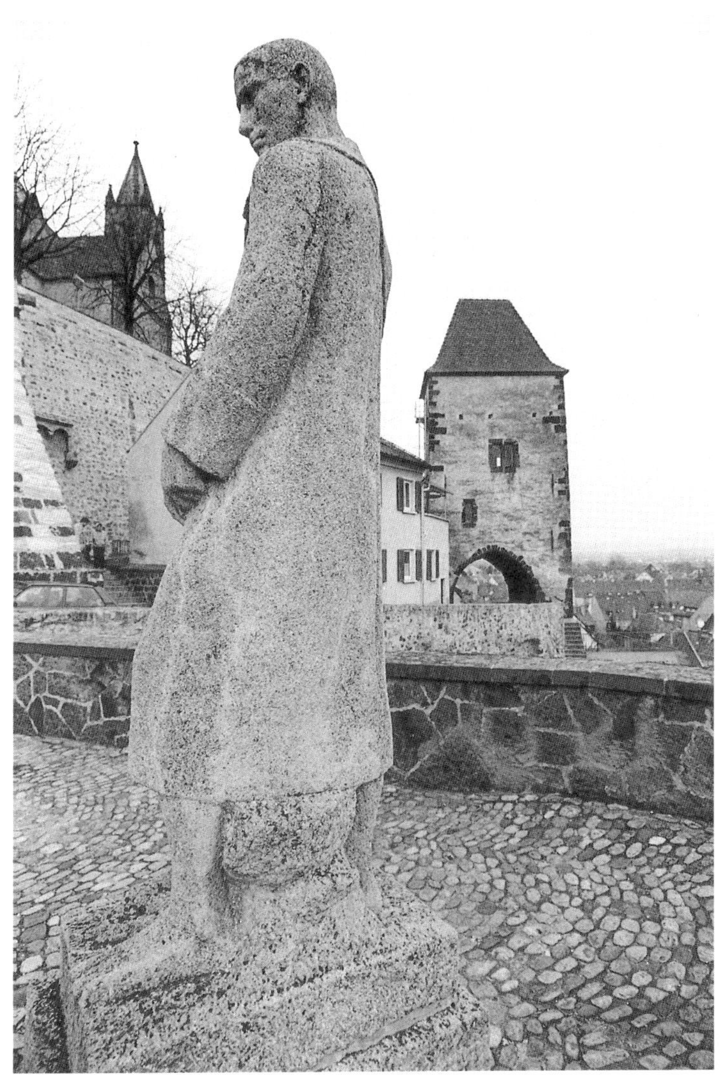

apparent only with certain subjects, such as landscapes with large areas of blue sky where there may be a noticeable falling off in brightness at the edges of the frame, particularly at maximum aperture. Stopping down by two stops should cure the vignetting effect.

Distortion is a reproduction fault which, in accordance with optical laws, increases with the angle of view and causes straight lines to be reproduced curved. But with the extreme wide-angle lenses that go with the Leica R7, distortion is minimal and can be disregarded in the majority of situations. It is only likely to be noticeable at the edges of the frame with subjects that have clear straight lines, such as in architectural photography.

A focusing screen with grid divisions is best with extreme wide-angle lenses, not only for aligning the camera, but also for focusing, because focusing is possible at any point on the groundglass screen.

Careful use of the exposure meter is even more important than usual when taking landscape photographs with extreme wide-angle lenses. Because of the very wide angle of view the sky will often take up a large part of the frame. With a high degree of contrast between sky and landscape, the integral metering system can be deceived, causing the foreground of the landscape to be underexposed. Depending on the subject contrast and the amount of sky in the photograph, an exposure compensation of between +1 and +2 EV may be required. When using selective metering, particularly if the horizon is located in the lower half of the image, make sure that the metering area does not capture too much sky. In this case the right choice of metering method would be a substitute measurement of an area corresponding to a grey card and subsequent locking of the exposure, or better still a two-point measurement.

Super-Elmar-R 15mm, f/3.5

This is without doubt an extraordinary lens. It is not a fish-eye, its 110° angle of view in the diagonal produces an image with very little distortion. For a lens of this focal length the Super-Elmar-R 15mm,f/3.5 is also extremely well corrected in other respects. Its sharpness and contrast are considerable even at the maximum aperture, and the vignetting effect usually found in this focal length range is largely eliminated when stopped down to f/5.6 or smaller apertures. Its very good reproduction quality is maintained even in the close-up range. At the

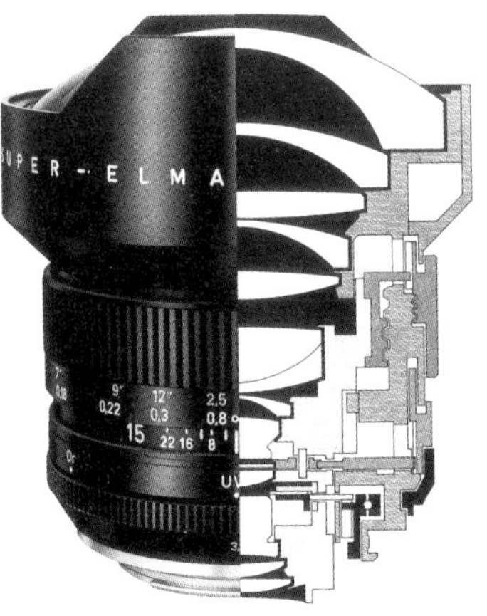

closest focusing distance of 16cm the reproduction ratio is 1:3, which allows models, for example, to be photographed with a pronounced wide-angle characteristic. The lens has many possible applications, but the breathtaking perspective can probably be put to best creative use in landscape and architectural photography. It is also ideal for interiors.

The Super-Elmar-R 15mm,f/3.5 comes with an integral filter turret containing four filters: UV, yellow, orange, and blue. The UV filter should be in place all the time, unless one of the other filters is to be used because these filters are part of the optical construction of the lens.

It is not possible to provide an effective lens hood in this focal length range because of the extreme angle of view. The small fins are there to protect the exposed front element. Providing shade with a hat or other object isn't without risks either – all too often you will end up getting the hat in the angle of view instead of the reflections you intended to prevent!

Elmarit-R 19mm,f/2.8

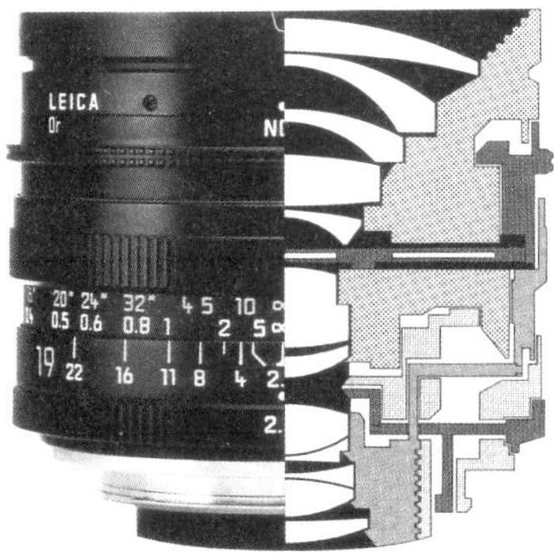

Compared to its predecessor, the new Elmarit-R 19mm,f/2.8 has become 17mm slimmer, even with its integral filter turret, similar to that on the 15mm Super-Elmar-R. The optical performance has been further improved, distinguished by good contrast and excellent flatness of field, and is maintained even in the close-up range, thanks to internal focusing. Closest focusing distance is 30cm, providing a reproduction ratio of 1:11, allowing model photography with a realistic impression. The lens is very well-suited to landscapes, photojournalism, industrial, and architectural photography. Its great depth of field and high speed make it excellent for interior work in low light or for snapshots, conveying a sense of being in the thick of events. The clip-on lens hood has its own rectangular protective cap.

Super-Angulon-R 21mm,f/4

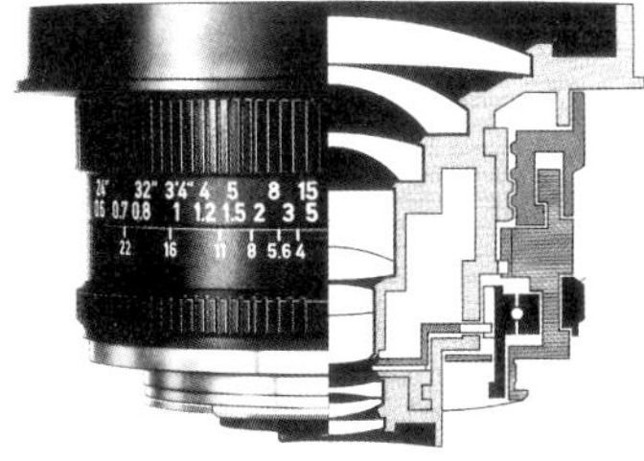

The Super-Angulon-R 21mm,f/4 is an extreme wide-angle lens of more modest maximum aperture and with excellent reproduction characteristics. The whole image area is illuminated evenly, even at maximum aperture. The sharpness and contrast are excellent and do not decrease towards the image

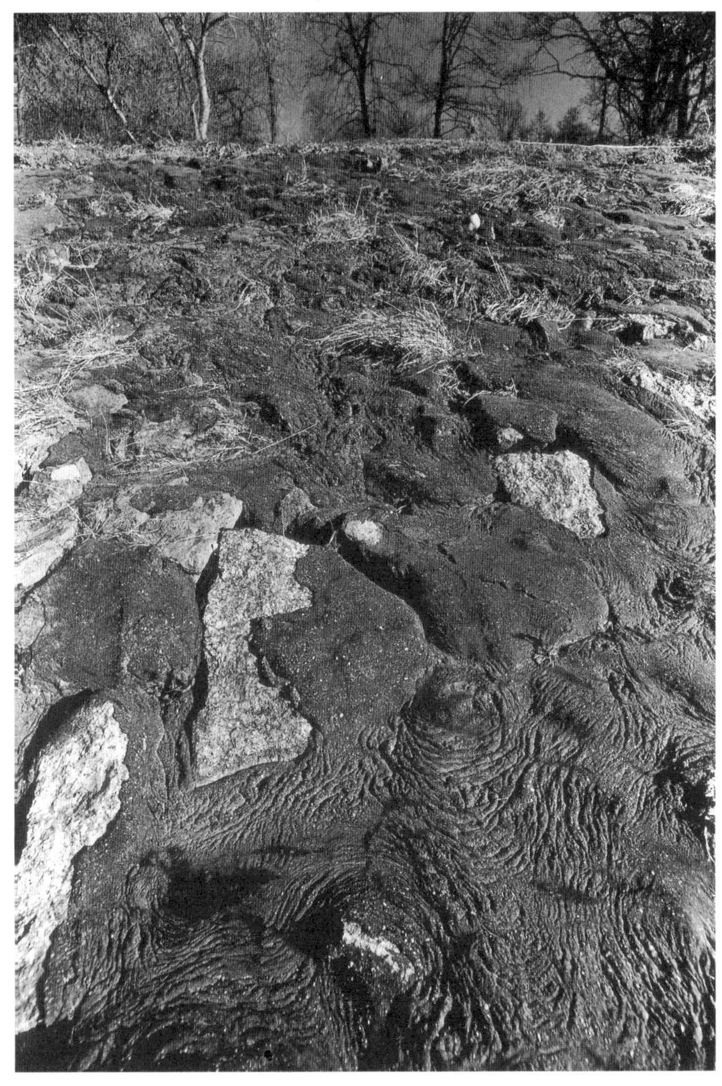

Great depth of field at close range is available with the Elmarit-R 19mm,f/2.8.

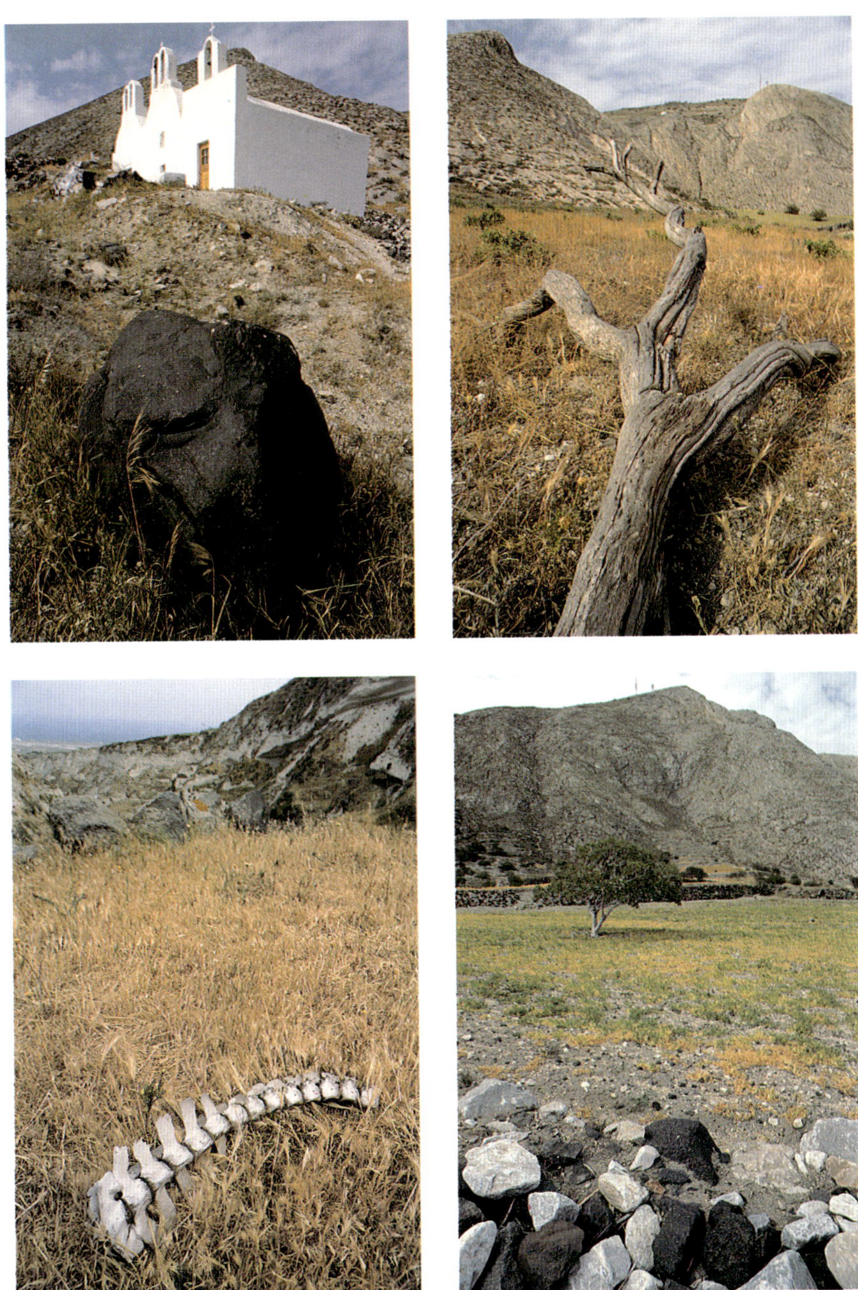

A great deal of emphasis on the foreground with a receding background is a characteristic of extreme wide-angle lenses.

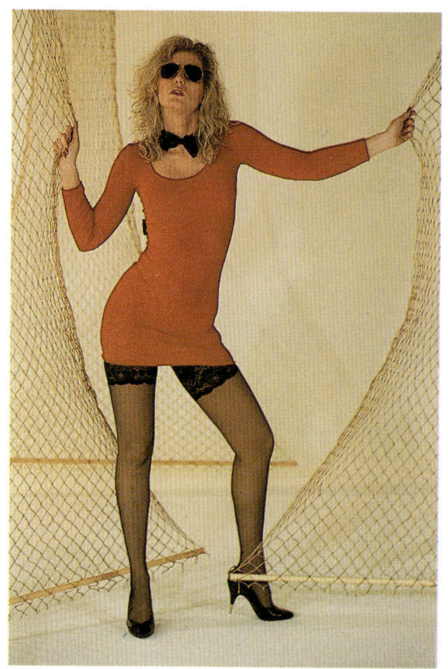 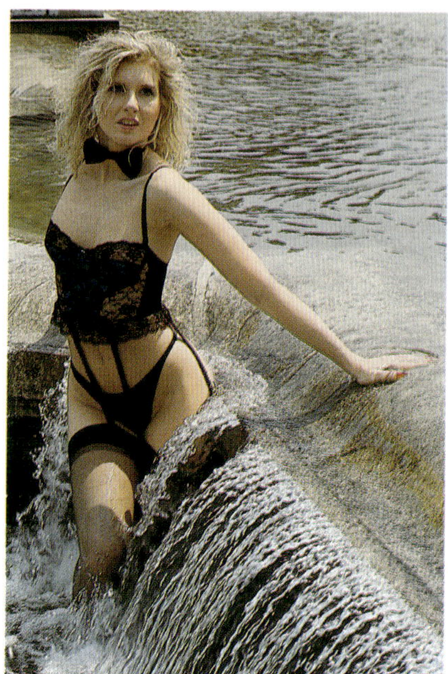

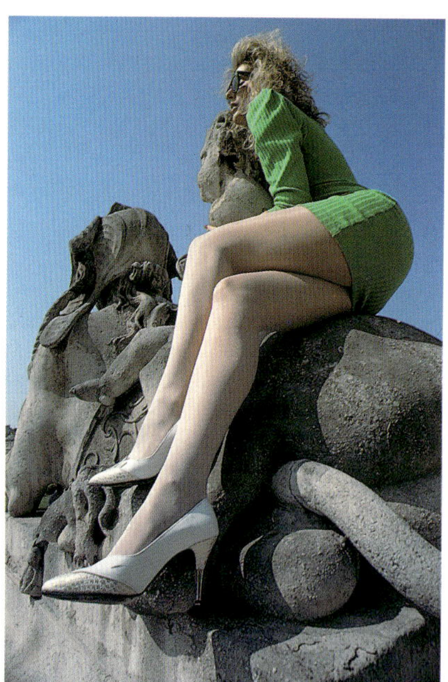 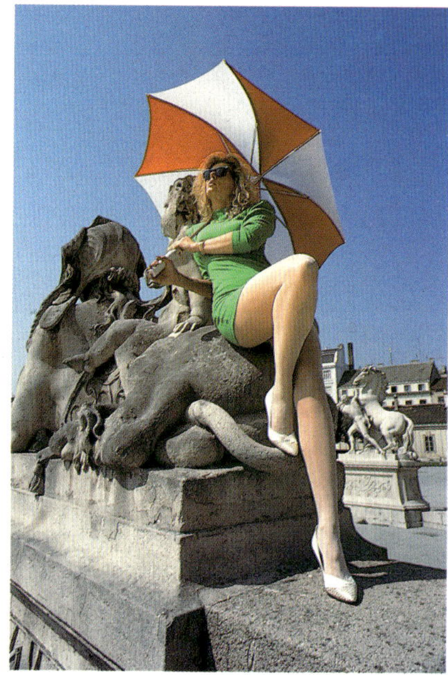

The Leica system is ideal for professional glamour photography. Motorized film transport and the handgrip are a valuable help for these applications. The high-quality Leica R lenses lend the shots a remarkable brilliance, which cannot be fully appreciated in the reproductions here.

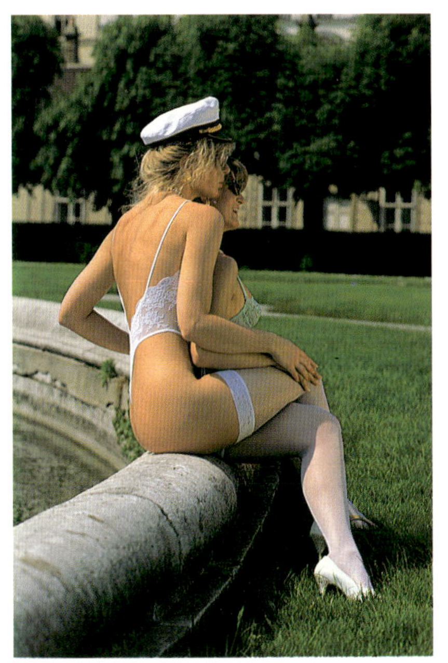
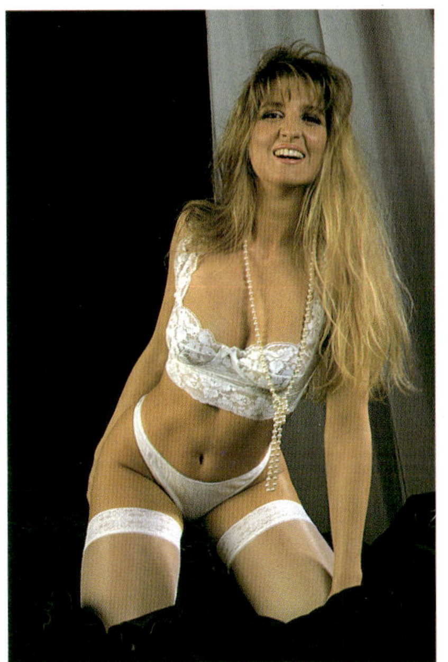
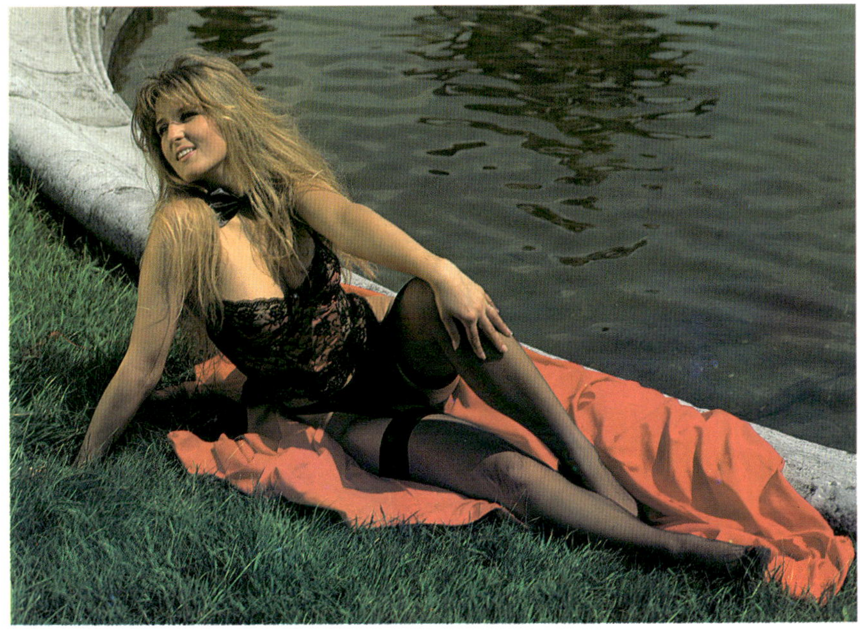

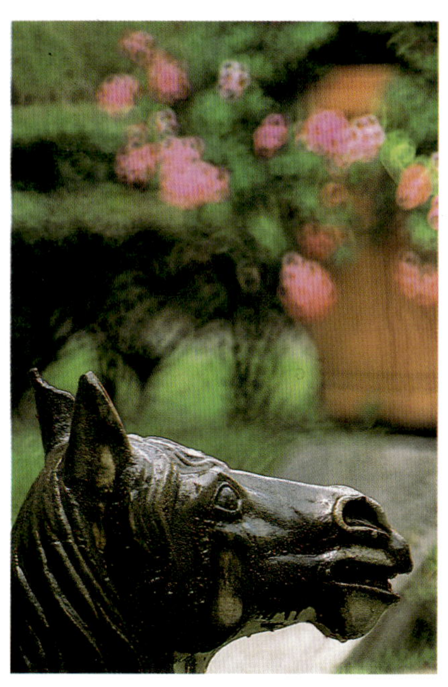
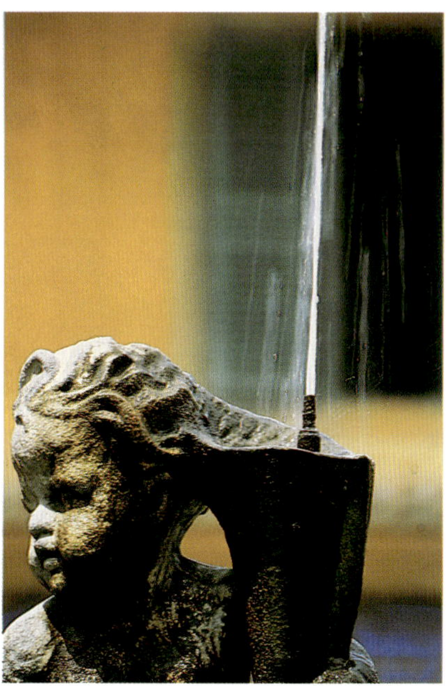
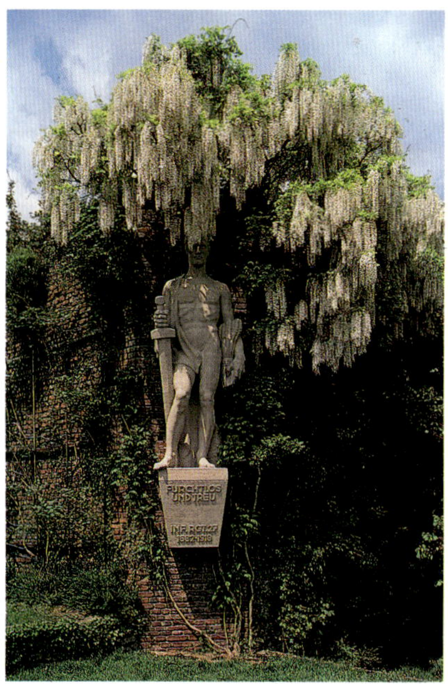
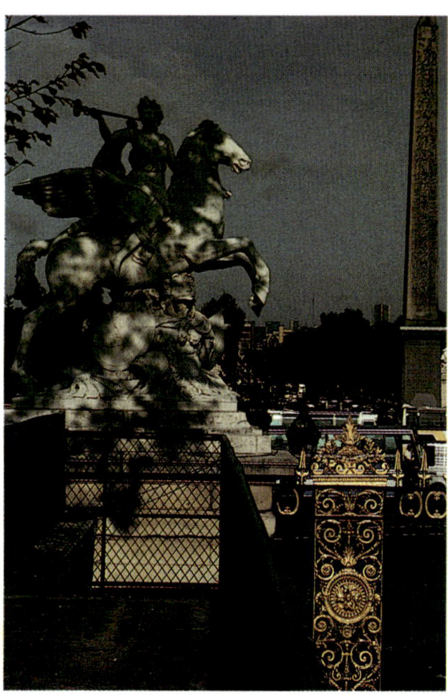

Each subject needs to be carefully and thoughtfully exposed if it is to be reproduced to maximum effect.

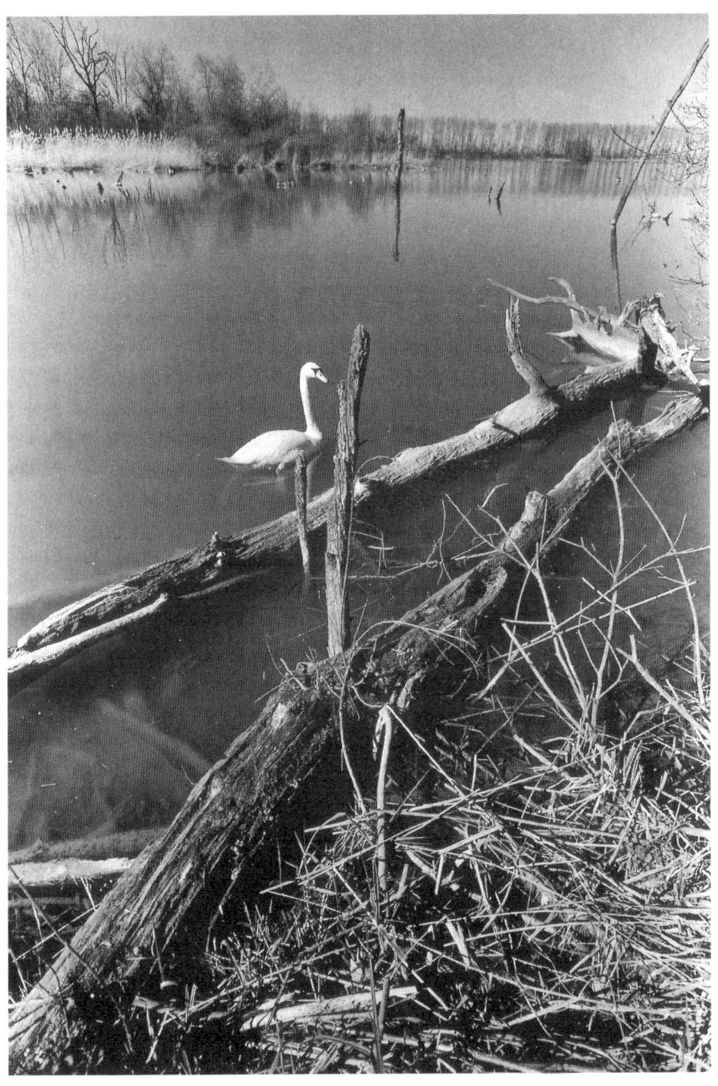

The Super-Angulon-R 21mm,f/4 gives this picture an impression of great space.

edges. Distortion is fairly slight and can be ignored in photographic practice. At the closest focusing distance of 20cm the lens achieves a reproduction ratio of 1:6. The excellent optical performance is also maintained in the close-up range. Weighing only 410g, it is an ideal travel lens and covers the same applications as the 19mm Elmarit.

The medium wide-angle Range (24mm to 28mm)

The medium wide-angle range with focal lengths of 24mm and 28mm forms the transition between the extreme and the classical wide-angle lenses. This central position accounts for the universal usefulness of both these lenses. Their relatively wide angle of view lends the results a clear wide-angle character, without over-emphasizing the perspective. Provided the camera is aligned accurately, the photographs produced will appear balanced, even though the angle of view is one-and-a-half times to twice as wide as our normal angle of vision. But if the camera is tilted, or if you shoot from a very low position, the perspective will still appear exaggerated.

Because of their great depth of field and their relatively high speed the Elmarit-R 24mm,f/2.8 and Elmarit-R 28mm,f/2.8 are ideal lenses for photojournalism. Landscapes, townscapes, snapshots, or staged portraits are other applications where both lenses will show their strengths.

Elmarit-R 24mm,f/2.8

Despite its fairly high speed the Elmarit-R 24mm,f/2.8 delivers very good sharpness and contrast, which are maintained even in the close-up range thanks to floating elements. The closest focusing distance is 30cm. Even at maximum aperture illumination into the image corners is fairly even, and distortion should only become noticeable at the image edges of critical subjects. Professional photographers like to use the Elmarit-R 24mm,f/2.8 for available-light interior photography. The over-emphasis on the foreground and receding effect of the background is not as radical as with extreme wide-angle lenses, but still clearly noticeable.

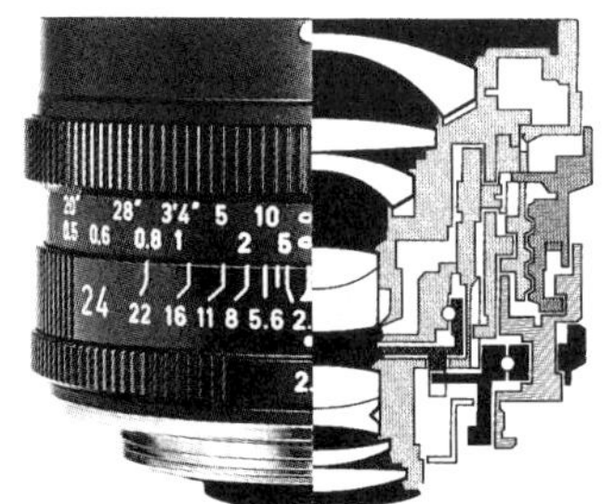

Elmarit-R 24mm,f/2.8

Series 8 filters can be inserted into the lens hood supplied with the lens (the polarizing filter can still be rotated). The internal thread has a diameter of 60mm (although vignetting can occur if screw-on filters in thick mounts are used).

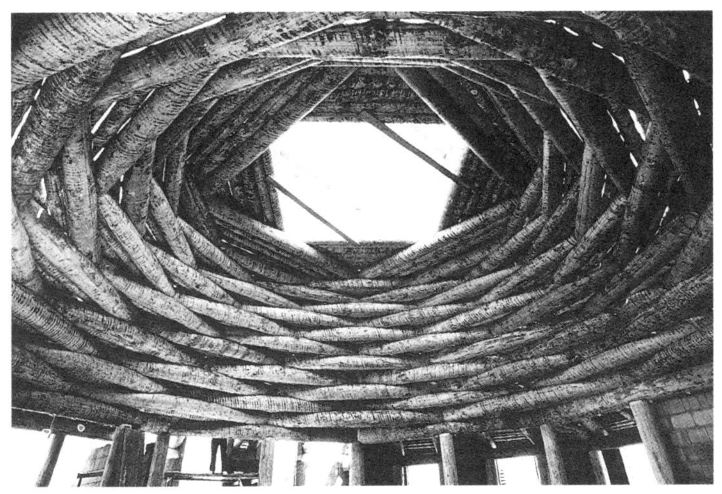

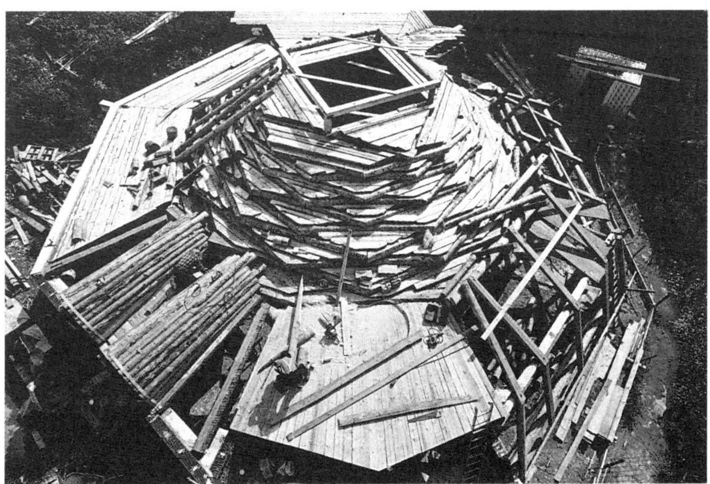

Two shots documenting the construction of an 'eco-house': the interior shot was taken with the Elmarit-R 24mm,f/2.8, the exterior with the Elmarit-R 28mm,f/2.8 (from a crane).

Elmarit-R 28mm,f/2.8

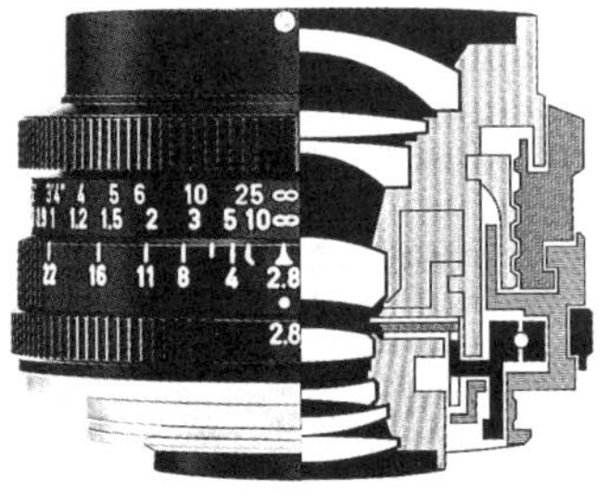

Many photographers consider the Elmarit-R 28mm,f/2.8 to be a universal wide-angle lens. With an angle of view of 76° it has a wide-angle effect that many people find pleasant. Handling the lens is easier because a slight tilt on the camera is not so disasterous as with shorter focal lengths. Even at the maximum aperture the lens is well-corrected for the range between 1.5m and infinity. The lens is characterized by faultless brilliance and reproduction of detail. The inherent slight distortion can normally be ignored in practice. Stopping down to f/5.6 or f/8 will eliminate slight vignetting. The lens achieves a reproduction ratio of 1:8 at the closest focusing distance of 30cm, but it is not specifically corrected for the close-up range, so when shooting at distances below 1.5m stop down to f/8 or f/11 to maintain its very good reproduction quality.

At a length of just 40mm and a weight of 310g the Elmarit-R 28mm,f/2.8 is an ideal travel lens and very useful all-rounder.

The classical wide-angle range (35mm)

A focal length of 35mm was for a long time regarded as the standard for a wide-angle lens because there weren't any others, or at least none that were sufficiently well-corrected. But now we have well-corrected wider-angle and extreme wide-angle lenses, and familiarity with pictures taken with them has caused a change in the way we view photographs. Consequently, photographs taken with a 35mm lens are no longer perceived as typically wide-angle, but rather as 'normal'. So the 35mm lens lost its appeal as a wide-angle lens, and at the same time started to appeal as a standard lens. With an angle of view of 64° the 35mm lens captures a substantially wider view than the 50mm standard lens, whilst reproducing a 'normal' perspective. The depth of field is greater than that of the 50mm lens, focusing is less critical, and the danger of camera shake is less. Snapshots, photojournalism, landscapes intended to convey a realistic impression, group photos of people, staged portraits where the surroundings are to be visible, still life photos with larger objects, and architectural photography at eye level are the domain of the 35mm focal length.

Summilux-R 35mm,f/1.4

The Summilux-R 35mm,f/1.4 is specifically designed for so-called available-light photography. Great brilliance and good rendering of detail distinguish the lens, even at maximum aperture. At maximum aperture there is a slight reduction in sharpness towards the image edges, but it is fully eliminated from f/5.6 onwards. The good sharpness and contrast performance is maintained even in the close-up range, thanks to a floating elements construction. For a super-fast lens of this focal length the distortion is minimal. Vignetting is fairly slight at the maximum aperture and no longer visible from f/4 onwards. There is no flare, even when a light source is located in the image area.

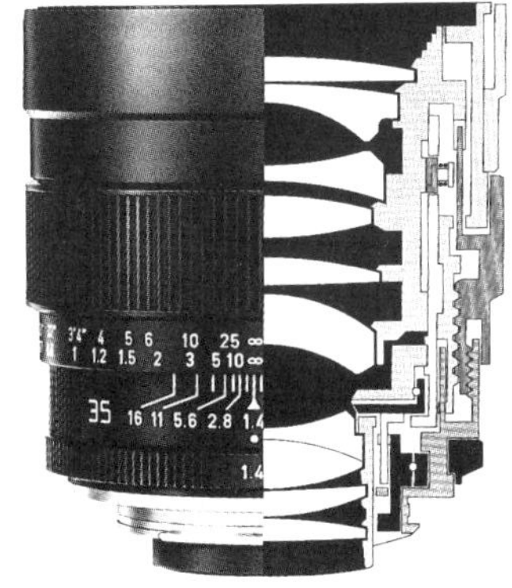

The telescopic lens hood is integral and screw-in 67mm filters can be used, but filters in thick mounts, for example polarizing filters, can cause vignetting that will still be visible in a framed slide.

Summicron-R 35mm,f/2

The Summicron-R 35mm,f/2 also counts as a fast, high-performance lens. It is optimally corrected in a range from infinity to 1.4m and if stopped down delivers a respectable performance down to 30cm. Vignetting and distortion are not unpleasantly noticeable. Flare caused by light sources within the image area is so slight that it can be ignored in practice.

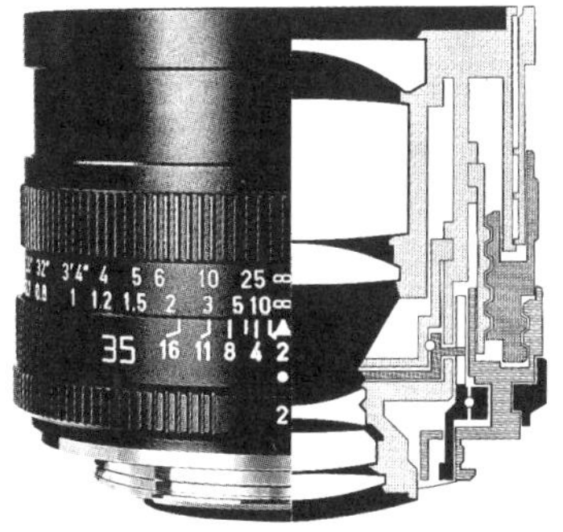

Elmarit-R 35mm,f/2.8

The Elmarit-R 35mm,f/2.8 possesses good optical properties, but is also compact and light, making it a good travel lens. It is an inexpensive alternative to the faster 35mm lenses for photographers who can do without a high maximum aperture. Even at the maximum aperture the Elmarit-R 35mm,f/2.8 offers good sharpness and contrast performance, which reaches its maximum at f/5.6. The barrel-shaped distortion that is inevitable with retrofocus lenses is so slight that it only becomes noticeable at the image edges of architectural subjects, if at all. Vignetting can become visible at f/2.8 with critical subjects, such as an evenly-lit light-coloured wall or a blue sky dominating the subject, but is eliminated

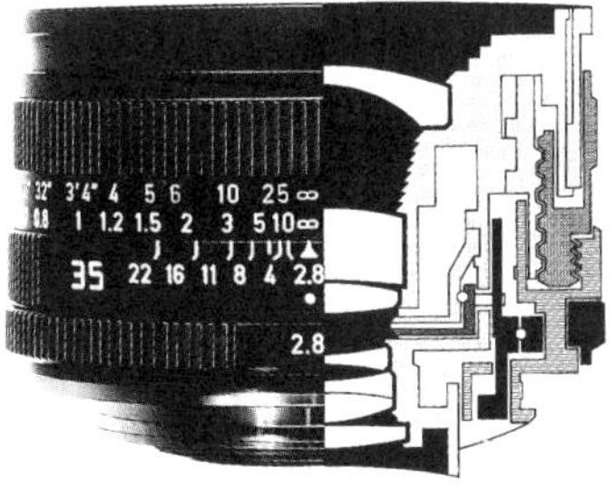

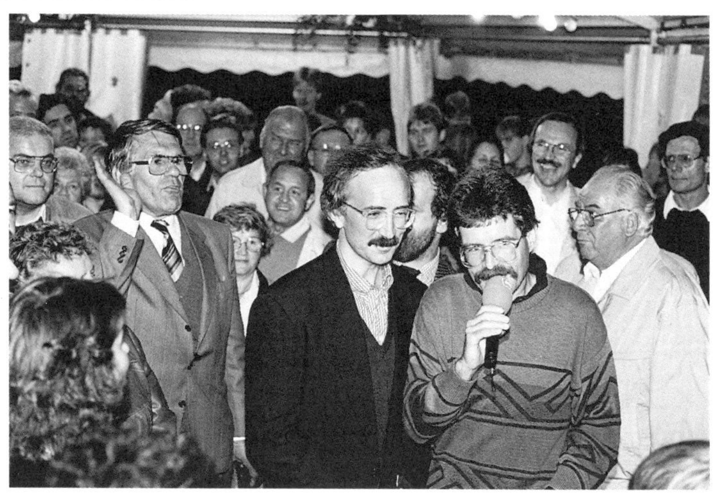

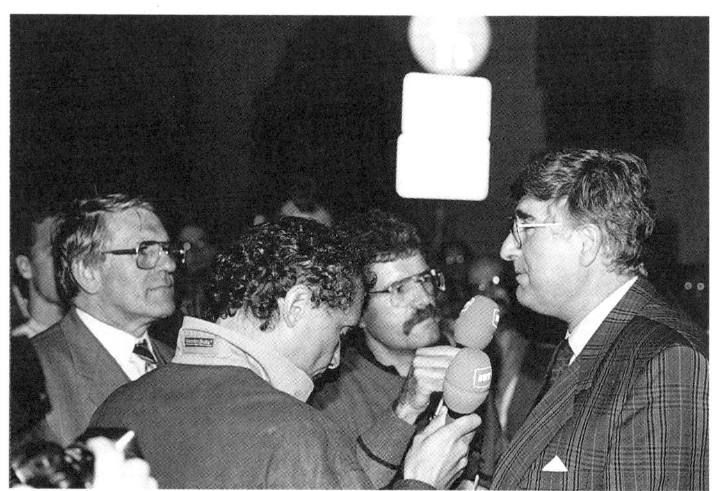

from f/5.6 onwards. It lacks the speed of the other two 35mm lenses, but its light weight make it an ideal travel lens.

The standard range (50mm to 60mm)

A focal length of 50mm is regarded as standard for the 35mm format. The 45° angle of view is roughly the same as the angle of vision at which our eyes perceive things in focus. The fashionable view that picture composition with standard lenses is tame and boring is still widely held because of the novelty offered by very short and very long focal lengths. But this view is strongly challenged by the work of photographers like Henri Cartier-Bresson who made photographic history with rangefinder Leicas with standard lenses.

The Leica R lenses with focal lengths of 50mm or 60mm can be used for almost all applications: photojournalism, snapshots, travel photography, still-lifes with large objects, architectural details, staged portraits, and child or group photographs. The standard lenses are compact, light, and inexpensive, and as in the good old days, every beginner should still start off with one of these lenses.

Summilux-R 50mm,f/1.4

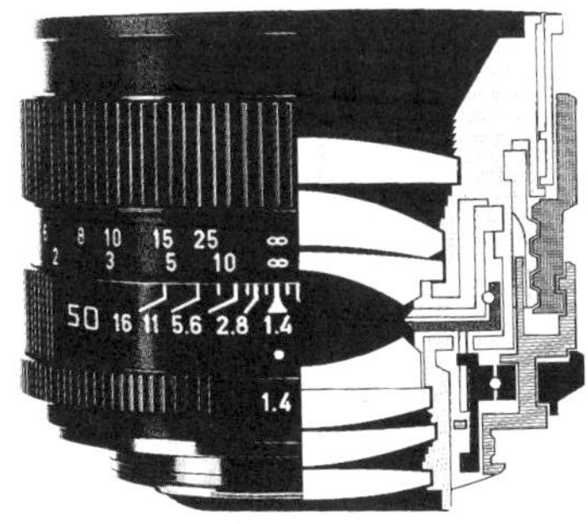

The Summilux 50mm,f/1.4 is a superfast lens with a very good optical performance. It proves once again that the large maximum aperture of Leica lenses not only provides a brighter viewfinder image to aid focusing, but also yields faultless results. The very good rendering of contrast at the maximum aperture can be improved only slightly by stopping down to f/2. The lens is practically free of distortion and the slight vignetting caused by the high maximum aperture is eliminated from f/4 or f/5.6 onwards. The lens is ideal for available-light photography, for photojournalism in interiors, or for snapshots. The Elpro attachments can be screwed into the filter thread, but at the maximum aperture the mount of the close-up attachments can cause vignetting.

Summicron-R 50mm,f/2

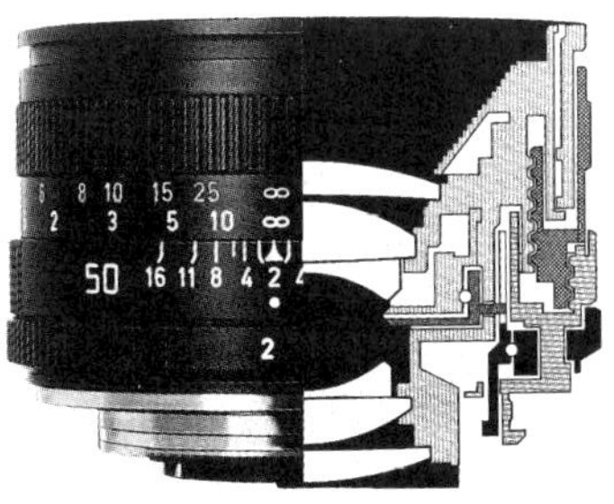

The Summicron-R 50mm,f/2 is a fast universal lens with excellent sharpness and contrast rendering across the whole focusing range. Over greater distances the lens offers an excellent reproduction quality, even at the maximum aperture, and this quality can be maintained in the close-up range by stopping down to f/5.6 or f/8. Vignetting and distortion can be ignored in practice. The Elpro Close-up Attachment 1 provides very good reproduction quality and a reproduction ratio of 1:3.8, the Elpro Close-up Attachment 2 takes it down to 1:2.6. The lens can also be used with a bellows unit (with reproduction ratios of up to 2.9:1, or as much as 3.16:1 with the Elpro 2). This is the cheapest and lightest Leica R lens.

Macro-Elmarit-R 60mm,f/2.8

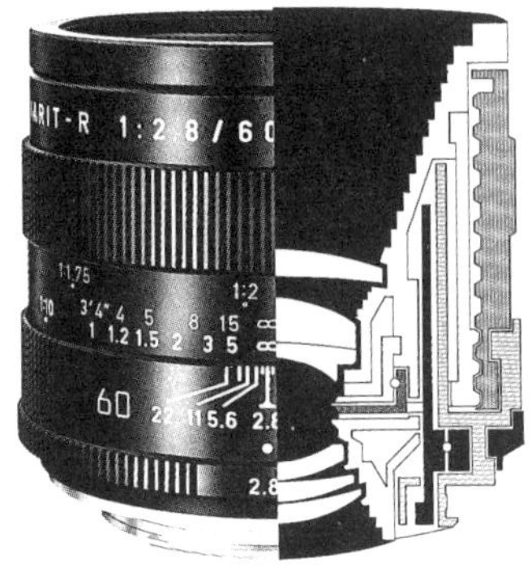

The Macro-Elmarit-R 60mm,f/2.8 is not only corrected for the close-up range, but also performs well at infinity. The sharpness and contrast performance is very good across the whole focusing range, even at the maximum aperture, reaching a peak at f/5.6. Vignetting and distortion are so slight that they can be ignored in practice. With this lens you can work in the same areas as with the Summicron-R 50mm,f/2. The fact that the angle of view is slightly smaller makes hardly any difference and can even be an advantage with detailed work. If you can do without a high speed and want to work in the macro range, this lens is an excellent all-rounder.

The strengths of this lens become particularly apparent at reproduction ratios between 1:20 and 1:10, where maximum reproduction quality is achieved at f/4, although it is still very good at maximum aperture. At the closest focusing distance of 27cm the lens achieves a reproduction ratio of 1:2; the actual working distance from the front of the barrel is 15cm. The Macro-Adapter-R reduces the distance setting to 24cm, which corresponds to a reproduction ratio of 1:1 with a working distance of 10cm. See the table of close-up accessories for reproduction ratios that can be achieved with further accessories.

The medium telephoto range (80mm to 135mm)

Telephoto lenses with focal lengths between 80mm and 135mm are amongst the most popular of all lenses. They are easy to handle and have many applications. Their relatively tight angle of view encourages the photographer to concentrate on the essentials. The framing is easier to check than with wide-angle and standard lenses because a smaller part of the subject is framed at a larger reproduction ratio for the same camera distance. The shallow depth of field can be used in conjunction with a wide aperture to increase the overall effect of the photograph. In this way a sharp main subject can be made to appear three-dimensional in front of an unsharp background. For this reason, and the fact that these focal lengths enable portrait sitters to be placed further from the camera, giving a more natural perspective to the face, 80 and 90mm lenses are used as portrait lenses.

Focal lengths between 80mm and 135mm compress the subject space to some extent, but not so much as longer focal lengths so it is still perceived as natural. Lenses in this range are ideal for detailed work, still-life, landscapes – rendering good detail of small areas of image,

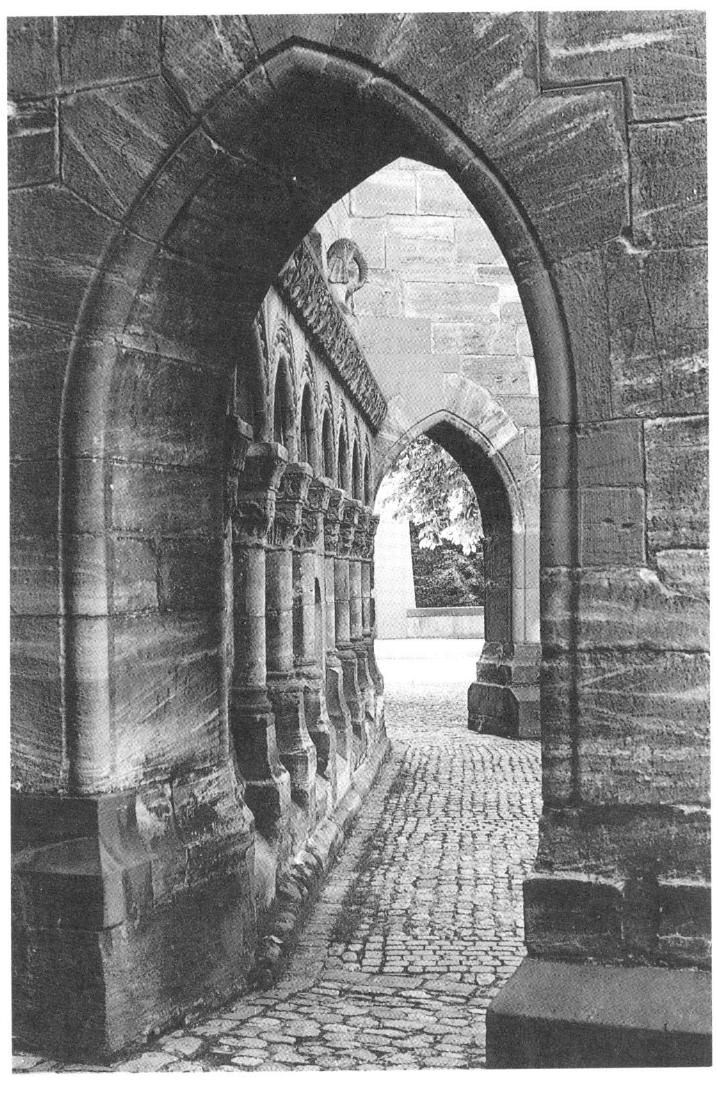

The Macro-Elmarit-R 60mm, f2.8 can also be used as a standard lens at greater range with equally good reproduction

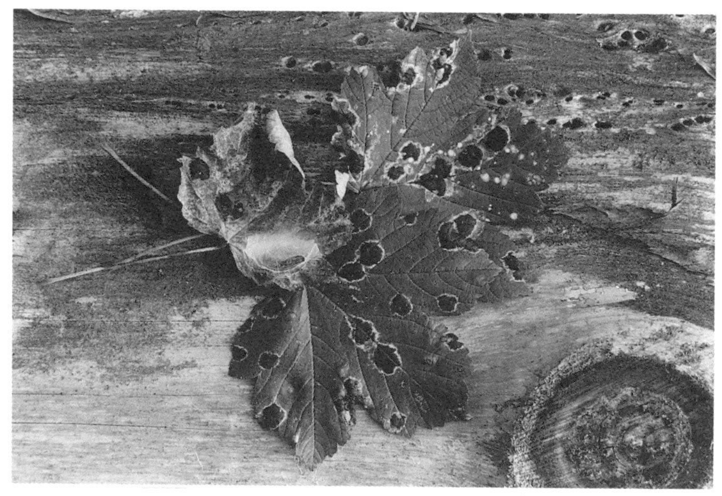

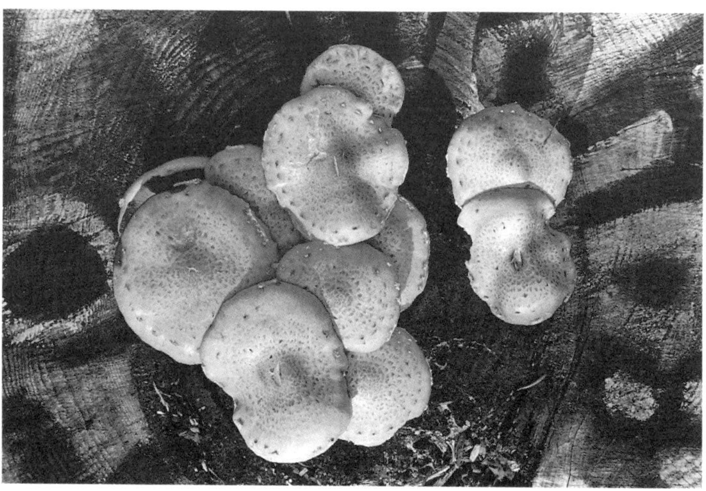

Frame-filling details and still-lifes are in the domain of medium telephoto lenses.

and also architectural photography for both close-up detail and for photographing buildings from a greater distance to avoid having to tilt the camera. They are popular for photojournalism, travel and fashion photography, and for snapshots from a discreet distance.

Summilux-R 80mm,f/1.4

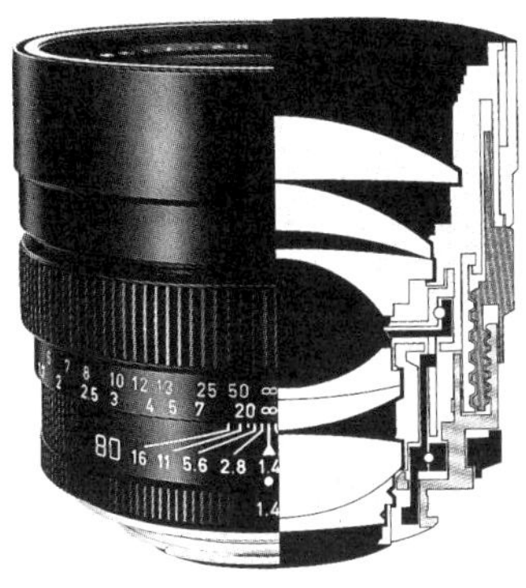

The Summilux-R 80mm,f/1.4 is a super-fast lens with very good reproduction quality at infinity, even at maximum aperture. At close range, and f/1.4, the curvature of the image inherent in the system causes slight unsharpness in the image corners, but in pictorial photography this will only be noticeable on clearly structured subjects and is eliminated by stopping down to f/8. Vignetting is very slight and becomes invisible if the lens is stopped down by one or two stops. The lens comes into its own with high-contrast subjects, which are rendered in fine colour details and tonal gradations. Light sources within the image area do not cause flare. The bright, high contrast viewfinder image and the shallow depth of field at f/1.4 aid accurate focusing, even in low light. The lens is therefore ideal for portraits, photojournalism, and theatre photography, particularly if existing lighting moods are to be captured.

Summicron-R 90mm,f/2

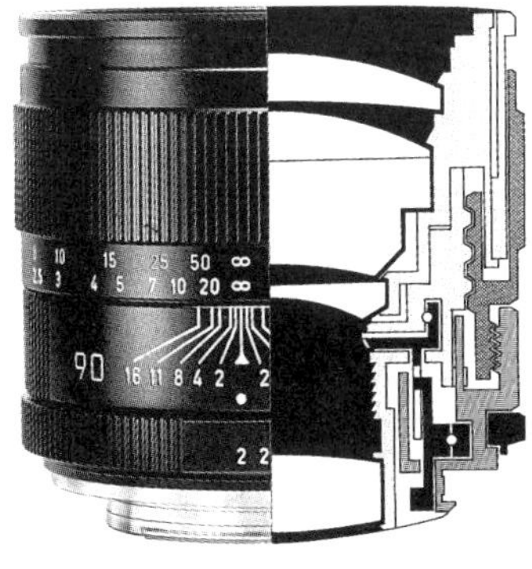

The Summicron-R 90mm,f/2 is a fast, high-performance lens with excellent sharpness and contrast rendering. It is also surprisingly compact – just 61mm long. At longer distances the excellent reproduction performance, evenly distributed across the entire image area, is maintained right to maximum aperture. If a comparably good reproduction quality is to be achieved right into the image corners at distances below 2.5m, the lens needs to be stopped down to f/8. Vignetting and distortion are negligible across the whole focusing range, and the same goes for flare. The closest focusing distance of 70cm produces a reproduction ratio of 1:6. With the close-up attachment Elpro 3 the lens can achieve a reproduction ratio of 1:3, when it should be stopped down to a medium aperture. The Summicron-R 90mm,f/2 is excellent for portraits, photojournalism, theatre photography, detail shots, snapshots at

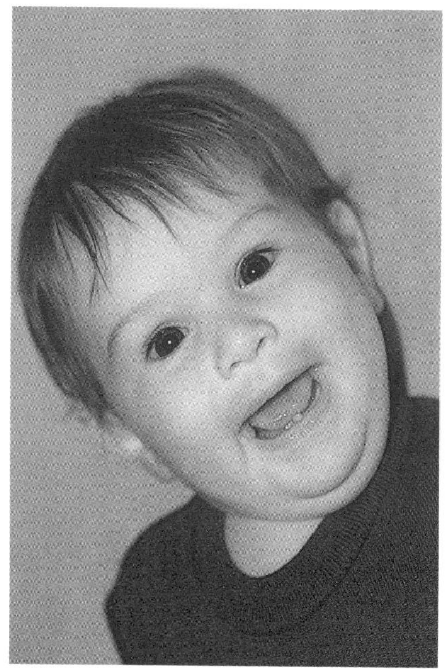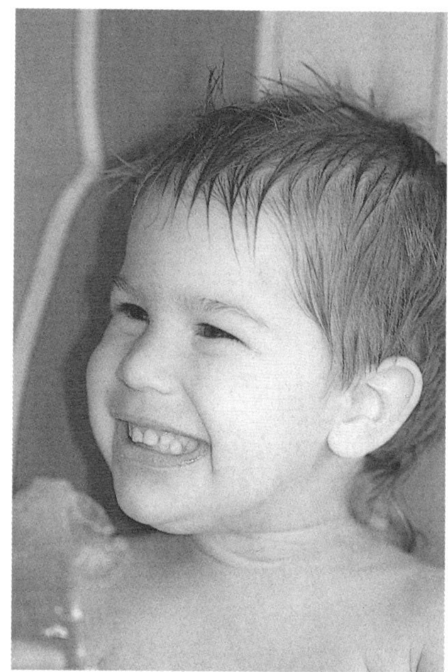

The Summicron-R 90mm,f/2 is not only an ideal lens for classical portraits, but also for photographs of children.

medium range, available-light work, still-lifes, landscapes with good resolution of detail, and architectural photography.

Elmarit-R 90mm,f/2.8

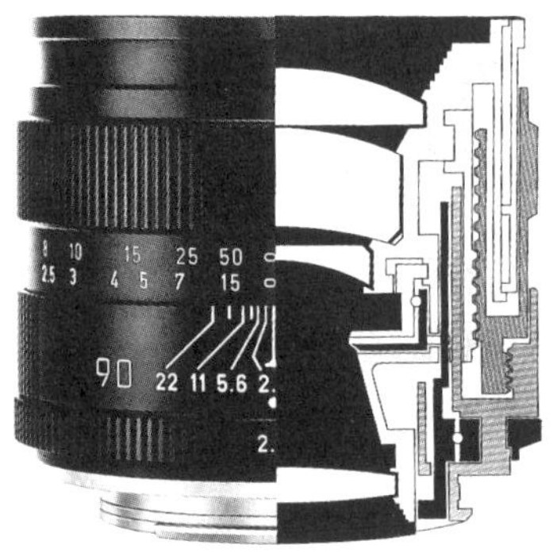

The Elmarit-R 90mm,f/2.8 is also very well corrected at the maximum aperture. At f/4 the lens reaches its optimum sharpness and contrast performance. The correction in the close-up range is also excellent, reaching its maximum reproduction quality from f/5.6 and smaller. The minimal vignetting and distortion are of no consequence in pictorial photography. With the close-up attachment Elpro 3 the lens can reach a reproduction ratio of 1:3 and should be stopped down to f/5.6 for best reproduction quality. Applications are similar to those of the Summicron, bearing in mind the lower maximum speed.

Apo-Macro-Elmarit-R 100mm,f/2.8

Because of its apochromatic correction the Apo-Macro-Elmarit 100mm,f/2.8 offers excellent sharpness and contrast rendering across the whole focusing range, even at the maximum aperture. Stopping

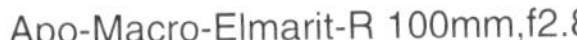

Apo-Macro-Elmarit-R 100mm,f2.8

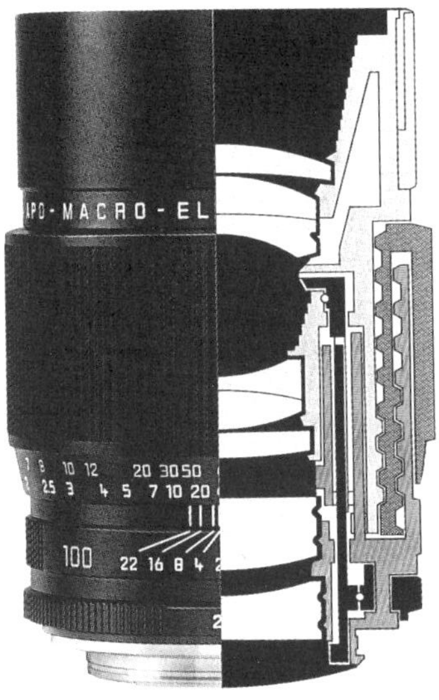

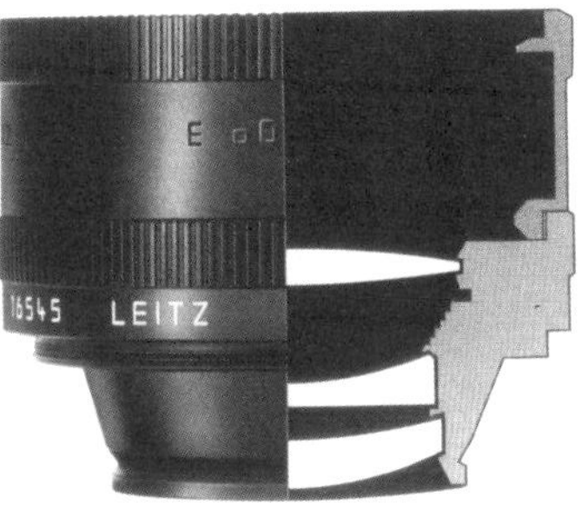

Elpro 1:2-1:1 for the Apo-Macro-Elmarit-R 10mm,f/2.8

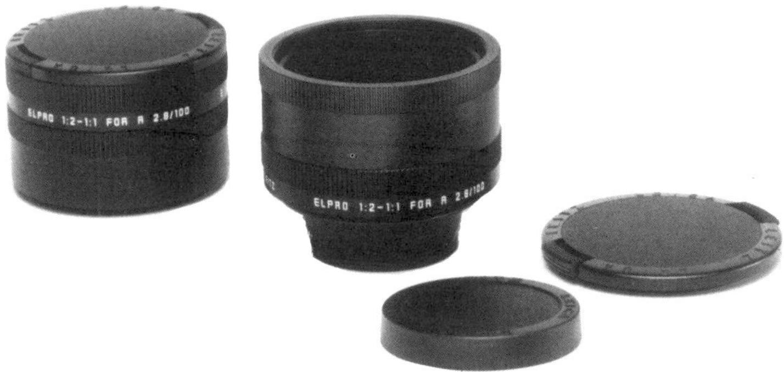

The Lens hood of the Elpro 1:2-1:1 can be screwed onto the rear of the Elpro and then, with the front and rear caps in place, it forms a convenient protective container for it.

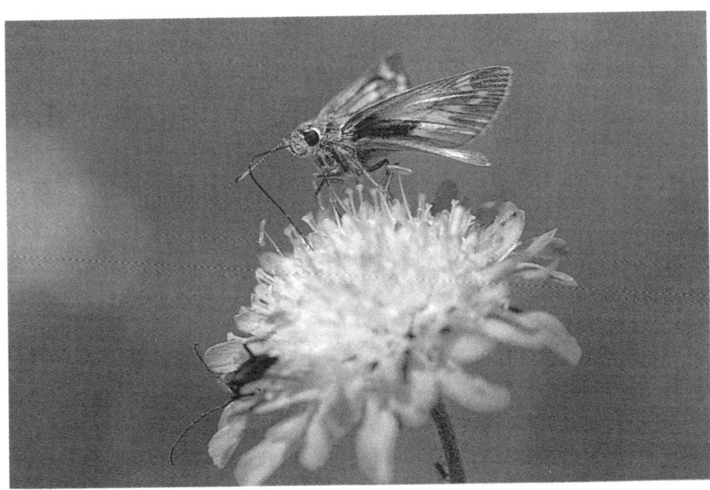

Leica R macro lenses make photography in the close-up range very easy, and give excellent reproduction quality

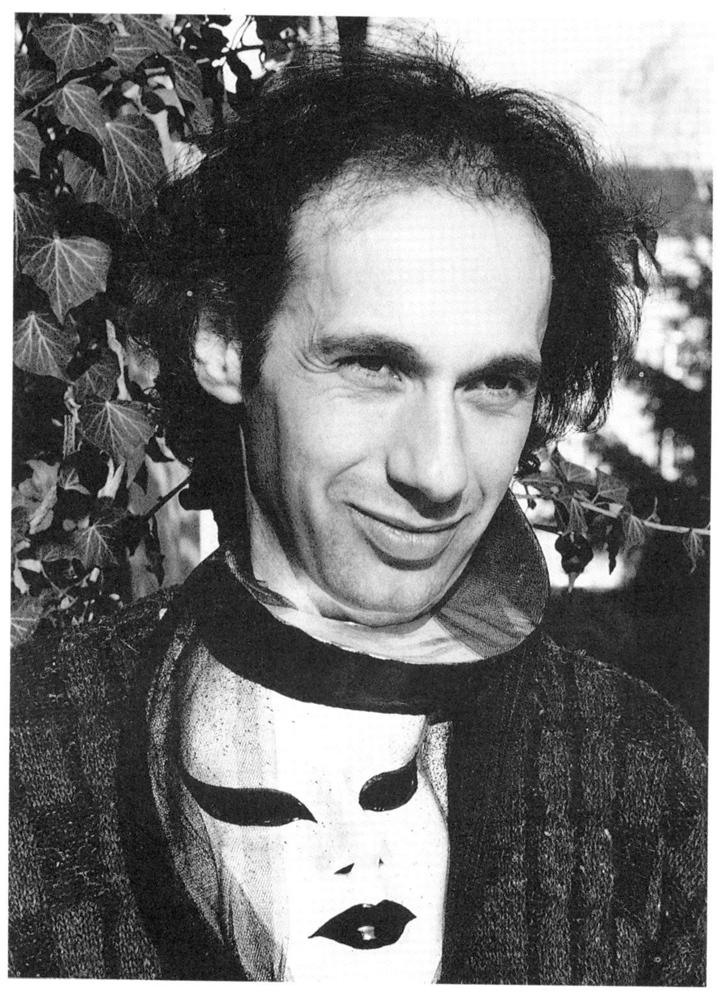

The Apo-Macro-Elmarit-R 100mm,f/2.8 is also suitable for portraits

down to f/4 or f/5.6 achieves only a slight improvement. It is excellent for all the applications covered by the 90mm lenses, limited only by its maximum aperture of f/2.8. Only the Apo-Extender-R 2x can be used with this lens, no other extender is suitable: the Extender-R 2x reduces the reproduction quality, while the Apo-Extender-R 1.4x can damage the lens.

The excellent reproduction properties are fully maintained through the whole focusing range, down to a reproduction ratio of 1:2. If used with the Elpro 1:2-1:1, specifically designed for use with this lens, reproduction quality is maintained down as far as 1:1. No other close-up accessories should be used. Markings on the lens barrel indicate the reproduction ratio at any setting.

Macro-Elmar-R 100mm,f/4

The Macro-Elmar-R 100mm,f/4 is available in two versions, with or without a helical focusing mount. That without the mount is for use on the focusing bellows. Both lenses are well-corrected for the whole focusing range, but the maximum reproduction quality is reached at reproduction ratios between 1:5 and 1:10. At f/8 the sharpness and contrast rendering is on a par with that of other Leica R lenses, even at greater range. This means that the lens can be used in portrait or landscape photography, but hand-held photography with bellows is awkward. These lenses are really more suitable for macro photographers who occasionally venture into landscape or portrait photography, rather 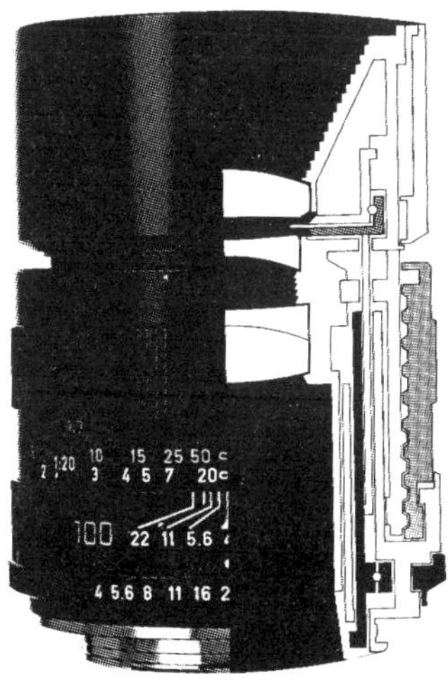 than portrait and landscape photographers who take the odd macro picture.

The lens is well-corrected for the whole range, but the reproduction quality reaches its peak at reproduction ratios between 1:5 and 1:10. In the helical mount it can achieve a reproduction ratio of 1:3. The Macro-Adapter-R extends this to 1:1.6. The long focal length of this lens allows a greater distance between lens and subject. The working distance, at 1:3 reproduction, is 39cm, and with the Macro-Adapter-R, at 1:1.6 reproduction, it is 25cm. This relatively large working distance makes for easier lighting of the main subject and enables small animals and botanical subjects to be photographed at greater range.

Elmarit-R 135mm,f/2.8

The Elmarit-R 135mm,f/2.8 with an angle of view of 18° has a more noticeable telephoto effect than the other lenses in this group. Even at

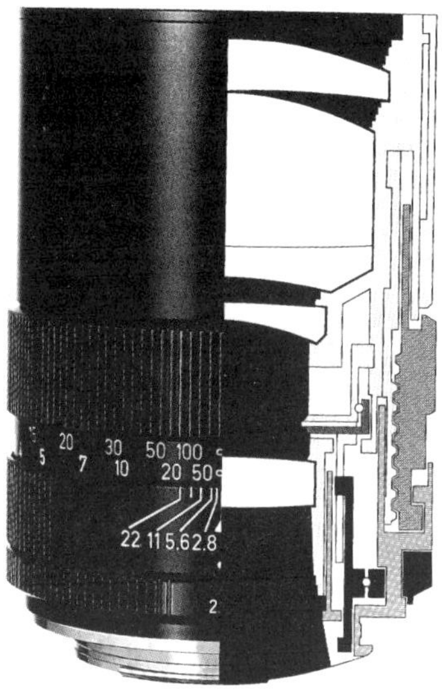
Elmarit-R 135mm,f/2.8

the maximum aperture the lens offers good sharpness and contrast rendering in the infinity range, reaching its peak at f/4. Stopping down further can only improve the reproduction quality in the close-up range. At the closest focusing distance of 1.5m the lens achieves a reproduction ratio of 1:9. With the close-up attachments Elpro 4 and Elpro 3 the close-up range goes down as far as 1:4.4 and 1:2.8 respectively, with good reproduction quality. Vignetting and distortion are negligible.

The Elmarit-R 135mm,f/2.8 is still one of the most popular lenses. It is very well-suited to portraits, architectural work, snapshots at greater range, detail photography, and still-life. The lens can also be used for plant and animal photography, as well as landscape details and because of its compact construction and low weight it is also ideal for travel photographers.

The classical telephoto range (180m to 280mm)

Lenses with focal lengths between 180mm and 280mm show a pronounced telephoto characteristic: compression of space, tightening of the angle of view, and a shallow depth of field. They allow frame-filling photography of small objects at medium range without any problem. But the focal lengths are not enough to shoot at great range. You can, for example, take frame-filling photographs of animals in the zoo, but not (or only rarely) of animals in the wild. The 180mm telephoto offers 3.6x and the 280mm 5.6x the magnification of a standard focal length. Standard binoculars, by comparison, offer around 8x the magnification of normal vision.

The lenses in this telephoto range are well-suited to landscapes, for example frame-filling photographs of a mountain or rockface, or to bring out the structures of a landscape by compressing the space. In architectural photography details at a greater distance (eg of a roof gable), or whole rows of houses, can be compressed into a tight space. With telephoto lenses in this range you can take portrait photographs without being noticed or take photographs at concerts, if permitted. But in some sports and in animal photography these lenses usually capture too much of the surroundings of the main subject.

The classical telephoto range is covered by five Leica R lenses, including two with apochromatically corrected optics. The 180mm and 250mm telephotos are still quite compact and easy to handle, but you shouldn't attempt hand-held photographs at shutter speeds slower than 1/500 sec. The widely used rule of thumb that shake-free hand-held photographs can be achieved with shutter speeds corresponding to the reciprocal of the focal length does not apply if absolute maximum sharpness is required.

Elmarit-R 180mm, f/2.8

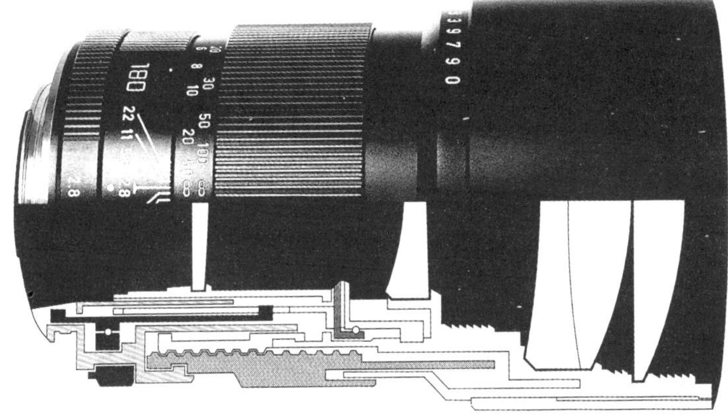

The Elmarit-R 180mm,f/2.8 is a fast telephoto lens with very good sharpness and contrast performance, which can be achieved even at the maximum aperture at greater distances. In the close-up range the curvature of field at the maximum aperture causes slight unsharpness in the image corners, but this can be eliminated by stopping down to f/4 or f/5.6. Vignetting and distortion are so slight that they will not be noticeable in the final results. With a length of about 12cm and a maximum diameter of 7.5cm the lens is surprisingly compact for its focal length and its speed. A combination of the Leica R7 and the Elmarit-R 180mm,f/2.8 is well-balanced and sits well in the photographer's hand, so you can take portraits without being noticed. The high speed produces a bright viewfinder image and therefore aids precise focusing, even in low light (although the uniform groundglass focusing screen is recommended). The lens is excellent for available-light photography, theatre and concert work, landscape photography, and animal photography at closer range. At the closest focusing distance of 1.8m the lens achieves a reproduction ratio of 1:8, which is particularly useful for detail photography at greater range, and everyday applications in architectural and industrial photography.

Apo-Telyt-R 180mm, f/3.4

The Apo-Telyt-R 180mm,f/3.4 is without doubt a superior lens. Originally computed for special photographic applications (such as surveillance and control photography), the lens offers rendering of

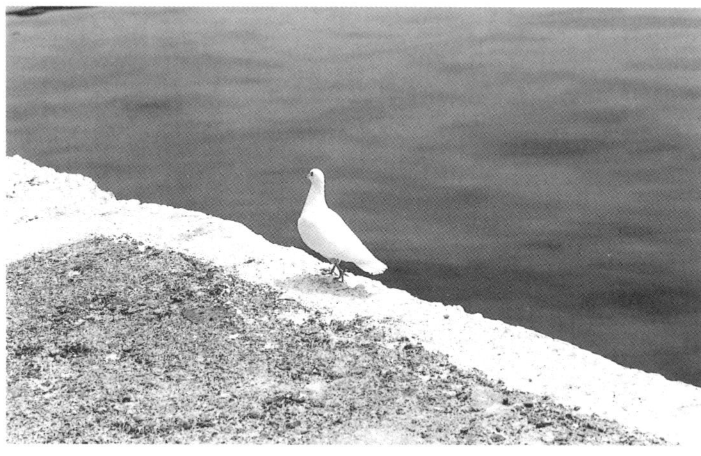

Apo-Telyt-R
180mm,f/3.4

Hand-held shot
with the
Apo-Telyt-R
180mm,f/3.4

details and a brilliance that is unsurpassed in this focal length. The sharpness and contrast in the infinity range are so high right into the image corners, even at the maximum aperture, that it cannot be improved to any real extent by stopping down. Due to the high degree of correction a slight vignetting can occur in the image corners at the maximum aperture when shooting evenly lit monochrome areas (e.g. a light-coloured wall or a blue sky), although this disappears if the lens is stopped down to f/5.6 or f/8. Distortion does not affect pictorial photography adversely.

The extraordinary reproduction quality of the Apo-Telyt-R 180mm,f/3.4 only becomes fully exploitable if it is used with a high-quality slow film and the camera is mounted on a sturdy professional tripod, and making use of the R7's independent mirror release. But if you do want to use this compact and handy lens for hand-held work, use the fastest shutter speed you can. It is suitable for almost any application, eg portraits, available-light photography, theatre and concert work, architectural details, animal photography at close range, and landscape photography.

Elmar-R 180mm,f/4

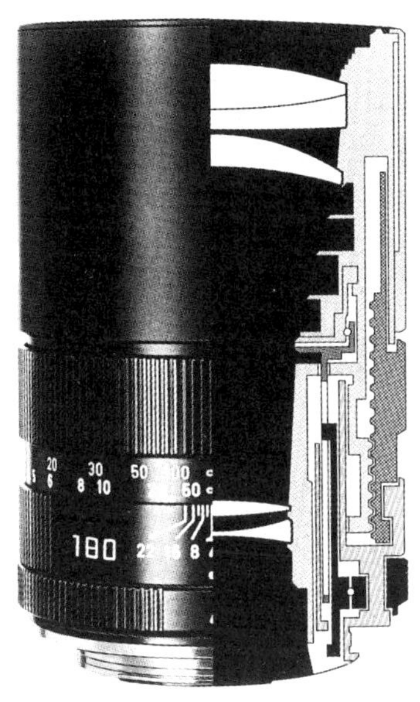

The Elmar-R 180mm,f/4, the third lens in the 180mm focal length group, renders sharpness and contrast very well at maximum aperture in the range between 3m and infinity, and this can be maintained in the close-up range by stopping down to f/5.6 or f/8. Otherwise the reproduction characteristics of the Elmar-R 180mm,f/4 largely correspond to those of the Elmarit-R 180mm,f/2.8. Because of its optical construction it achieves a reproduction ratio of 1:7 at the closest focusing distance of 1.8m. With a length of 100mm the lens is just 7mm longer than the 135mm Elmarit, and 190g lighter. This makes it an ideal travel lens. If you can do without the faster speed, the Elmar-R 180mm,f/4 will also provide you with an alternative in terms of cost compared to the other 180mm lenses.

Telyt-R 250mm,f/4

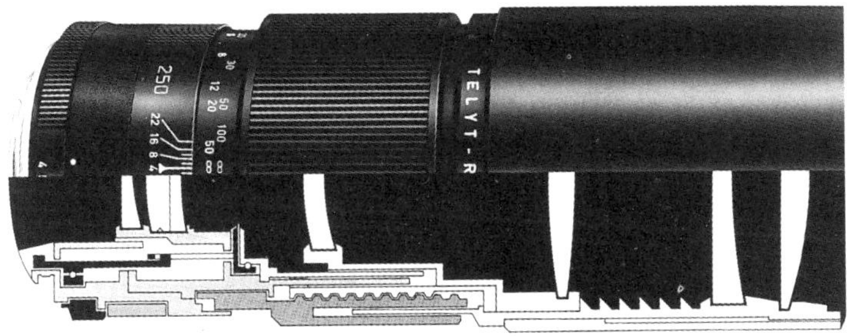

The Telyt-R 250mm,f/4 offers very good sharpness and contrast rendering in the range between 4m and infinity, even at the maximum aperture. In the closer range the lens reaches its maximum reproduction quality at f/5.6 or f/8. Distortion is negligible and the slight degree of vignetting, caused through the compact construction of the lens, can be eliminated by stopping down slightly. The closest focusing distance of 1.7m corresponds to a reproduction ratio of 1:5.2. With the Extender-R 2X the lens can achieve a reproduction ratio of as much as 1:2.6, which is quite unusual for a lens with this focal length. The lens is fairly compact and handy, with a very short focusing travel, allowing hand-held photography at fast shutter speeds (1/500 sec, or better still 1/1000 sec). This means that snapshots and portraits can be attempted at greater

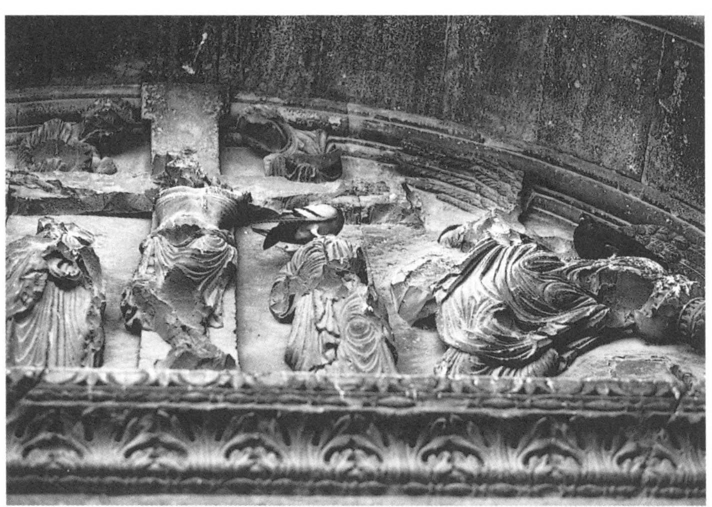

The Telyt-R 250mm,f/4 is a useful lens for the recording of architectural details.

range. Landscapes and architectural details, animal photography at close and medium range, and indoor sports photography are further applications. The lens is equipped with a revolving tripod mount, which engages in the landscape and portrait format positions.

Apo-Telyt-R 280mm,f/2.8

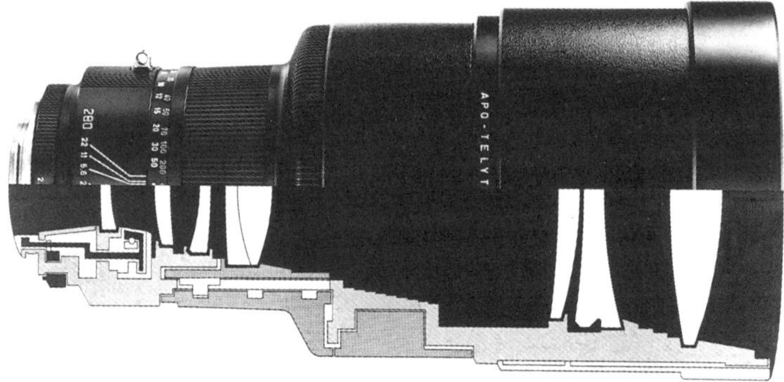

The Apo-Telyt-R 280mm,f/2.8 is a super-fast telephoto lens with outstanding reproduction quality. The excellent rendering of sharpness and contrast is achieved at the maximum aperture at long and medium range, and is not really improved further by stopping down. At shooting distances below 5m the lens should be stopped down to f/4 to compensate for curvature of field in the image corners. Vignetting and distortion are so slight that they do not appear in practice.

Precise focusing and shake-free shutter release are pre-requisites if the outstanding reproduction quality of the Apo-Telyt-R 280mm,f/2.8 is

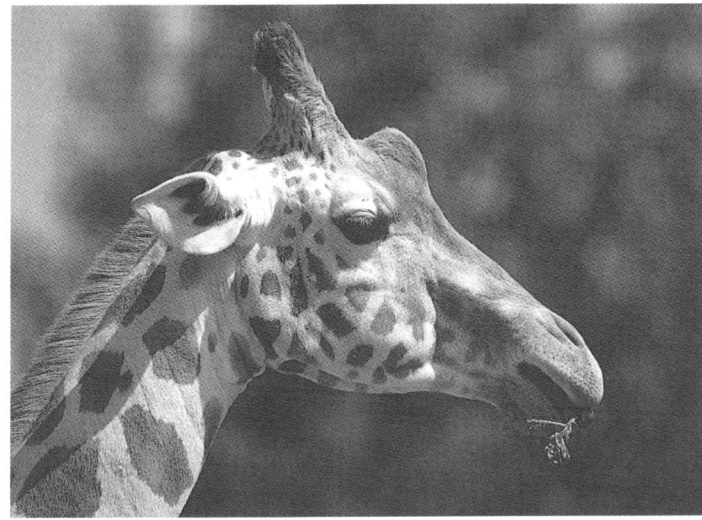

Animal portraits in the zoo can easily be obtained with the Apo-Telyt-R 280mm,f/2.8 on a monopod.

to become fully utilized. Thanks to the palm grip supplied with the lens, it sits well in the hand, despite its weight of 2.7kg. The diameter of the non-slip focusing ring increases along its length and can be operated with the thumb both when the camera is mounted on a monopod (using the thumb of the hand that is holding the monopod) and with the palm grip attached. The shallow depth of field at the maximum aperture causes a clearly visible separation of sharpness and unsharpness, so the uniform groundglass focusing screen is the one most recomended for use with this lens.

Regardless of whether the lens is used on a tripod or with the palm grip, the camera/lens unit can be rotated in the tripod mount and engages in either the landscape of portrait format position (there are also two intermediate positions with a difference of 15° between them). The easy handling of this lens with the palm grip attached makes it very tempting to shoot with the camera hand-held. But the outstanding

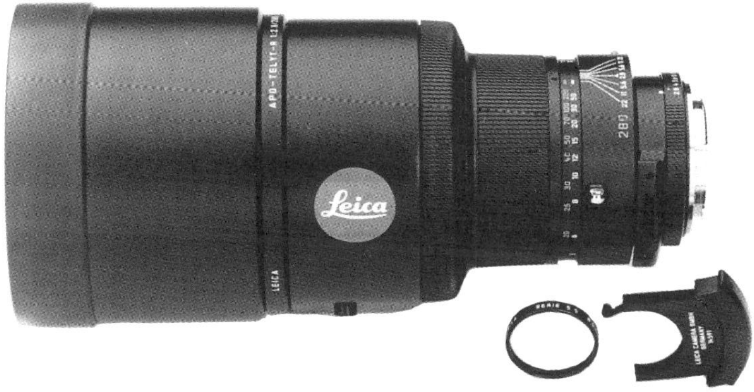

The new model of the Apo-Telyt-R 280mm,f/2.8 is equipped with a filter compartment for Series 5.5 filters.

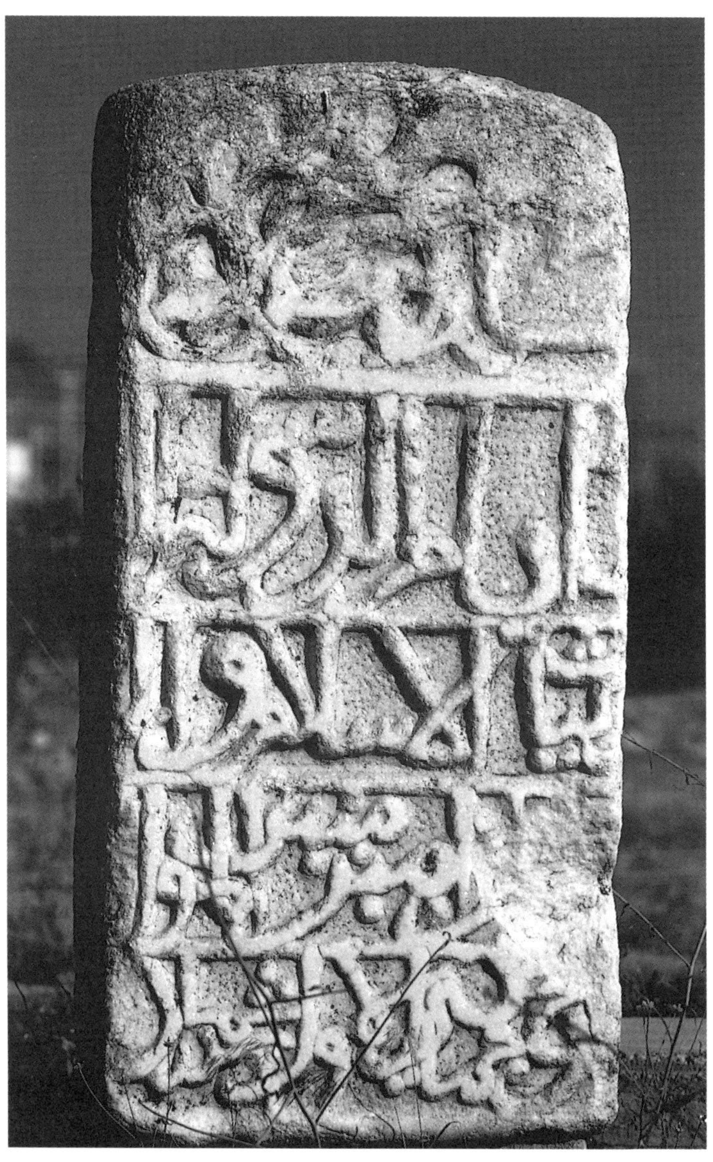

The shallow depth of field produced by long focal length lenses causes the main subject to appear three-dimensional against the background.

optical performance can only be realized if it is supported on a sturdy professional tripod and using the R7's independent mirror release. Where this is impractical in sports and animal photography support the lens on a monopod.

The lens is supplied with a colourless neutral-density filter with a filter factor of 1. The makers say that this filter should always be attached to the lens to protect the front element.

The Apo-Extender-R 1.4X has been specially computed for the Apo-Telyt-R 280mm,f/2.8. The Extender turns the Apo-Telyt-R 280mm,f/2.8 into a 400mm,f/4 telephoto lens, whose excellent reproduction quality is maintained at medium and greater distances. In the close-up range the lens should be stopped down by one or two stops to maintain the reproduction quality at its highest level.

The Apo-Extender-R 2X doubles the focal length and reduces the speed by a factor of four, so the Apo-Telyt-R 280mm,f/2.8 becomes a 560mm,f/5.6 telephoto lens. The apochromatic correction is fully maintained. With the non-apochromatic Extender-R 2X the reproduction quality is not as good, but it is still considerable, particularly if the lens is stopped down by one or two stops.

The Apo-Telyt-R 280mm,f/2.8 is ideal for interior sports photography, for theatre and concert photography, for detail photography at great range (eg in architectural photography), and for animal photography (even in the wild when using an extender).

The extreme telephoto range
(350mm to 800mm)

Lenses with focal lengths between 350mm and 800mm can bridge great shooting distances. They are ideal for animal, sports, and landscape photography. The characteristic of long focal lengths is a greatly enlarged reproduction of a subject, as well as an extreme compression of perspective. These properties can also be used in creative or experimental photography.

Even when working from a sturdy professional tripod, movement blur, caused by a gust of wind or vibration of the mirror (unless working with the independent mirror release), can become noticeable. With the exception of the Telyt-S 800mm,f/6.3, the telephoto lenses for the Leica R7 are designed in such a way that they can also be used hand-held. The excellent sharpness produced by the Leica telephoto lenses only becomes fully visible on shake-free exposures and with accurate focusing, so the uniform groundglass screen is a must. The telephoto lenses for the Leica R7 can be focused beyond infinity, which is particularly important when using extenders.

Amongst this focal length group are the rapid-focusing lenses, Telyt-R 400mm,f/6.8 and Telyt-R 560mm,f/6.8, and the MR-Telyt-R 500mm,f/8 mirror lens, which are covered in the next chapter.

Telyt-R 350mm,f/4.8

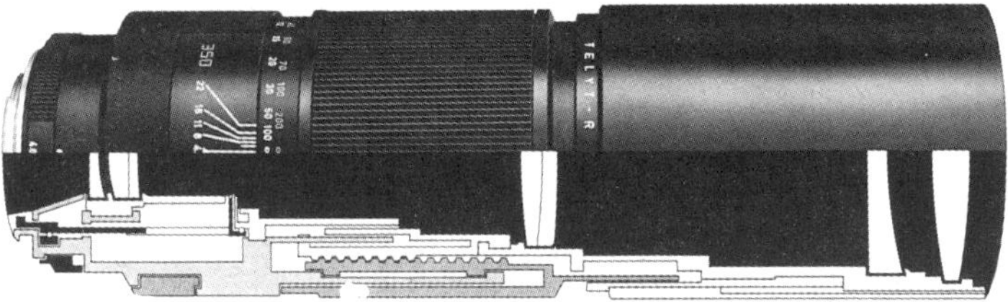

The Telyt-R 350mm,f/4.8 provides very good resolution of detail and reproduction of contrast. The remaining colour aberrations that are inevitable with long focal length non-apochromatic lenses only become visible in the image corners on clearly structured subjects, such as buildings, and at maximum aperture. To keep the lens compact slight vignetting was accepted, but this is only apparent with evenly lit bright subjects in the image corners. Stopping down to f/8 reduces vignetting and the remaining colour aberrations to a minimum. The same goes for the close-up range, where top optical performance is also reached from f/8 onwards. With the Extender 2X the focal length is doubled to 700mm. However, this also reduces the speed to f/9.6.

Like the Telyt-R 250mm,f/4, the Telyt-R 350mm,f/4.8 has a very short focusing travel. This allows for fast focusing, particularly important for sports photography. The rotating tripod mount on the lens makes

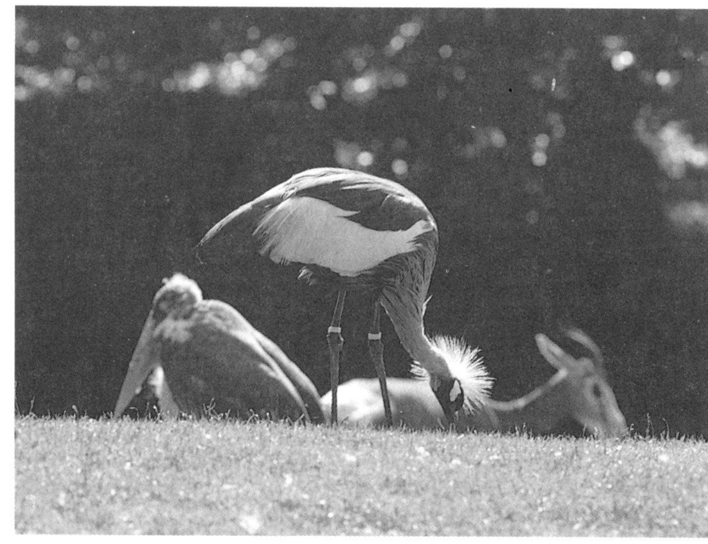

This shot with the Telyt-R 350mm,f/4.8 was taken in an open-air enclosure.

switching between landscape and portrait formats easy. Apart from sports photography the Telyt-R 350mm,f/4.8 is very well-suited to animal and landscape photography.

Apo-Telyt-R 400mm,f/2.8

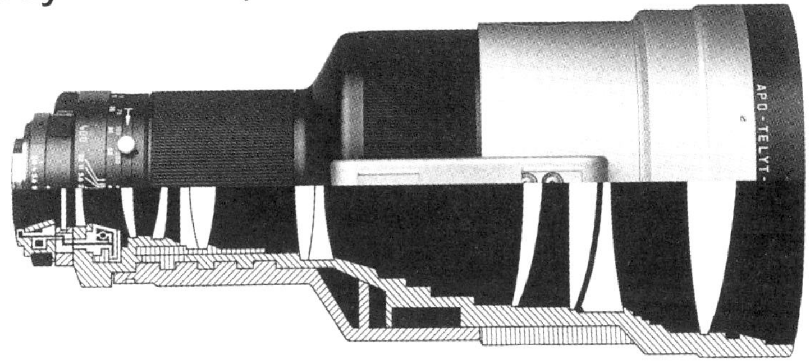

The Apo-Telyt-R 400mm,f/2.8 is an apochromatically corrected tele-photo lens with extraordinary optical characteristics. The rendering of sharpness and contrast at medium and greater distances is outstanding, even at maximum aperture, so much so that it can hardly be improved by stopping down. At the closest focusing distance the lens reaches maximum reproduction quality when stopped down by one or two stops. Field flatness is very good, providing faultless reproduction of detail right into the image corners. Vignetting and distortion are minimal.

The lens is equipped with a slip-in filter holder for Series 5.5 filters. A neutral density filter is supplied with the lens and, because it is taken into account in the lens computation, it has to be in place at all times, unless of course another filter is required. Leica has developed a circular polarizing filter, specifically for this lens, which is inserted in the filter compartment and can be turned from the outside.

The lens has been designed for hand-held photography in the same manner as the 280mm Apo-Telyt, but the slightest movement blur destroys its extraordinary sharpness. Use a monopod, or for critical results with a static subject a sturdy professional tripod and the inde-pendent mirror release function.

The closest focusing distance is 4.7m. For sports photography from the edge of the pitch it is possible to preselect a certain distance setting, for example to the nearest goal. In this way the sports photographer is free to focus across the whole pitch, whilst reserving the ability to rapidly adjust to the pre-selected setting if interesting action in the goal area arises. The lens is also ideal for animal photography in the wild, or for frame-filling pictures of important details in a landscape. But it is also very well-suited to fashion or advertising photography where its shallow depth of field and telephoto character can be used for unusual results.

The Apo-Extender-R 1.4X turns the 400mm Apo-Telyt into a 560mm, f/4, and the Apo-Extender-R 2X converts it to a 800mm, f/5.6, retaining apochromatic correction and excellent reproduction quality, even at the maximum aperture. With the Extender-R 2X the apochromatic correction is not fully maintained and stopping down by one or two stops is necessary.

The lens hood supplied with the Apo-Telyt also protects the front element against mechanical damage and should always be kept in place.

Telyt-S 800mm, f/6.3

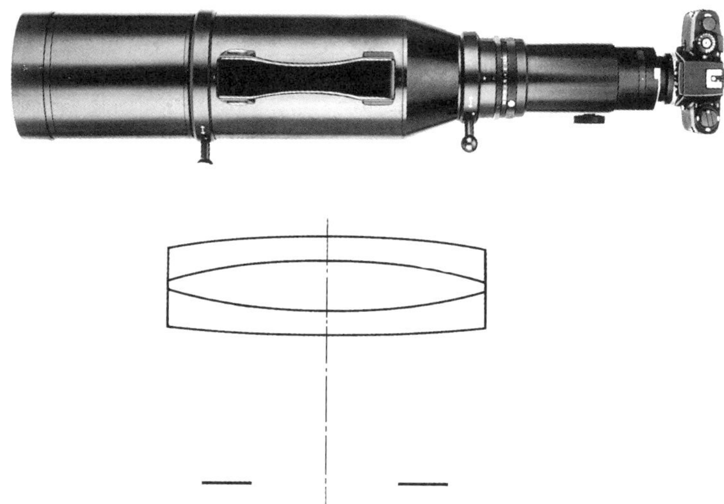

The Telyt-S 800mm, f/6.3 is a distance lens specifically developed for specialist applications, such as documentary photography and surveillance of subjects that are difficult of access. The sharpness and contrast reproduction of this lens are unsurpassed in this focal length and it possesses almost apochromatic properties. The smallest details are clearly resolved. Vignetting and distortion are so slight that they can be ignored. The lens consists of only three elements cemented together, a construction made possible by using specially developed optical glass with extraordinary properties produced in the Leica laboratory.

The lens does not have an automatic spring-back diaphragm, but the pre-selected aperture can be used in aperture priority mode. A filter compartment, built into the lens, accepts series 7 filters. Focusing is carried out by means of a knob with parallel action. The tripod mount allows easy switching from portrait to landscape format, and vice versa. The carrying handle of the lens also acts as post-and-notch sight for rapidly aligning the lens on its 'target'. It should only be used on a very sturdy tripod with an additional monopod to support the barrel, which has a socket for the purpose. When shooting with the Telyt-S 800mm,f/6.3 and the R7 use the independent mirror release if possible. For transport purposes the lens can be disassembled into five components, which fit into the aluminium case supplied.

The zoom lenses

Considerable thought is required when considering whether to add zooms to a Leica outfit. Leica recognized this a long time ago, and its range of zoom lenses shows wise restraint. The zoom lenses available for the Leica R7 are subject to Leica quality requirements, which means that no extreme focal length ranges are offered. The optical performance of the three Leica zoom lenses is good. But how good, you may ask. The belief is widely held that today's zooms offer the same reproduction quality as fixed focal lengths, but this is true only if average fixed focal length lenses are used in the comparison. Compared to the optical quality of the fixed focal length Leica R lenses, the zoom lenses, particularly at their maximum aperture and at the extremes of their focal length range, cannot compete, although at f/8 or f/11 and with average subjects the reproduction quality of the zooms is comparable, although a reduction in optical performance in the image corners is still noticeable. Zoom lenses are also slower than fixed focal lengths, leading to slower shutter speeds and a slight reduction in the creative possibilities of the depth of field. Moreover, the construction of zoom lenses gives rise to a greater degree of vignetting and distortion than comparable fixed focal length lenses.

On the other hand, zoom lenses offer a number of advantages. They cover a wide focal length range and consequently, from a creative point of view, replace several lenses. Lens changing is usually avoided, so opportunities are not missed, and there is no need to carry around several lenses. There is a considerable financial saving too if one zoom is bought in place of several individual lenses.

Zoom lens advocates claim they allow the photographer to select any image area within the focal length range without changing the shooting position. But frame-filling photographs do not replace the conscious search for the best camera position and for interesting perspectives. Consequently many zoom photographers are unwilling to search for pictures by making conscious use of focal length.

Vario-Elmar-R 28-70mm,f/3.5-4.5

With the Vario-Elmar-R 28-70mm,f/3.5-4.5, focal length and focusing are adjusted by two separate rings. The speed of the lens varies with the focal length, which enabled its design to be compact and lightweight. At the 28mm setting the maximum aperture is f/3.5, which is continuously reduced down to a speed of f/4.5 at 70mm but this is automatically taken into account by the TTL metering system of the Leica R7.

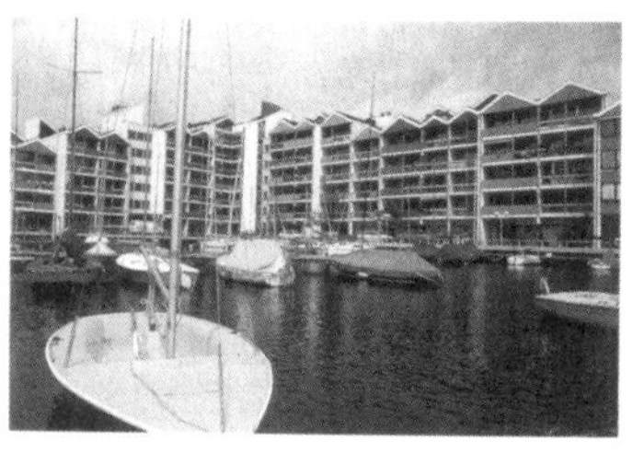
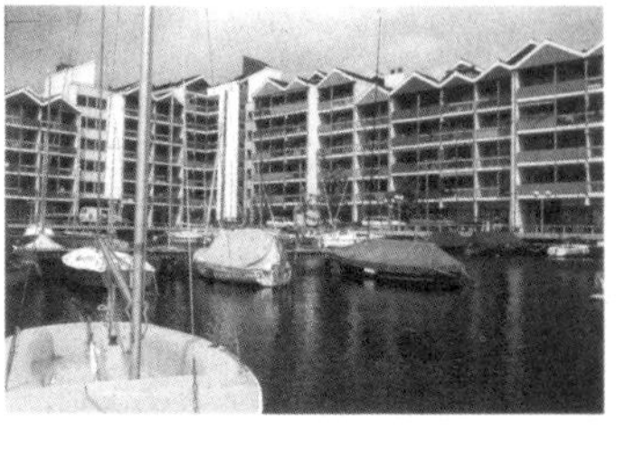

The Leica zoom lenses between them cover a wide range of focal lengths.

The engraved aperture values refer to the 28mm focal length. As the focal length is increased the front element moves into the lens barrel. This, in conjunction with the telescopic lens hood, protects the front element against stray light in a way that is appropriate to the changing focal length. A polarizing filter cannot really be used because its mount causes vignetting at the shortest focal length and at longer focal lengths retraction of the front element prevent its being rotated.

At the maximum aperture the Vario-Elmar-R 28-70mm,f/3.5-4.5 offers good contrast and sharpness, which can be improved further by stopping down by one or two stops. A reduction in sharpness and contrast becomes noticeable in the image corners at close range, but can be largely eliminated by stopping down to f/11. At short focal lengths it exhibits barrel distortion, and at longer ones pin-cushion distortion. Focal lengths just under 50mm are almost free of distortion. Vignetting, especially at short focal lengths, can be reduced considerably by stopping down to f/5.6 or f/8. The Vario-Elmar-R 28-70mm,f/3.5-4.5 is well-suited to landscape and travel photography.

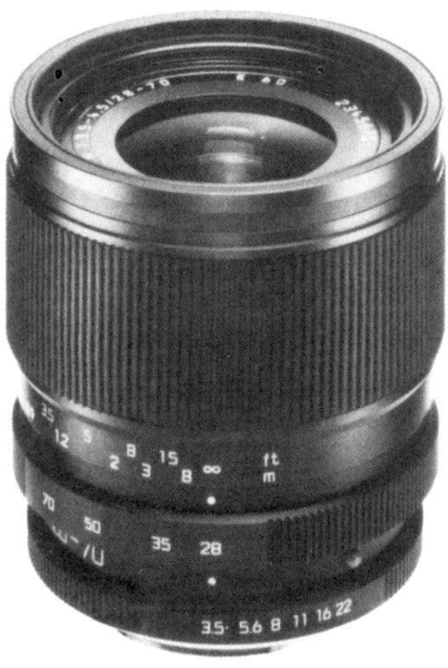

Vario-Elmar-R 28-70mm,f/3.5-4.5

Vario-Elmar-R 35-70mm,f/3.5

The Vario-Elmar-R 35-70mm,f/3.5 is a two-ring zoom with parallel focusing action, so that polarizing and graduated filters can be used. The maximum aperture of f/3.5 is constant across the whole focal length

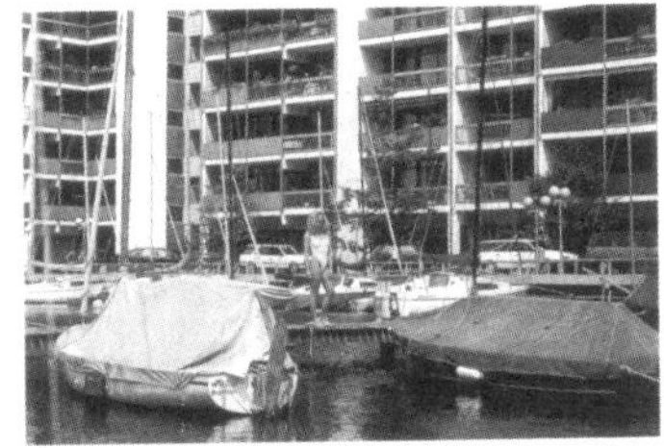
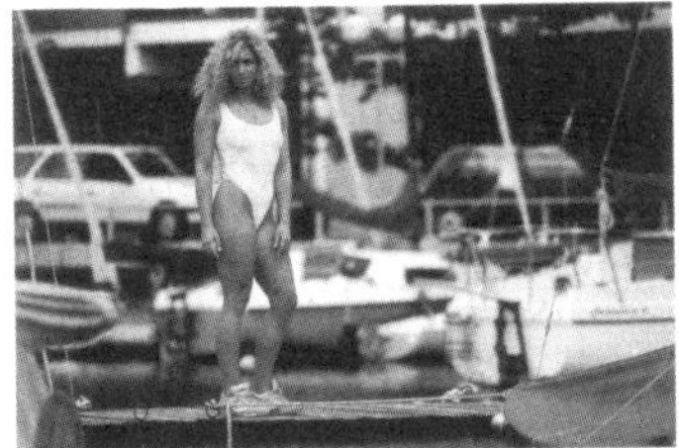
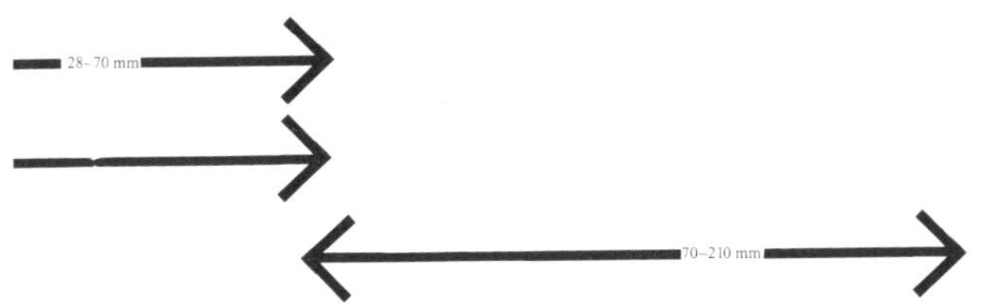

range. At the maximum aperture and medium and longer range the sharpness and contrast performance is good and can be improved by stopping down to f/5.6 or f/8. At closer range there is slight curvature of field. The barrel-shaped distortion at short focal lengths and pin-cushion distortion at longer focal lengths – inevitable with zoom lenses – are so slight that they will hardly be noticeable in practice. The slight vignetting at the maximum aperture is largely eliminated by stopping down to f/8. The preferred applications of this all-round-lens are travel and landscape photography.

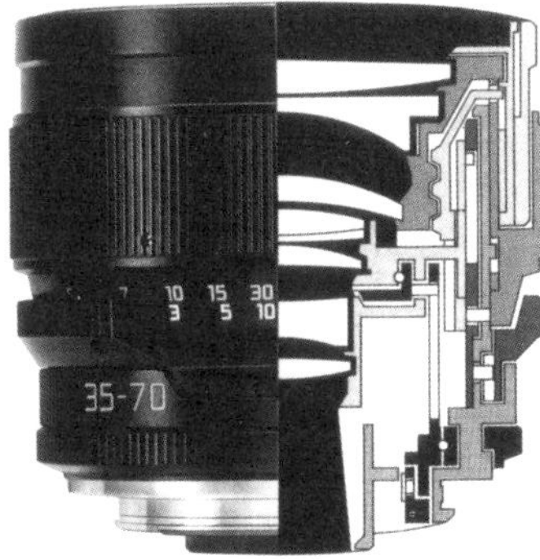
Vario-Elmar-R 70-210mm,f4

Vario-Elmar-R 70-210mm,f/4

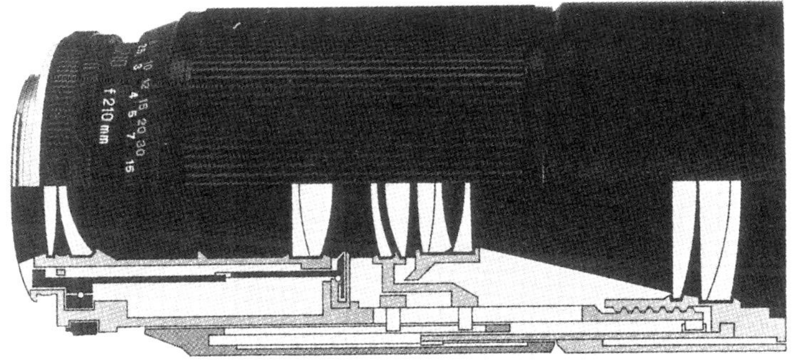

The Vario-Elmar-R 70-210mm,f/4 is a slide zoom with a constant maximum aperture across the whole focal length range. At medium and long distances it offers good sharpness and contrast, even at the maximum aperture, which can be further improved by stopping down to f/5.6 or f/8. At close range and maximum aperture it shows slight curvature of field which is unimportant in pictorial photography. The barrel distortion at shorter focal lengths and pin-cushion distortion at longer focal lengths is so slight with this lens that it can be ignored in pictorial photography. Vignetting is only visible on even, light-coloured subjects, but can be reduced considerably by stopping down to f/8 or f/11.

The Vario-Elmar-R 70-210mm,f/4 is a good complement to the Vario-Elmar-R 28-70mm,f/3.5-4.5 or the Vario-Elmar-R 35-70,f/3.5. Its particular strengths are landscape and travel photography, as well as portrait, sports, and animal photography at medium range.

7. Specialist Leica R lenses

The rapid-focus lenses

The Telyt-R 400mm,f/6.8 and Telyt-R 560mm,f/6.8 lenses are equipped with the Novoflex rapid-focusing handgrip. Both lenses consist of only two cemented elements, employing special Leica glasses, but they are highly corrected achromatically, producing very sharp and brilliant images. Slight curvature of field, characteristic of the design, is of no consequence when the lenses are used on subjects for which they were intended, such as wild-life and sport.

The Novoflex rapid-focusing handgrip and shoulder stock permits hand-held photography of rapidly moving subjects. The lenses will probably be used at maximum aperture to ensure the fastest possible shutter speed. The Novoflex rapid-focusing handgrip has two pistol grips, the rear one of which can be attached to a shoulder stock. In the neutral position the lens is set at its closest focusing distance by means of spring tension. By pressing the handgrips together, the optic is moved along the optical axis to focus. If desired, a pre-selected distance setting can be fixed by means of a dial on the handgrip.

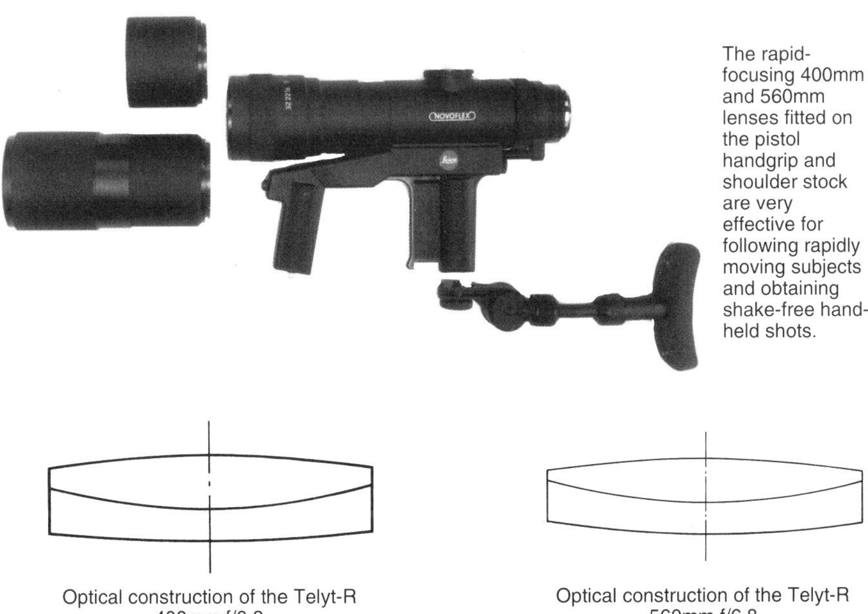

The rapid-focusing 400mm and 560mm lenses fitted on the pistol handgrip and shoulder stock are very effective for following rapidly moving subjects and obtaining shake-free hand-held shots.

Optical construction of the Telyt-R
400mm,f/6.8

Optical construction of the Telyt-R
560mm,f/6.8

The Telyt-R 400mm,f/6.8 can be focused to 7.5m, while the Telyt-R 560mm,f/6.8 focuses down to 13m. An extension tube brings the closest focusing distance of the 400mm lens to 2.4m and that of the 560mm to 4.15m.

A release button on the forward grip connects to the camera by a cable release or electronic cable connection, provided a motor drive or winder is attached to the camera. Exposure lock is also possible with selective metering if a cable release is used. The camera can be rotated to select landscape or portrait format. Filters fit into a special compartment.

The mirror lens

The MR-Telyt-R 500mm,f/8 is a cata-dioptric, or mirror lens in which the light rays fall onto a ring-shaped concave main mirror at the back of the lens, which concentrates them onto a small secondary mirror in front, from which they are reflected back and focused onto the film by a number of lens elements. The lens is very light-weight and compact for its focal length and particularly attractive for travel photographers.

Because of their construction mirror lenses cannot have an iris diaphragm. The stated maximum aperture refers to the size of the entry pupil and corresponds to an aperture value of f/8. Exposure can only be adjusted by means of the shutter speed and there

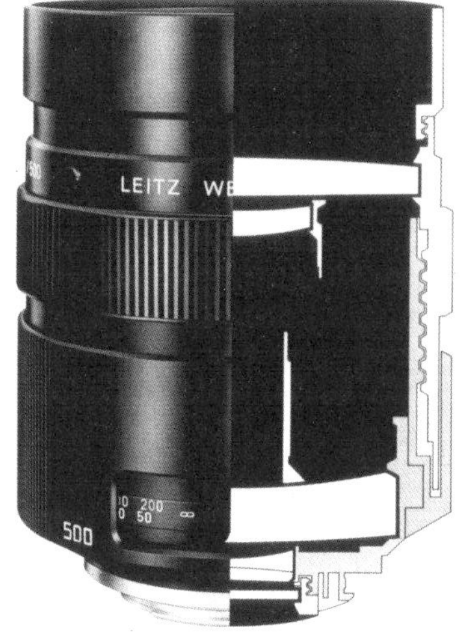

MR-Telyt-R 500mm,f/8

is no control over depth of field. If the light intensity is too bright, even for 1/2000 sec, the neutral density filter, with a filter factor of 4x, supplied with the lens has to be attached.

Because of its mirror construction the MR-Telyt-R 500mm,f/8 is largely free of chromatic aberration. Sharpness and contrast are correspondingly high, almost reaching the level of apochromatically corrected lenses at medium and long distances. No focus correction is necessary for infra-red photography. The closest focusing distance is 4m with a slight reduction in performance at close range.

As the depth of field cannot be extended by stopping down, focusing is more important than usual. The uniform groundglass focusing screen is definitely recommended. The slightly darker viewfinder image does, however, make accurate focusing more difficult, particularly in low

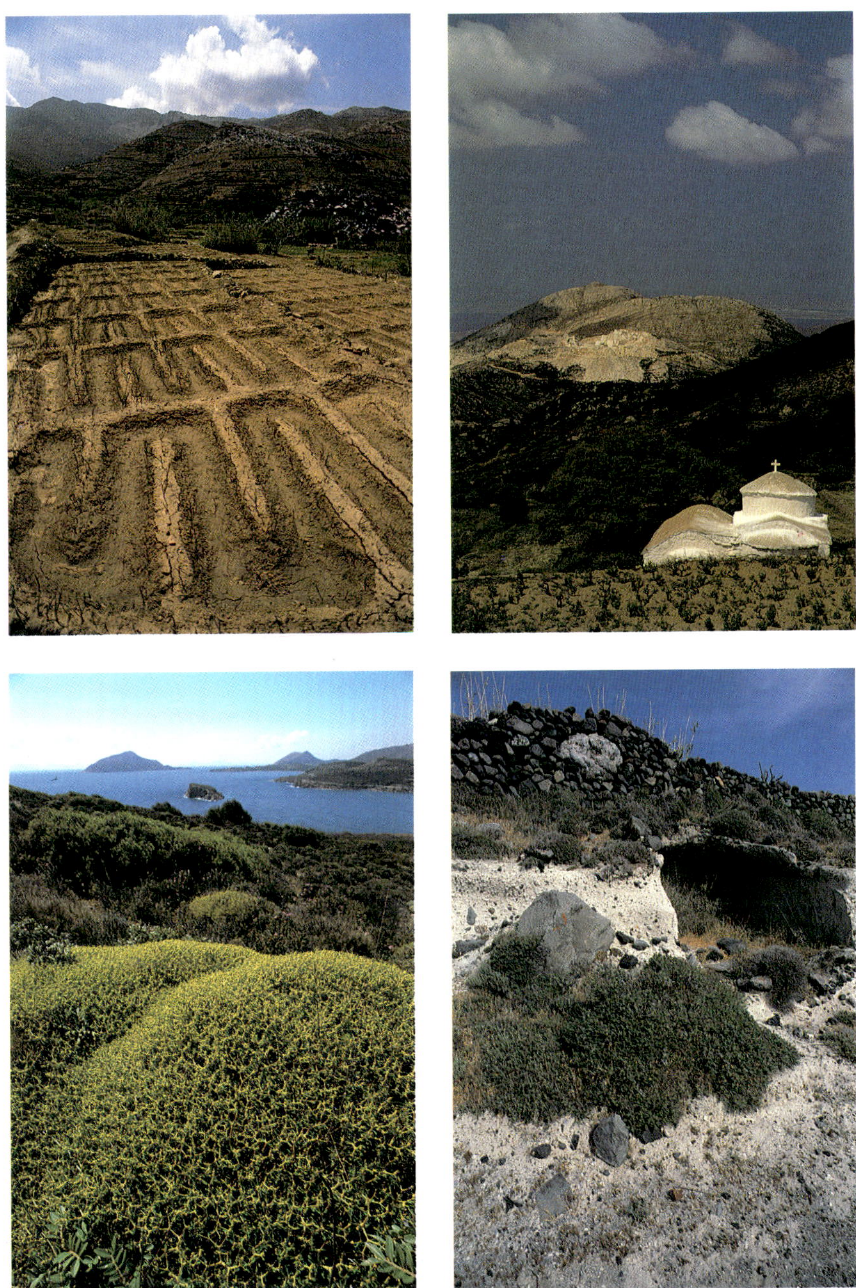

Wide-angle lenses can produce landscape pictures with great emphasis on the foreground (left), but with everything in focus. Medium long focus lenses can be used to pick out the middle distance (right), with everything in focus to the horizon. The former can produce a feeling of tension, the latter is more restful.

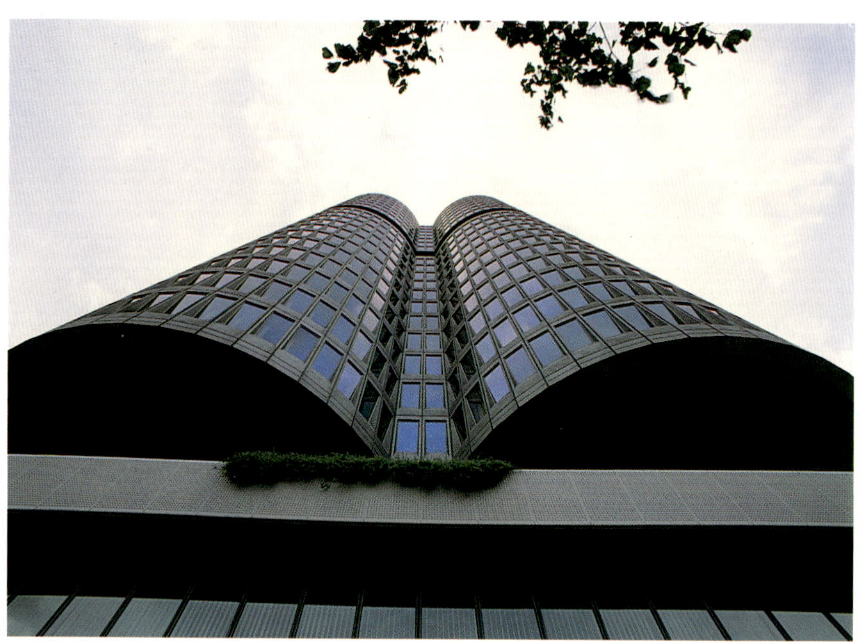

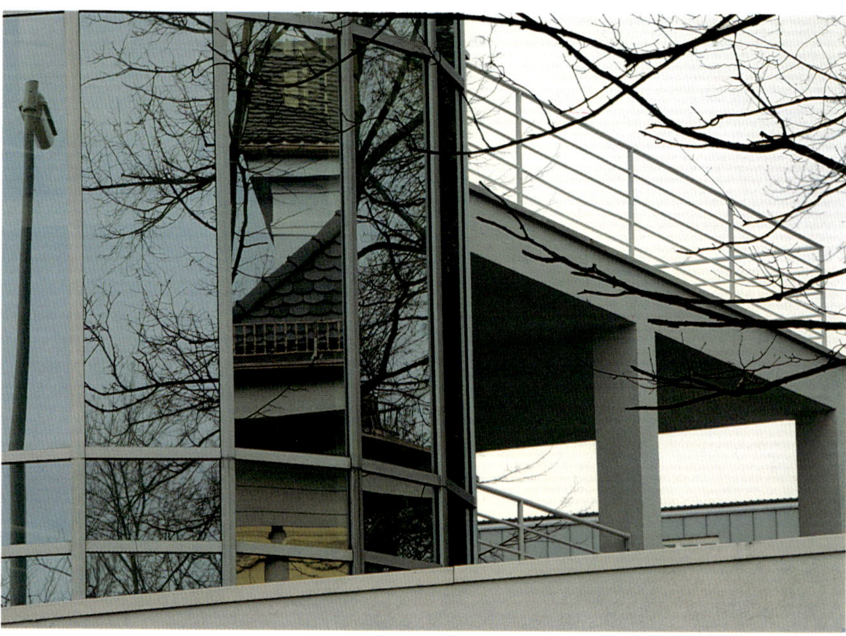

Architectural photography is not limited only to accurate reproduction of buildings in terms of perspective, as evidenced by these interpretative architectural shots.

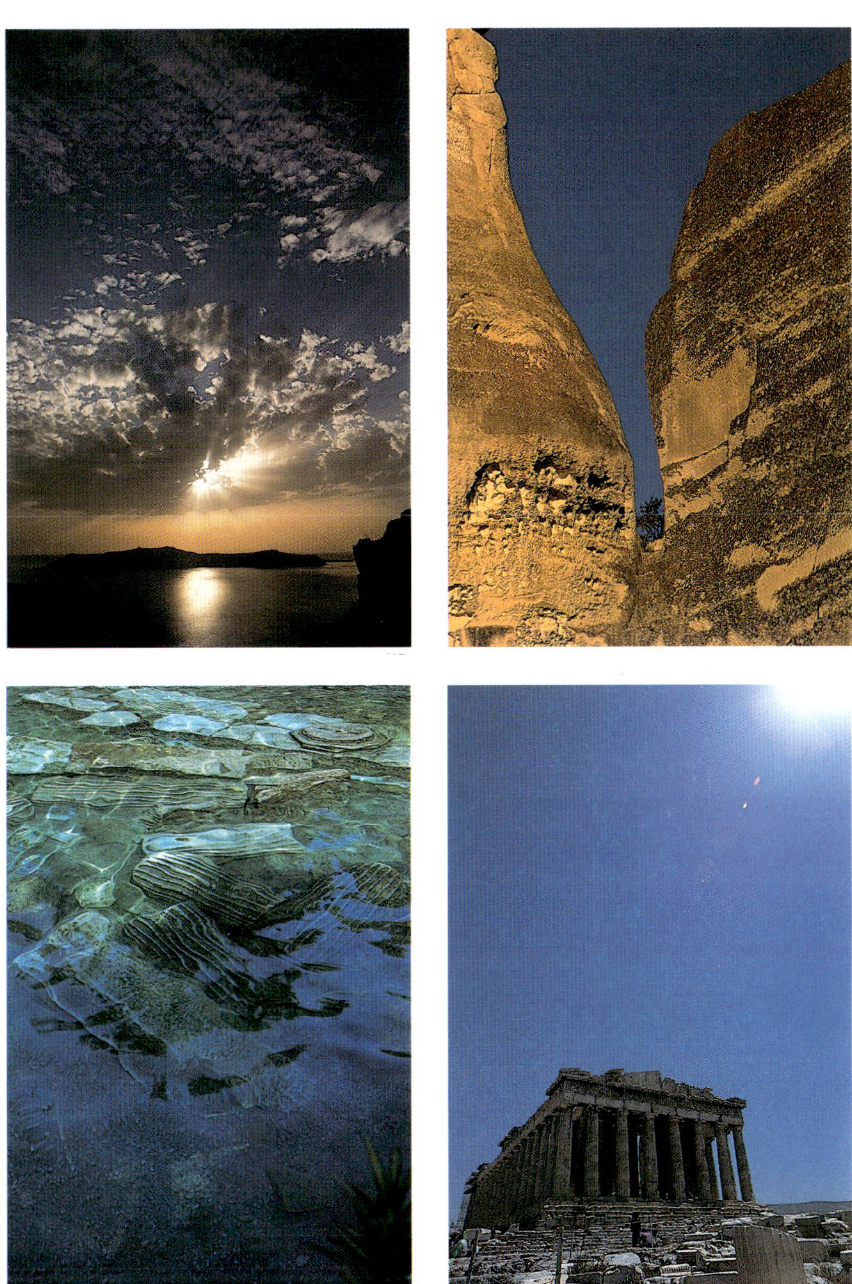

Polarizing filters are amongst the most important in professional photography. They remove reflections from non-metallic surfaces (water) or provide the right mood for a picture.

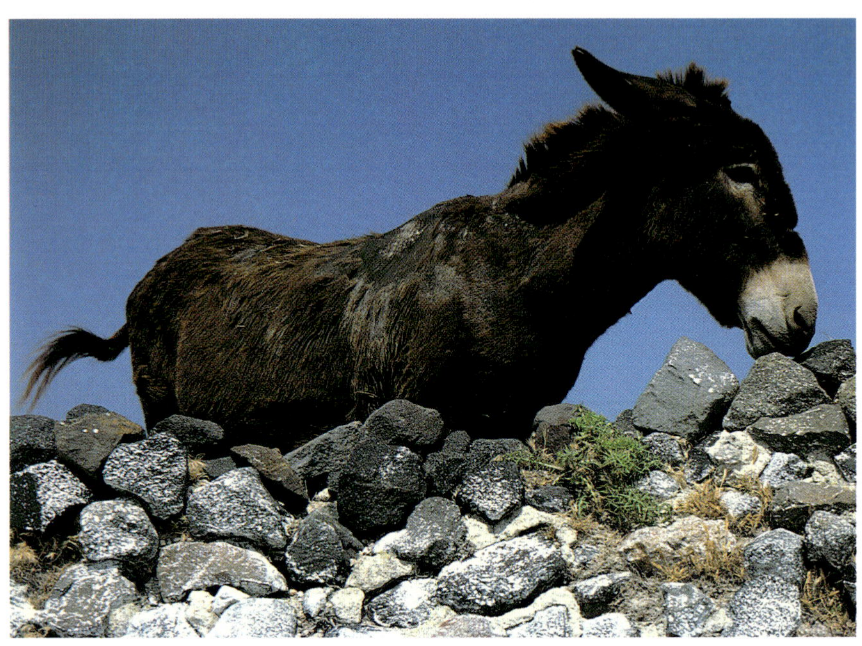

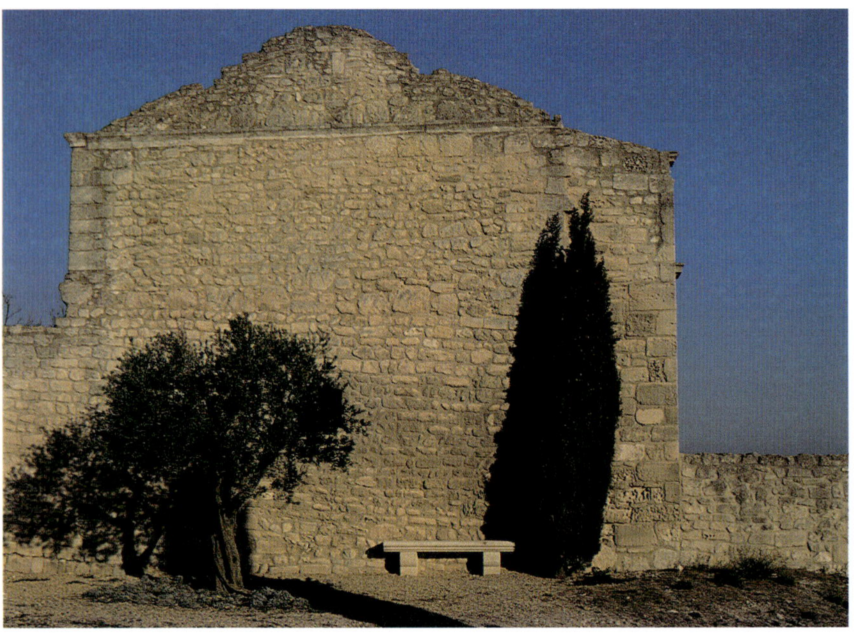

Polarizing filters can be used to produce a richer reproduction of colour, which can often increase the effect of a picture.

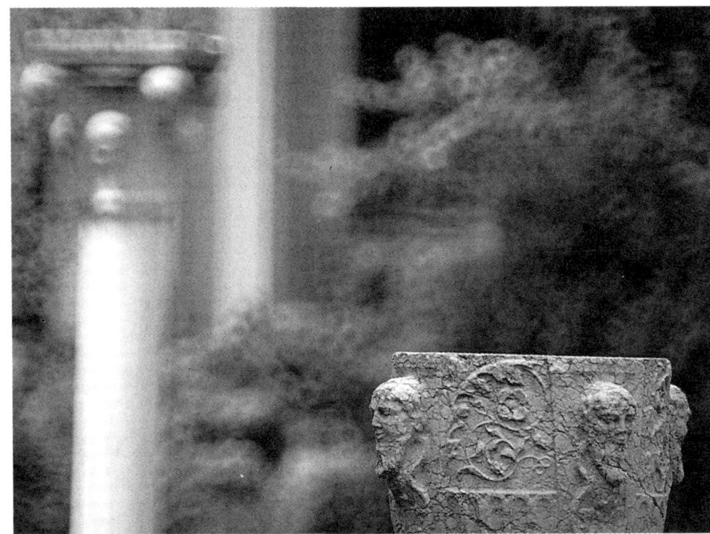

The ring-shaped blurred images of small details in the out-of-focus areas in the picture are typical for a mirror lens.

light. The low weight of the lens means that it has a very low inertia and therefore is even more prone to shake than heavier lenses.

An out-of-focus point in the image from a mirror lens appears as a ring rather than a disc. This is most noticeable with bright points of light in a picture, such as with sunlight reflected on water. The effect can be used as a deliberate stylistic tool in picture composition.

Perspective control lenses (Shift Lenses)

Used purposefully and with skill, converging verticals can increase the effect of a picture; used badly, or resulting from carelessness, they can ruin one. Converging verticals occur, for example, when a tall building is photographed from street level with the camera tilted, so that parallel lines converge towards the top of the frame. There are many ways of avoiding converging verticals, but most have a snag. Converging verticals can only be properly avoided if the film plane is aligned so that it is parallel with the subject plane, and this is only possible, as far as 35mm cameras are concerned, with shift lenses (also called PA lenses, for perspective adjustment; or PC lenses, for perspective correction). These are wide-angle lenses with an over-large image circle. The optic can be mechanically shifted from its normal axis so that it will reproduce a portion of the image that would otherwise be outside the image area of a conventional lens with the same focal length. It is important that the camera is aligned precisely before the shift is carried out. This can best be achieved using the focusing screen with grid divisions. Depending on the shooting distance, a small shift of only a few

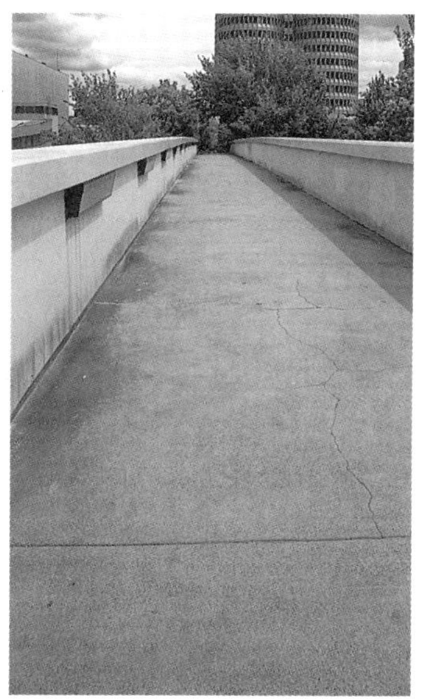
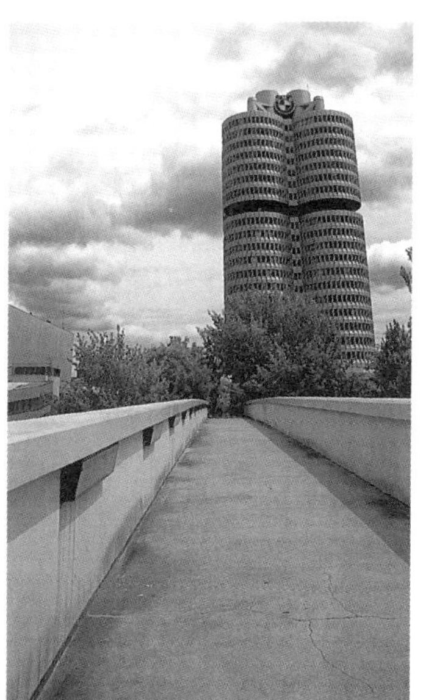
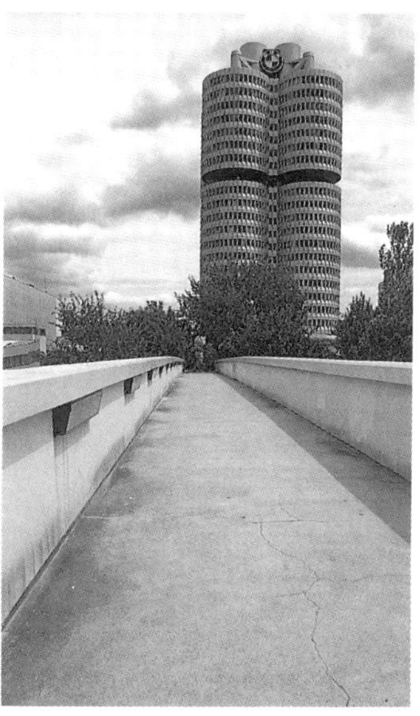

PC-Super-Angulon-R 28mm,f/2.8. Top left:
Film plane parallel with the subject plane, no
adjustment on lens.

Top right: Camera tilted to include tower; film
plane no longer parallel with the subject plane,
no adjustment on lens.

Right: Camera level but an upward vertical shift
of 10mm applied to lens; film plane now
parallel with the subject plane, whole of tower
in view, no converging verticals.

millimetres may be enough to move the image area by several metres. The shift in the image area is visible in the viewfinder of the Leica R7, and can also be calculated using the following formula:

Lens shift (in mm) x shooting distance (in m) / focal length (in mm) = shift in the image area (in m) in the subject plane parallel to that of the shift.

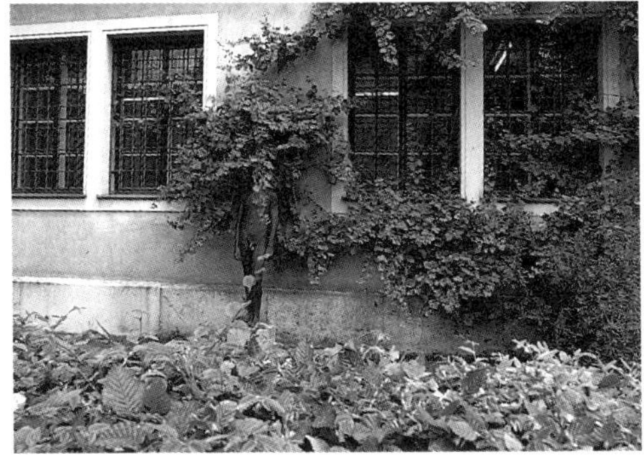

A

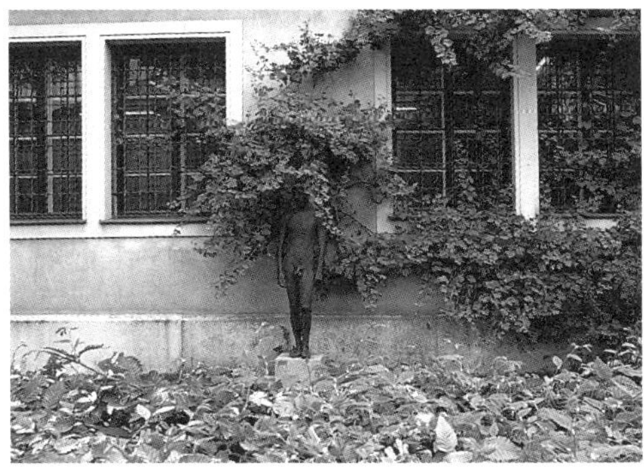

B

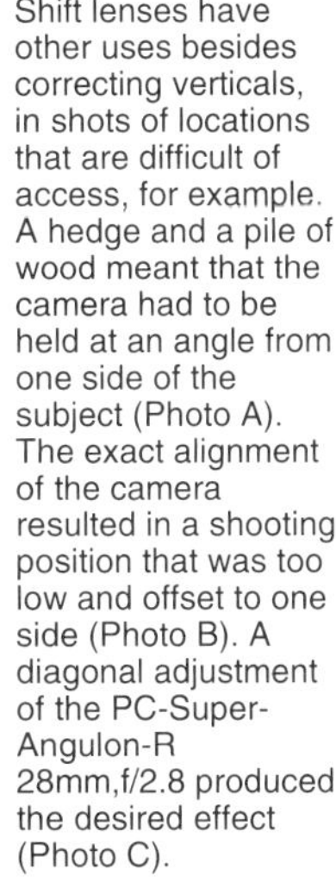

Shift lenses have other uses besides correcting verticals, in shots of locations that are difficult of access, for example. A hedge and a pile of wood meant that the camera had to be held at an angle from one side of the subject (Photo A). The exact alignment of the camera resulted in a shooting position that was too low and offset to one side (Photo B). A diagonal adjustment of the PC-Super-Angulon-R 28mm,f/2.8 produced the desired effect (Photo C).

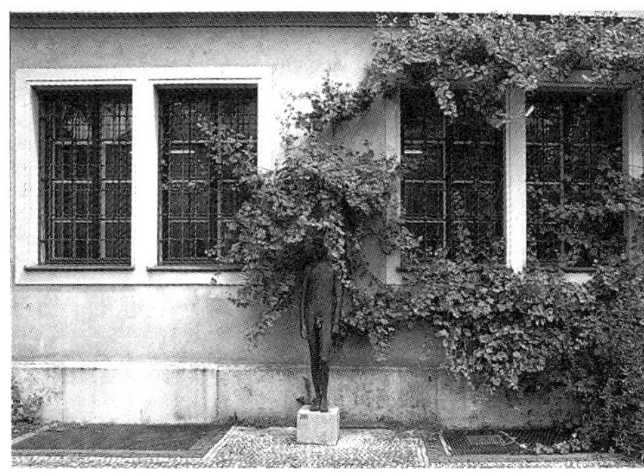

C

Here is an example for the PC-Super-Angulon-R 28mm,f/2.8, with a shift of 11mm and a shooting distance of 50m:

11mm x 50m / 28mm = 19.65m.

Thus an 11mm shift of the lens will cause the image area to be shifted by almost 20m in the subject plane.

The shift can be vertical, horizontal, or diagonal. A horizontal or diagonal shift is most effective if the camera has to be held side-on, for example to avoid a reflection or to get around an obstacle, or to reproduce an object without the receding backgrounds associated with normal perspective. Architectural photography is the obvious domain of shift lenses. A shift lens cannot be fitted with an automatic springback diaphragm so you have to work with the working aperture.

PC-Super-Angulon-R 28mm,f/2.8

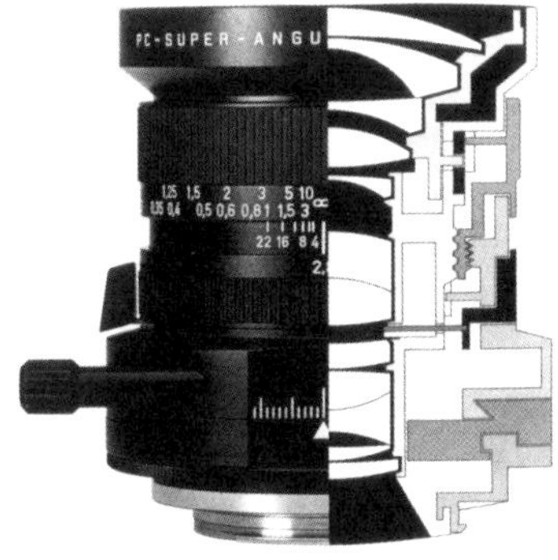

The PC-Super-Angulon-R 28mm,f/2.8 has an effective image circle diameter of 62mm, almost 20mm more than the diagonal of the 35mm film format. This means that the optical axis can be shifted by 11mm in the horizontal or the vertical and by 9.5mm in the diagonal. The shift is effected by a dovetail slide with smooth and precise movement. The degree of shift can be read off a millimetre scale. Click-stops mark the central position and the 9.5mm position. The lens can be turned to the left or right by 360°. Click-stops mark the positions 0°/360°, 45°, 90°, 135°, 180°, 225°, 270°, and 315°.

In the normal setting the PC-Super-Angulon-R 28mm,f/2.8 offers good sharpness and contrast, even at the maximum aperture, which can be further improved by stopping down to f/4 or f/5.6. For medium shifts, f/8 or the smallest aperture f/11 should be selected. For shifts greater than about 9mm an exposure compensation of +½ is necessary.

PA-Curtagon-R 35mm,f/4

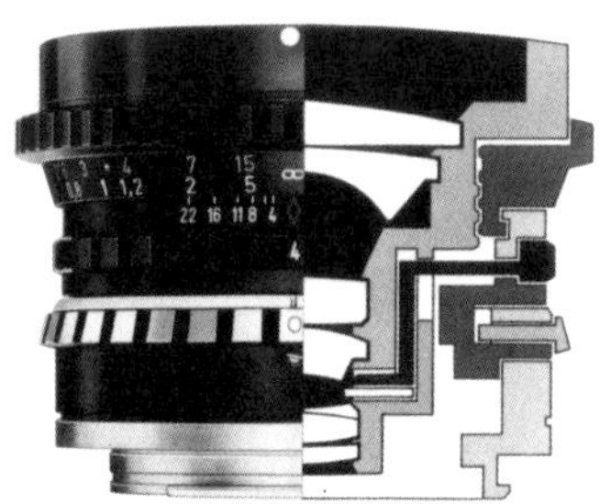

The PA-Curtagon-R 35mm,f/4 has an effective image circle diameter of 57mm, ie 14mm more than the 35mm format diagonal. By means of a special ring the lens can be shifted by 7mm in each direction. The horizontal and vertical positions are click-stopped, but the direction

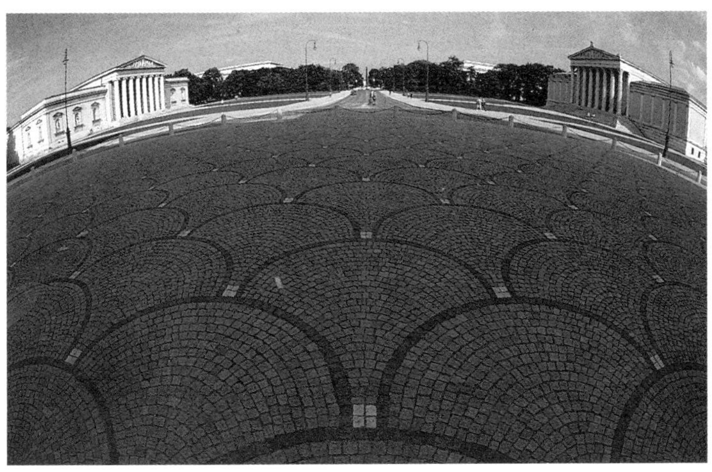

A typical shot with a fisheye lens, easily recognizable from the extreme angle of view and the curved reproduction of straight lines.

Only locals will realize that this shot was taken with the fisheye: the edge of the lake at Nymphenburg Castle is actually straight, not curved as shown in this photo. The line of buildings on the far side of the lake is reproduced as straight because it passes through the centre of the field of view.

of shift can also be turned to the left or right by 360°, so you can shoot
at any intermediate position. The shift from the optical axis is indicated in millimetres, from 0 to 7, on the setting ring.

This lens offers very good sharpness and contrast, even at the maximum
aperture, which can be further improved by stopping down by one or
two stops. At maximum shift stopping down to f/11 is recommended.

The fisheye lens

The special characteristic of the Fisheye-Elmarit-R 16mm,f/2.8 is the
barrel-shaped distortion of straight lines not running through the image
centre. The effect increases with the distance of lines from the centre.
Lines passing through the centre are reproduced straight. The lens offers
good detail and brilliance, even at the maximum aperture, but the reproduction quality can be further improved by stopping down to f/5.6. It
has an integral filter turret with four
filters.

The Fisheye-Elmarit-R 16mm,f/2.8
covers the whole 35mm film format.
Apart from the distortion, the large
diagonal angle of view of 180° has a
panoramic character. But watch out
that the tips of your shoes don't appear
in the photograph – as this can happen
only too easily. Use selective metering
for high contrast subjects – the
different partial contrasts captured by
the wide angle of view can confuse
the exposure meter. This lens is particularly suitable for landscape photography or experimental architectural
photography.

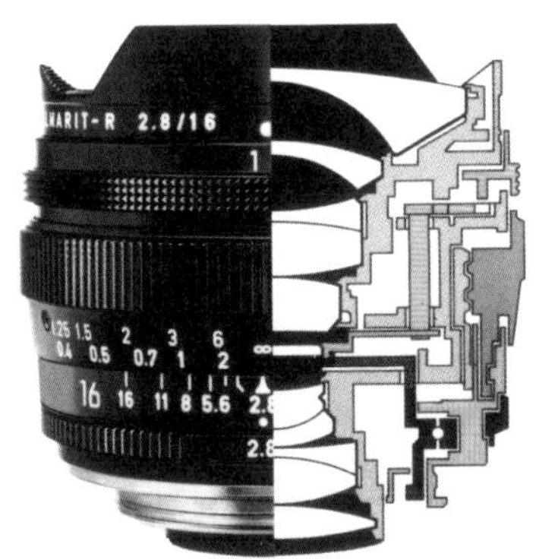

Fisheye-Elmarit-R 16mm,f/2.8

Extenders

The Leica R extenders are high-quality optical systems consisting of 5
or 7 elements. They increase the focal length of the lenses they are used
with by the stated factor, 1.4x or 2x, but at the same time reduce the
speed by a factor of 2 or 4 respectively. Leica extenders are designed
for lenses with focal lengths from 50mm upwards and maximum apertures of f/2 or smaller.

The aperture values and depth of field scales engraved on the lens will
no longer apply to the new focal length. If, for example, the Summicron-
R 90mm,f/2 is turned into a 180mm,f/4 lens with the Apo-Extender-R
2X, the engraved aperture value f/8 corresponds to an actual aperture
value of f/16.

The extenders are useful not only for telephoto photography, but also in the close-up range. A doubling of the focal length at a constant closest focusing distance doubles the reproduction ratio.

The fully automatic spring-back diaphragm function of the Leica R lenses is maintained with the extenders in place, but in order to prevent incorrect exposures you should only select manual or aperture priority exposure modes with integral or selective metering.

Apo-Extender-R 2X

The Apo-Extender 2X has been designed for the apochromatic Leica lenses to maintain their apochromatic correction. It is not suitable for use with the following lenses: Telyt-R 400mm, f/6.8, Telyt-R 560mm,f/6.8, Vario-Elmar 28-70mm, f/3.5-4.5, and Vario-Elmar 70-210mm,f/4.

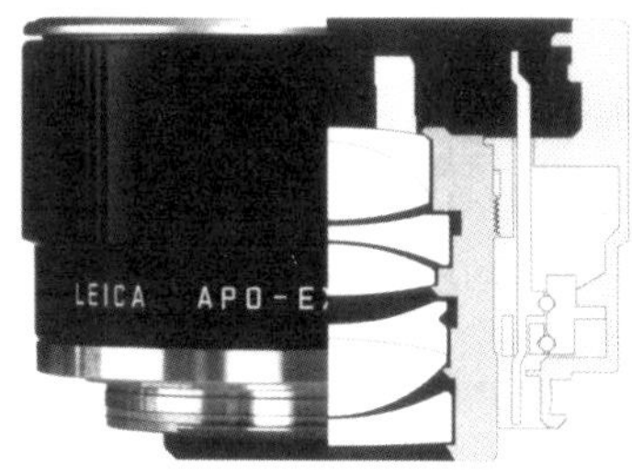

Apo-Extender-R 1.4X

The Apo-Extender-R 1.4X was specially designed for the Apo-Telyt-R 280mm, f/2.8 and the Apo-Telyt-R 400mm,f/2.8, fully maintaining the apochromatic correction of both lenses. The barrel of the Apo-Extender-R 1.4X protrudes at the front and can damage some lenses, but it can be used safely with the following: Macro-Elmar-R 100mm,f/4; Elmarit-R 180mm,f/2.8; Telyt-R 400mm, f/6.8; Telyt-R 560mm,f/6.8; and the Telyt-R 800mm,f/6.3.

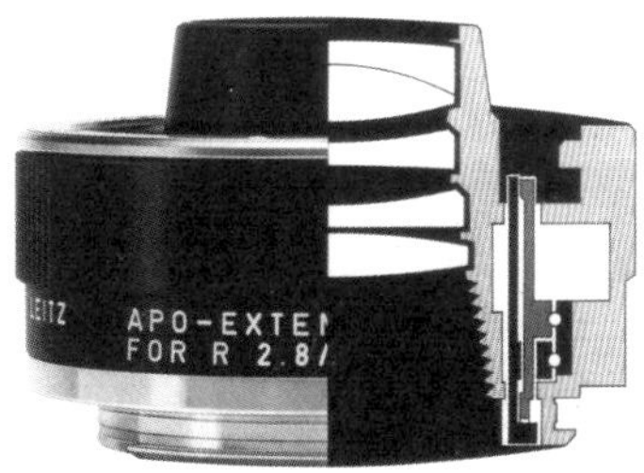

Extender-R 2X

The Extender-R 2X is a high-quality optical construction which can be used with all Leica R lenses of focal length 50mm and longer and with a maximum aperture no larger than f/2, At longer ranges the optical performance that can be achieved with the Extender-R 2X is very good, even at the maximum aperture, and can be further improved by stopping down by two stops. It is not recommended with the Vario-Elmar-R 70-210mm,f/4.

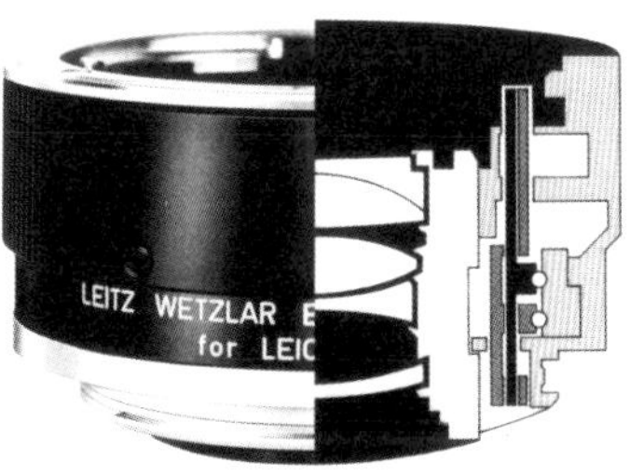

The Photar lenses

The Photar lenses, which are used with the bellows via an adapter, are magnifier lenses specifically designed for the job. They are available at three different focal lengths for different reproduction ratios: Photar 50mm,f/4 (up to 3.2:1), Photar 25mm,f/2 (up to 7:1), and Photar 12.5mm,f/2.4 (up to 15.5:1). The reproduction ratio of 15.5:1 that can be achieved with the Photar 12.5mm,f/2 magnifies a subject area of only 1.5x2.3mm to 24x36mm. These specialist lenses offer maximum reproduction quality at such reproduction ratios.

8. Accessories for the Leica R7

With an appropriate selection of lenses, the Leica R7 has everything you need to take photographs, but a sensible choice of accessories will extend the scope of the camera. They can open up new possibilities in close-up photography, or simply contribute to more effective operation in everyday photography. Leica supply accessories specifically designed to go with its own cameras and lenses. The most important accessory items abd their applications are described in the following pages. Many amateur photographers encumber themselves with so many accessories that that they inhibit their photography. Accessories should be chosen with great care and discrimination, for the sort of work you want to do, not because they look impressive and might come in useful one day.

Viewfinder accessories

The viewfinder image is crucial for accurate focusing of the lens, and therefore greatly influences image sharpness. But different photographic applications often require different focusing aids. In order to ensure optimum focus in every shooting situation, there are viewfinder accessories such as interchangeable focusing screens, anglefinders, and eye cups.

Interchangeable focusing screens

There are five different focusing screens for the Leica R7. Depending on the subject, reproduction ratio, lens focal length, and lighting conditions, one of them will be best to assist in accurate focusing. All are easily interchangeable by means of the tweezers supplied with each accessory screen. Never touch the screens with your fingers, and always exercise great care when changing the screens. On all focusing screens a central circle with a diameter of 7mm marks the selective metering area. Leica focusing screens are highly sophisticated designs and offer excellent optical quality.

The Universal Focusing Screen is supplied with the Leica R7 as standard so the camera is well-equipped for most, or at least the most common, photographic situations. A split-image wedge with a diameter of 3mm is located at the centre of the screen, and a microprism ring (consisting of four-sided microprisms) is located around this. The outer edge of this ring also marks the area for selective metering. The surrounding field looks like a ground-glass screen, but actually consists of minute triangular microprisms.

The split-image wedge helps even inexperienced photographers to focus quickly and easily on subjects with clear lines or contours in the

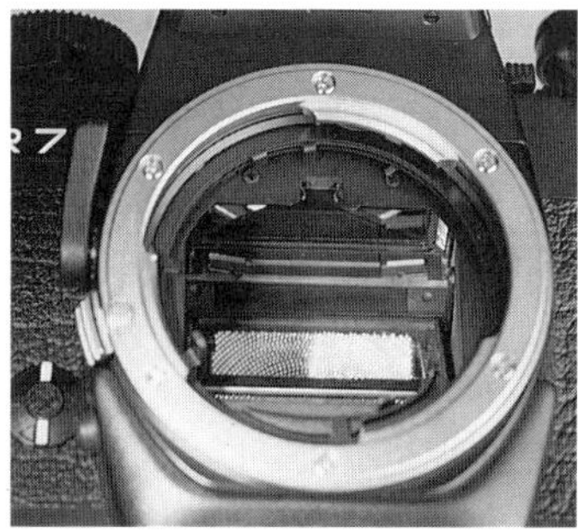

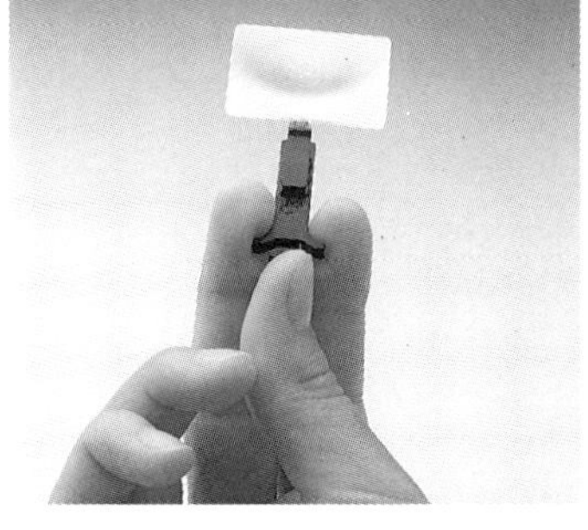

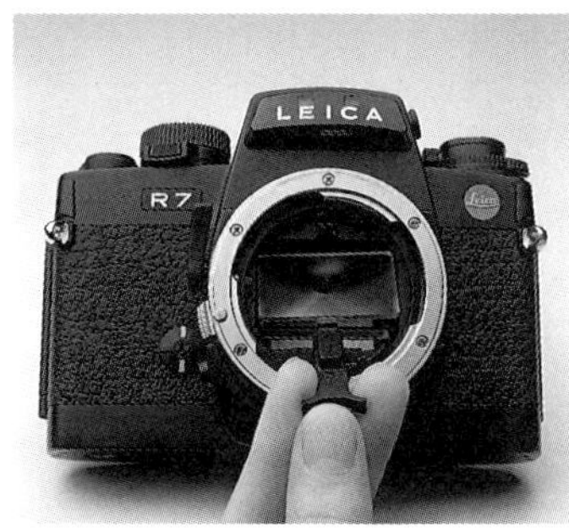

Changing the focusing screen must only be done with the special tweezers provided and with great care.

focusing plane. The metered portion of the subject is sharp if the partial images in the two halves of the split-image wedge fit together. The microprism ring aids focusing on areas or structures that do not have recognizable lines or contours. If the image is unsharp, the microprism ring 'flickers'. When the focus is found the flickering stops and the focused image portion is sharp and clearly visible. These two focusing aids can fail in the telephoto range, depending on the subject and lighting conditions. From a focal length of 180mm, in combination with apertures smaller than f/4, the metering circle begins to darken, so that focusing is no longer possible. In such cases you can only use the matte surrounding area, as on a classical groundglass screen, or change to another focusing screen.

The Microprism Screen is constructed in a similar way to the universal focusing screen, only without the split-image wedge. The central microprism circle corresponds to the selective metering area and the surrounding field consists of triangular microprisms. Focusing is carried out via the microprism ring, or – as with the universal focusing screen – via the surrounding area. If the subject portion on the screen is not sharp, the rectangular microprisms will flicker. If the image is sharp the flickering stops and the subject portion will be clearly visible. When accurate focus is found the microprism focusing screen allows the whole image to be viewed freely, without any focusing aids getting in the way.

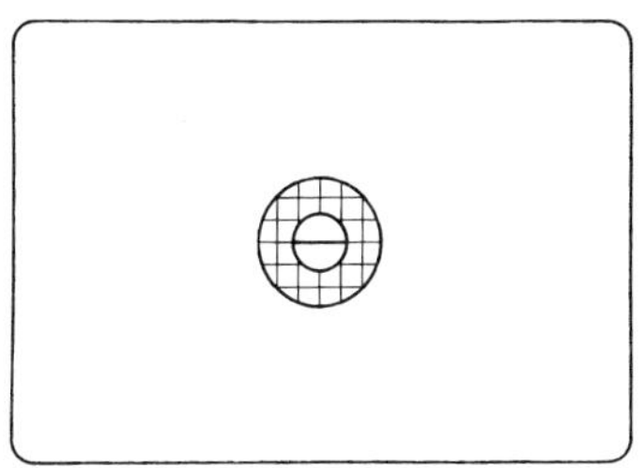

The universal focusing screen

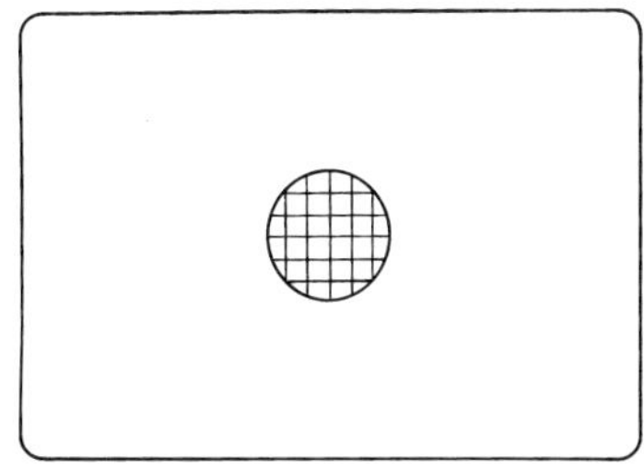

The microprism focusing screen

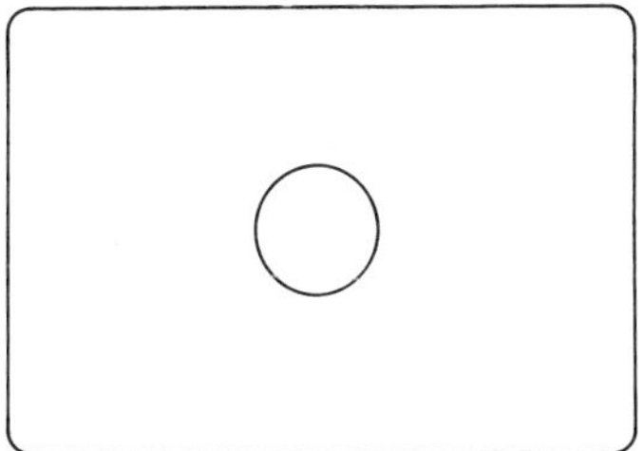

The groundglass matte screen

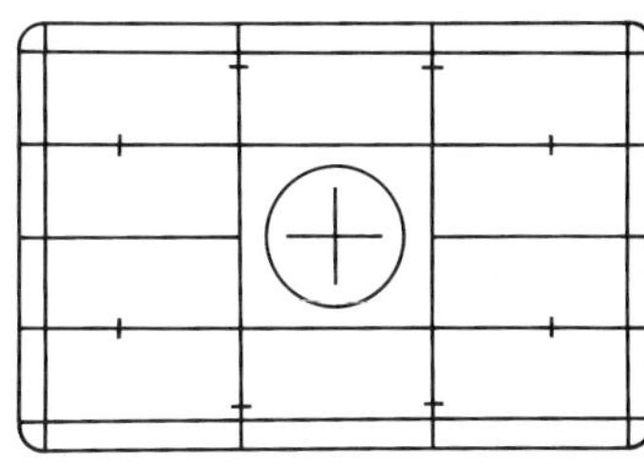

Groundglass matte screen with grid

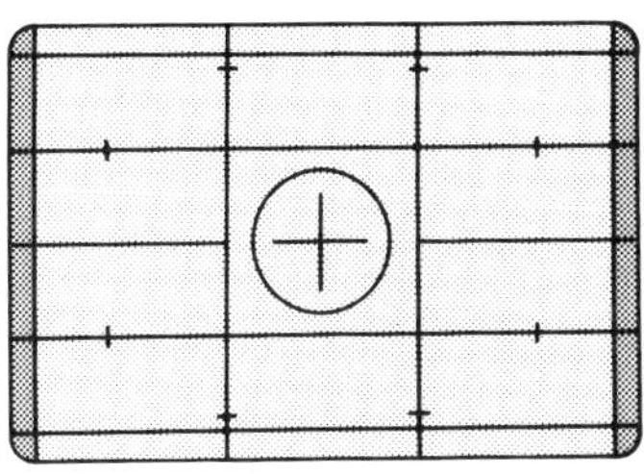

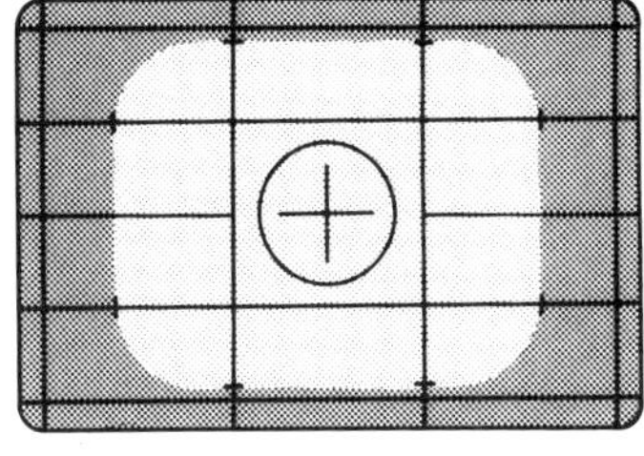

TV screen markings on the groundglass screen with grid divisions: the two outer vertical lines mark the cropping for frame-filling reproduction on a TV screen (left); the short cross-lines the title area according to DIN 108 (right).

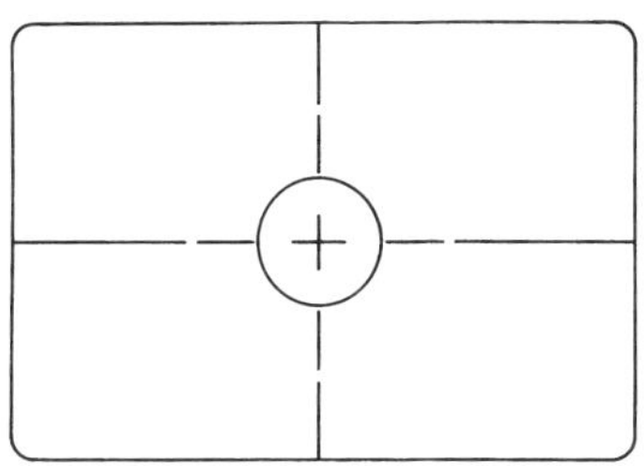

The clear glass screen
with crosshairs

But the transition from unsharp to sharp is less clearly visible than with the partial images produced by the split-image wedge. In low light or with macro work with long barrel extensions, accurate focusing is very difficult with this screen. Moreover, with slow telephoto lenses the microprism ring can darken from a focal length of 180mm.

The Uniform Groundglass Screen. Only the circle marking the selective metering area intrudes in the image formed on the universal groundglass screen. Focusing is done by sight and requires practice as the transition from unsharp to sharp is gradual rather than abrupt. The uniform groundglass screen provides a bright viewfinder image, which means that focusing is still easy even with slow lenses. The uniform groundglass screen is also very good for focusing with telephoto lenses with long focal lengths, as well as in the macro range.

The Uniform Groundglass Screen with Grid Divisions is a special version of the uniform groundglass screen for architectural and reproduction work. Vertical and horizontal lines divide the image area, the selective metering area is outlined by a circle, and cross-hairs define the precise centre. The two outer verticals mark the area (more precisely, the ratio between the sides) of the viewing screen, while the eight small cross lines indicate the proportions of the standard TV screen for making slides for TV transmission. In close-up and macro work the reproduction ratio can be determined through the viewfinder, directly on the groundglass screen because the two centre verticals are positioned at a distance of 10mm.

This screen provides a brilliant viewfinder image which can (depending on the maximum aperture of the lens and the light conditions) be up to two light values brighter than that of the universal focusing screen. It is ideal, if not indispensable (clip-on spirit level notwithstanding), for precise alignment of the camera for architectural, panoramic, and reproduction photography. It is also good for focusing with slow telephoto lenses or in low light.

Many photographers go for the uniform groundglass screen or the microprism screen because they find any markings in the viewfinder disturbs picture composition. However, this is down to individual preference. Some people use the uniform groundglass screen with grid division as a universal screen, making the most of the grid divisions for picture composition. The divisions not only help to avoid converging verticals, but also, in landscape photography for example, aid horizontal alignment of the horizon in the upper or lower third of the frame. You can also focus on any part of the screen, so you don't, for example, have to align the split-image wedge on a suitable outline at the side of the viewfinder, and then have to realign the camera to choose the framing. The uniform groundglass screen with grid divisions makes for easy working with almost any lens and in every subject area.

The Clear Glass Screen with cross-hairs, whilst not very suitable for pictorial photography, is ideal for photography with optical instruments, such as microscopes, astronomical telescopes, or endoscopes. Focusing takes rather longer and is complicated, but very precise, particularly at higher magnifications.

The Anglefinder R

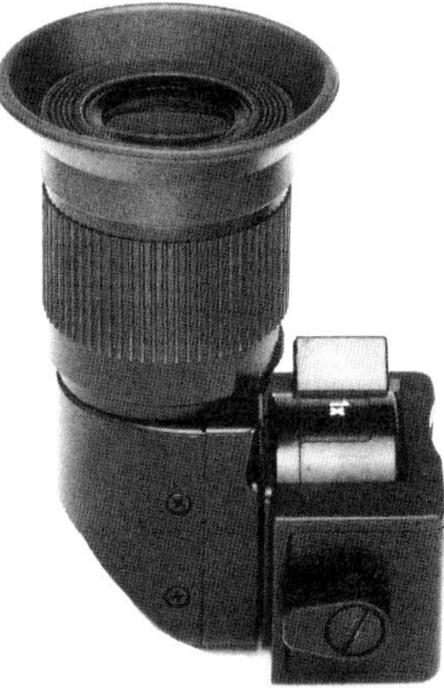

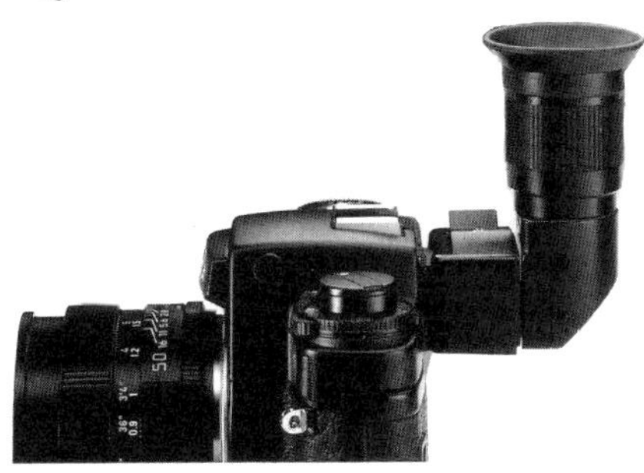

An anglefinder provides comfortable viewing from above or from the side. The Anglefinder R can be switched to give a 2x magnification.

The Anglefinder R is a welcome help for macro and repro photography, particularly when the camera is close to the ground or mounted on a repro stand. It provides a viewfinder image that is upright and the right way around. The Anglefinder R is pushed onto the eyepiece mount of the Leica R7 and can be rotated through 360° with a click-stop every 90°. In the basic setting (1X) the viewfinder image is marginally reduced, but the viewfinder indications are still visible. Switching to 2X causes the centre of the viewfinder image to be magnified 2x, which makes focusing easier. The integral dioptric adjustment allows corrections from −6 to +4 dioptres. The adjustment is carried out with the camera lens defocussed and until the selective metering circle is sharply defined.

Eyecup

The eyecup is pushed onto the eyepiece mount and protects the viewfinder eyepiece against strong side light. Spectacle-wearers also like to use the eyecup, in order to prevent scratching of their glasses. However, it can cause shading at the edges of the viewfinder, so that parts of the viewfinder image and the viewfinder indications are no longer visible.

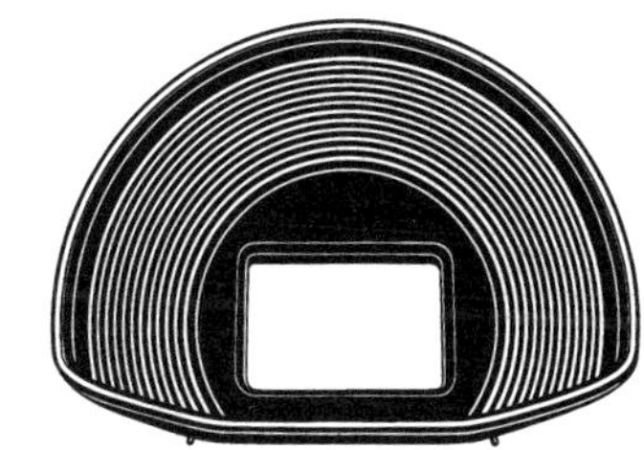

The eyepiece cup also serves to hold eyesight correction lenses

Eyesight correction lenses

The eyepiece of the Leica R7 is adjustable for the user's eyesight by
+/−2 dioptres. If a greater correction than this is required then it is
neccessary to fit additional eyesight correction lenses. Leica supply
these for plus or minus 0.5, 1.0, 1.5, 2.0 and 3.0 dioptres. They are held
in position by a special attachment which mounts on the eyepiece, or
by the eyecup. Either way they are securely locked in position. The
dioptre correction of the adjustable eyepiece and that of a correction
lens is additive, so it is possible to achieve a continuous range of correction from −5 to +5 dioptres.

Motor accessories

The motor drive is more than a 'film eater'. Used correctly it speeds up
the Leica. The vast majority of photojournalists and action photographers have motorized Leicas. But even in ordinary situations a
motor drive can bring benefits: the camera is always ready to shoot,
and you can make several exposures with the same framing, for example
for exposure bracketing, without taking the camera from the eye.

Motor Winder R and Motor Drive R

Two motors are available for the Leica R7, the Motor Winder R and the
Motor Drive R, both of which advance the film and cock the shutter.
Both Winder and Drive also automatically take on the power supply
to the camera, although the camera batteries have to remain in their
compartment. Both motors also work with all exposure modes.

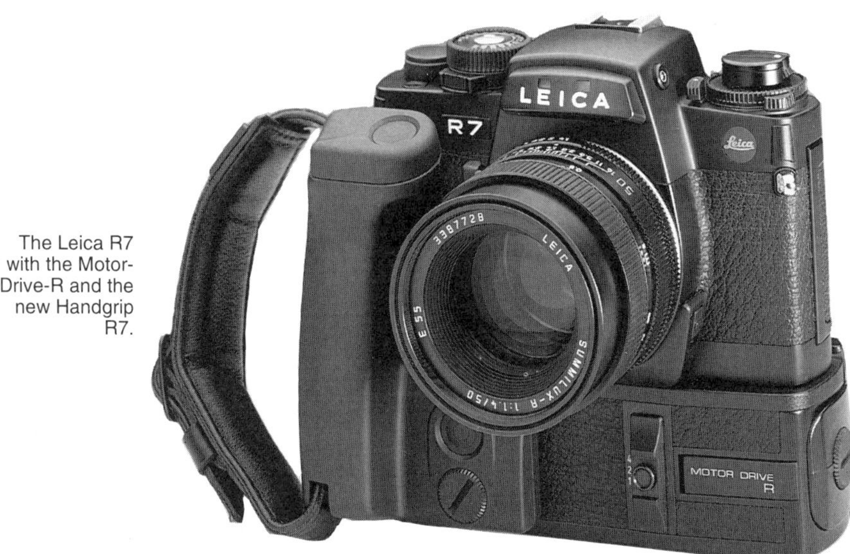

The Leica R7
with the Motor-
Drive-R and the
new Handgrip
R7.

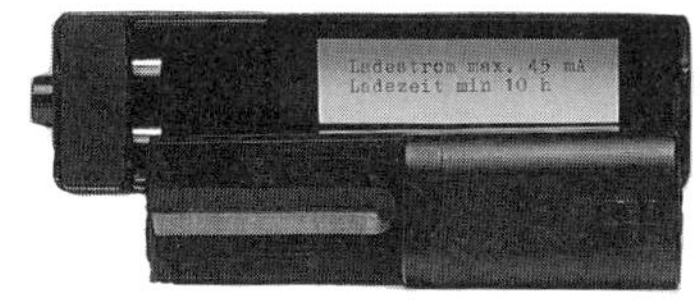
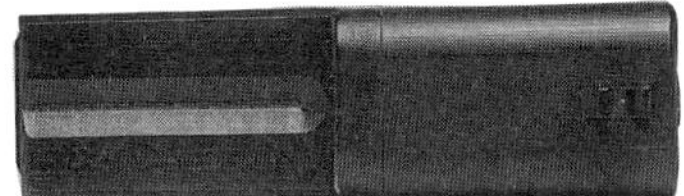
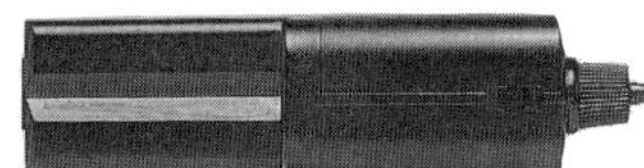

Additional battery/NiCd housings and the adapter for external power supply provide insurance for the reliable functioning of motor and winder on expeditions.

The Motor Winder R offers single-frame and continuous shooting at a frequency of up to two frames per second. Its operation is extremely quiet, thanks to the special low-noise drive system developed by Leica.

With the Motor Drive R the photographer can choose between several shooting frequencies: two or four frames per second as well as single-frame shooting. Thanks to a particularly sophisticated construction of the gears, the Drive is also relatively quiet.

The Winder is powered by six, and the Drive by ten standard AA batteries or equivalent NiCads. An additional battery housing is available for both motors. These housings facilitate speedy exchange of the whole set of batteries, which can be a useful facility during continuous use. The external power supply via the Adapter MD-R (Drive) or MW-R (Winder) guarantees full functioning, even in cold conditions. At temperatures around 20°C one set of batteries is sufficient to expose about 150 rolls of 36-exposure film.

Sequence shooting with the Motor Winder R and the Motor Drive R is only possible via the shutter-release button on the Winder (without handgrip) or Drive, or via both shutter-release buttons on the handgrip (more on this in a moment). With the relevant control unit, the remote control socket can also be used for sequence shooting. In selective metering mode the exposure can be locked via the camera shutter-

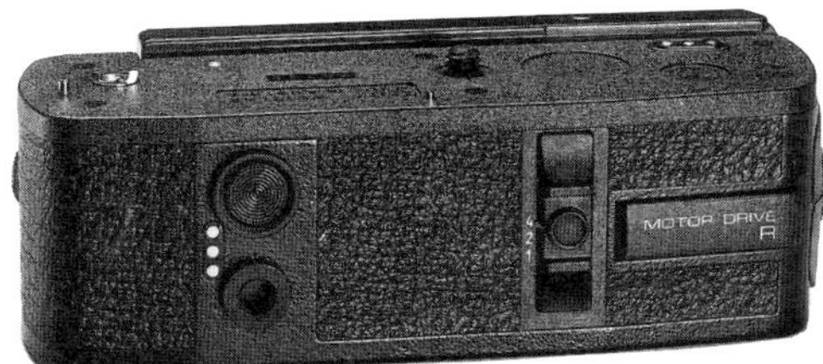

The two motorized film advance attachments for the Leica R7: the Motor Drive R above and the Motor Winder R below.

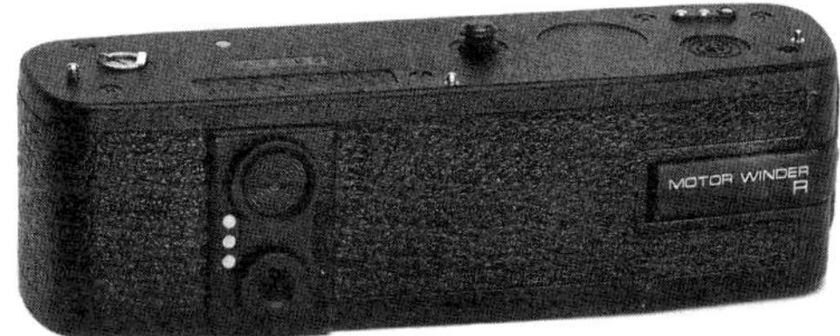

143

release button. With portrait format work it is advisable to use the shutter-release button on the Winder/Drive or the lower shutter-release button on the Handgrip R. Multiple exposures are possible at any time via the relevant button on the motor.

The Drive/Winder switches off automatically when the frame counter of the Leica R7 indicates frame number 36, but the film can be advanced manually beyond this by using the rapid advance lever. However, in motorized shooting mode the rapid advance lever always has to be set in the neutral position (folded in).

Handgrip R

The Handgrip R makes for easier handling in hand-held photographs, particularly in conjunction with the Motor Drive R or the Motor Winder R. The handgrip is equipped with two electrical shutter-release buttons, located to be within easy reach for use in either the landscape or portrait formats and so facilitating smooth shutter release. Thanks to an adjustable hand strap the camera can be held without tiring, even when at rest. The combination of camera, handgrip and winder or drive forms a functional unit facilitating dynamic photography.

Electronic control unit RC Leica R

The electronic control unit RC Leica R (remote control) can only be used in motorized shooting mode. This handy control unit allows remote and time-lapse sequences. The time-lapse function can be programmed for different intervals between 0.5 seconds and 10 minutes, and with the additional ST 16 M control unit, automatic time-lapse photography at intervals of up to 45 hours is possible. Used with an extension lead (cord) the RC Leica R has a range of more than 100m. A digital display signals that an exposure has taken place and indicates the number of exposures made.

It's best to use the RC Leica R with one of the automatic exposure programs and with the viewfinder eyepiece shutter closed. As the remote control is continuously powered by the power supply of the motor, it should not stay connected to the motor unnecessarily.

The RC Leica R can be used for botanical studies (plant growth, the opening of blossoms, etc.), record photography (phases of the moon or the sun), or as a remote control for animal photography.

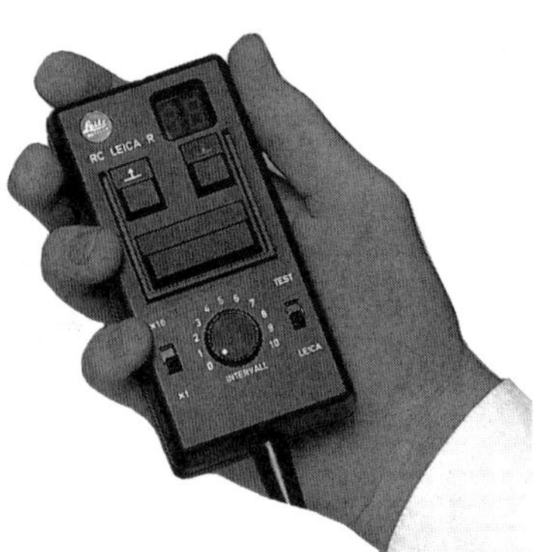

The electronic control RC Leica R.

Other accessories for motorized operation

Leica offers further accessories for motorized operation, such as the Tripod Holder R, the Electrical Release R and others.

The Tripod Holder R is intended mainly for use with long focal lengths or for working with the reproduction stand. It has two threaded bushes for the Motor Winder R or the Motor Drive R, but can also be used in conjunction with the Universal Handgrip.

The Electrical Release R is a pressure point switch for switching on the camera and locking the exposure in selective metering mode. In can be connected directly to the drive or winder via a plug.

The Electrical Cable Release R is intended for remote release of the camera and can be connected to the winder or drive via a plug. If used with several extension leads the cable release has a range of more than 100m.

Accessories for the close-up range

The close-up range with reproduction ratios between 1:10 and 10:1 goes beyond the closest focusing distances of most lenses. Moreover, lenses other than macro lenses are not corrected for the close-up range but for infinity, which can affect the reproduction quality. The loss in quality refers to the extremely high reproduction quality of the Leica lenses and is therefore relative. A Summicron-R 50mm,f/2, for example, used in conjunction with the bellows unit at a reproduction ratio of 1:1 can deliver photographs of higher quality than many a macro lens by independent manufacturers, but it does not reach the level of quality of Leica macro lenses. All the Leica macro lenses – the Apo-Macro-Elmarit-R 100mm,f/2.8, the Macro-Elmar-R 100mm,f/4 (available with helical focusing mount or lens head only for the bellows), and the Macro-Elmarit-R 60mm,f/2.8 – all offer excellent reproduction quality in the close-up range.

Specialist photographic accessories, such as close-up attachments, macro adapters, extension tubes, and bellows provide a high level of quality in the close-up range for some Leica R lenses. Moreover, close-up accessories can also substantially extend the applications of macro lenses.

Elpro close-up attachments

The Elpro close-up attachments are high-quality achromatic lenses designed for certain lenses or groups of lenses. The Elpro close-up attachments 1, 2, 3, and 4 consist of two cemented elements and change the focal length of lenses so that the reproduction ratio is increased whilst the setting distance of the lens helical mount remains constant. Unlike simple conventional supplementary lenses, the Elpro attachments improve the optical performance in the close-up range of a lens for which it is designed – provided the lens is stopped down by at least

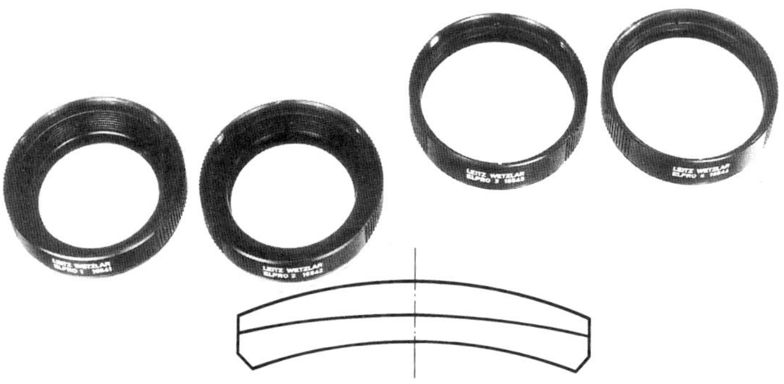

The Elpro close-up attachments are high-quality achromatic lenses consisting of two cemented elements.

two stops. They are an inexpensive alternative to the purchase of an additional macro lens for photographers who do not work in this range very often. These light-weight close-up attachments are hardly bigger than a filter and will fit in every photo bag, even when on holiday. But the Elpro attachments can also be of interest to photographers specializing in macro work. Unlike bellows units or extension tubes, Elpro attachments do not require an extension factor to be taken into account because they are screwed into the filter thread at the front of the lens. This means that the Elpro attachments produce a bright viewfinder image and facilitate shake-free hand-held results in the close-up range. Focusing is best done by means of a uniform groundglass screen (with or without grid division). All functions of the Leica R7 are fully maintained when Elpro attachments are used.

The Summicron-R 50mm,f/2 can be used with Elpros 1 and 2. The Elpro 3 was developed for the Summicron-R 90mm,f/2, and the Elmarit-R 90mm,f/2.8. The Macro-Elmar-R 100mm,f/4 (with helical mount) and the Elmarit-R 135mm,f/2.8 can be used with Elpros 3 and 4. But with these lenses the Elpro attachments can also be used in conjunction with the bellows unit, the macro adapter, or the extension tubes. The relevant tables provide information about possible combinations and reproduction ratios.

The Elpro 1:2-1:1, consisting of three freely moving elements and designed specifically for the Apo-Macro-Elmarit 100mm,f/2.8, occupies a special place. But as the question of an increase in the reproduction quality does not arise with this lens because it is already almost perfectly corrected for the close-up range, you have to be content with the fact that reproduction quality is largely maintained with this Elpro. But even then, for the highest demands of sharpness and contrast, right into the image corners, stopping down to f/5.6 or f/8 is advisable. However, this will not cause any great problems in the close-up range as one is normally seeking to increase the depth of field.

Macro Adapter R

The Macro Adapter R is an extension tube with automatic spring-back diaphragm which increases the barrel extension of a lens by 30mm. Exposure metering is carried out integrally or selectively at full aperture. The Macro Adapter R can be used with the Leica R7 in manual exposure mode or in aperture priority. But incorrect exposures can occur in the automatic program or in shutter priority. The extension factor caused by the increase in the length of the lens barrel is automatically taken into account by the TTL metering system.

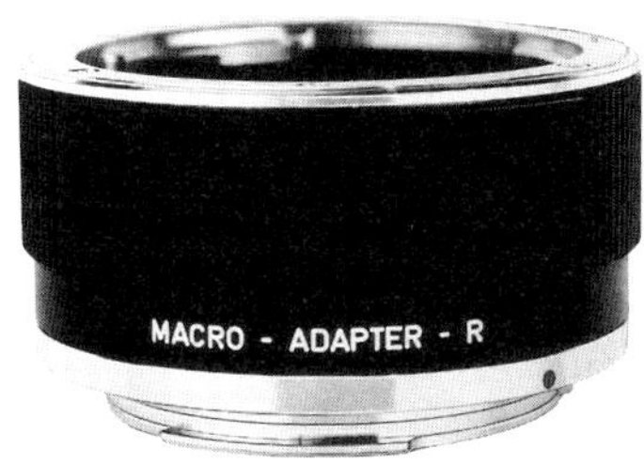

The Macro-Adapter-R, an extension tube with automatic springback diaphragm.

Lenses that are corrected for infinity should be stopped down to f/8 or f/11 when used in conjunction with the Macro Adapter R in order to maintain the good reproduction properties as far as possible in the macro range.

Extension tube combination for the close-up range

The extension tube combination for the close-up range consists of three extension tubes. The rear tube is connected to the camera, and the front tube to the lens. Both tubes can be connected together to achieve an increase in the length of the lens barrel of 25mm. If the centre tube is connected in between, the barrel is extended by 50mm, which corresponds to the focal length of the Summicron-R 50mm, f/2. This means that photographs at a reproduction ratio of 1:1 are possible with this lens (extension equal to focal length). If the helical extension of the Summicron-R 50mm, f/2 is also taken into account, a reproduction ratio of 1.1:1 can be achieved. This is important for frame-filling duplicates of framed slides (visible image format 23x35mm). But the extension tube combination can also be used with the macro lenses and all other lenses with focal lengths between 50mm and 350mm and a maximum aperture smaller than f/2. In this case lenses corrected for infinity need to be stopped down to f/8 or f/11 and, if possible, additional Elpro attachments should be used.

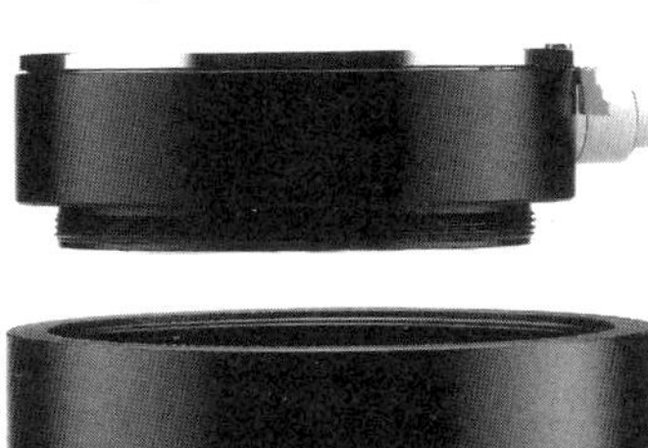

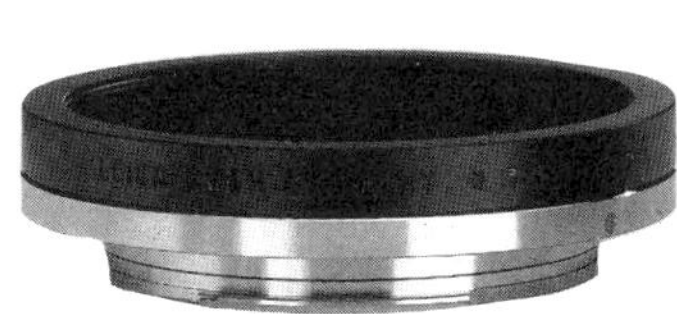

The extension tube combinations for the close-up range.

The extension tube combination offers only semi-automatic aperture transmission, so that the exposure is metered at the working aperture. The iris diaphragm can be closed to the pre-selected value by means of the stop-down lever on the front tube. This is more easily achieved with a double cable release, which closes the iris diaphragm to the pre-selected value immediately prior to the exposure. In this way you can also work in aperture priority mode (with integral or selective metering) without any problems. The threads of the extension tube combination are not 'aligned' and so the index mark on the lens can end up slightly shifted around the barrel. But this can be ignored as the aperture is not projected into the viewfinder and, because of the extension, the lens is easily visible from above. Theoretically several centre tubes can be connected together to achieve a greater reproduction ratio. Another possibility would be to connect the Macro Adapter R between camera and extension tube combination (with semi-automatic spring-back diaphragm; but if the adapter is connected between extension tube combination and lens, even the semi-automatic spring-back diaphragm no longer functions). But it is best to do without these additional possibilities if at all possible: the reproduction quality of lenses corrected for infinity is reduced as the reproduction ratio increases, the danger of stray light affecting the contrast increases, the extension factor becomes larger, and the shutter speeds become slower.

Focusing Bellows-R BR2

The Focusing Bellows-R BR2, introduced at the same time as the Leica R7, replaced the former Focusing Bellows R.

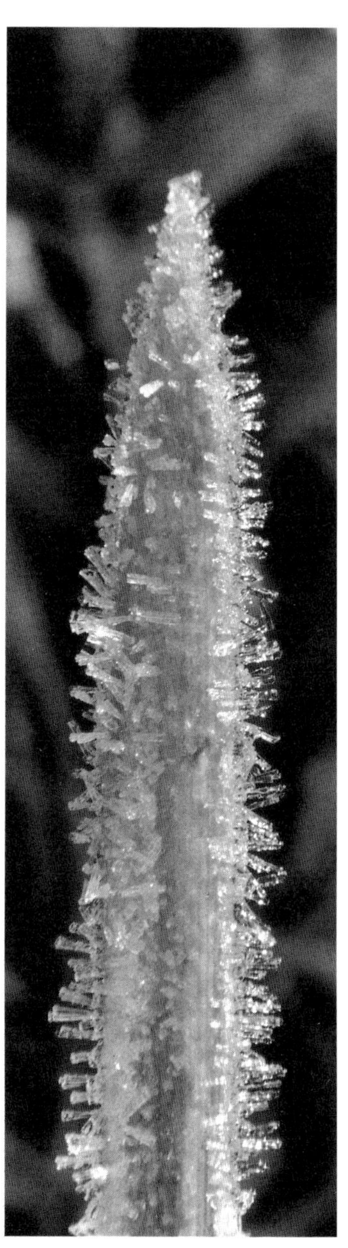

Taken with the Summicron-R 90mm, f/2 and the extension tube combination.

Close-up possibilities with the Automatic Bellows-R BR 2

Lens	Reproduction ratio	Distance from subject to front element in cm	Subject field in mm
SUMMICRON-R 1:2/50 mm	1 : 1 - 3,2 : 1	6,0 - 2,4	24 x 36 - 7,5 x 11,3
MACRO-ELMARIT-R 1:2,8/60 mm	1 : 1,2 - 3,2 : 1	7,2 - 2,2	29 x 43 - 7,5 x 11,3
SUMMICRON-R 1:2/90 mm ELMARIT-R 1:2,8/90 mm	1 : 1,7 - 2 : 1	21 - 10	41 x 61 - 12 x 18
MACRO-ELMAR 1:4/100 mm Lens head	1 : ∞ 1,1 : 1	∞ - 15	∞ - 22 x 33
MACRO-ELMAR-R 1:4/100 mm	1 : 1,9 - 1,9 : 1	26 - 12	46 x 68 - 13 x 19
ELMARIT-R 1:2,8/135 mm	1 : 2,6 - 1,3 : 1	48 - 23	62 x 94 - 18 x 28
ELMARIT-R 1:2,8/180 mm	1 : 3,4 - 1 : 1	77 - 33	82 x 122 - 24 x 36
APO-TELYT-R 1:3,4/180 mm	1 : 3,4 - 1 : 1	86 - 43	82 x 122 - 24 x 36
TELYT-R 1:4/250 mm	1:4,9 - 1:1	166 - 59	118 x 176 - 24 x 36
PHOTAR 1:2,4/12,5 mm	8,5 : 1 - 17,5 : 1	0,9 - 0,8	2,8 x 4,2 - 1,4 x 2,1
PHOTAR 1:2/25 mm	3,5 : 1 - 7,5 : 1	2,0 - 1,5	6,8 x 10,2 - 3,2 x 4,8
PHOTAR 1:4/50 mm	1,4 : 1 - 3,4 : 1	8,1 - 6,0	17 x 26 - 7,1 x 10,5

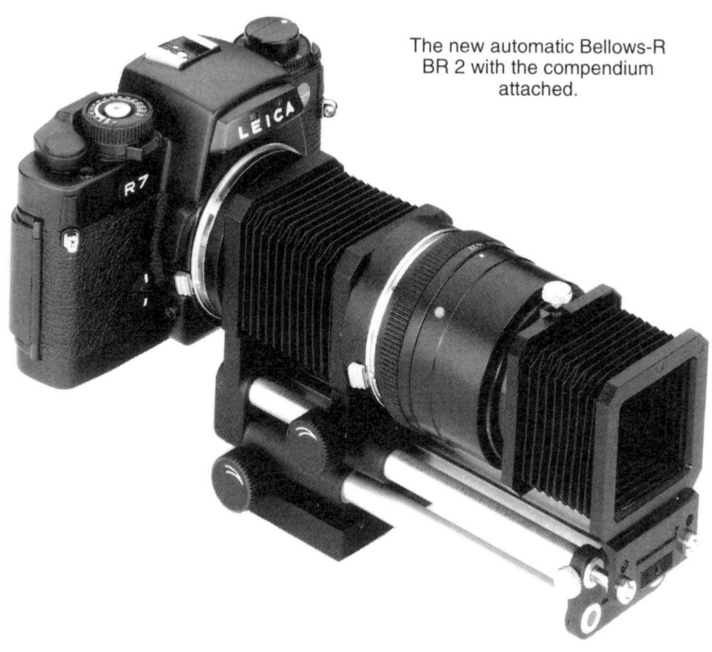

The new automatic Bellows-R
BR 2 with the compendium
attached.

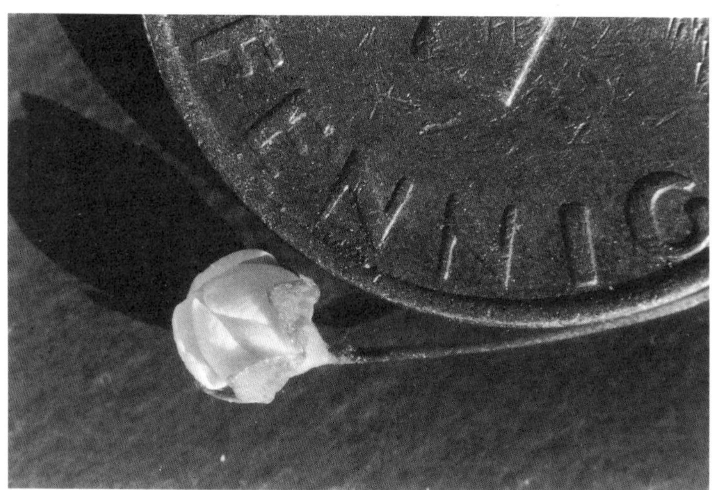

Taken with the Summicron-R 50mm,f/2 on the bellows attachment.

Their great advantage over the previous model is the spring-back diaphragm. They can be used in conjunction with Leica R lenses with focal lengths between 50mm and 350mm, as well as with Photar lenses, and provide continuous adjustment of the reproduction ratio. Because of the 100mm bellows extension, reproduction ratios of up to 4:1 can be achieved, depending on the focal length of the lens used, and in conjunction with Photar lenses even ratios up to 16:1 are possible. The Macro-Elmar-R 100mm,f/4 without focusing mount is specially constructed for use with the Focusing Bellows R, facilitating photographs not only up to a reproduction ratio of 1:1, but also at infinity. This latter is not possible with any of the other lenses because, even folded together completely, the bellows extension is 42mm.

The unit is connected between camera and lens and is sturdily constructed for vibration-free operation. The camera mount can be turned, which makes it considerably easier to switch between landscape and portrait format – without shifting the optical axis. In addition, a lockable focusing rail is attached to the bottom of the bellows. A millimetre scale (allowing repeat settings) and the reproduction ratios that can be achieved at 90mm, 100mm and 135mm focal length are engraved on a revolving rectangular scale.

In practice it is best to start by selecting the desired reproduction ratio via the very accurate bellows extension scale, then focus via the focusing rail. At reproduction ratios below about 1:4 focusing can also be achieved via the bellows extension.

Focusing Bellows R

This older unit does not have an automatic spring-back diaphragm nor an aperture simulator. To make the exposure, the lens aperture is set to the desired value, then the iris diaphragm can once again be opened for focusing via a lockable lever, but a double cable release makes for easier working. The exposure is metered at the working aperture, either manually or in aperture priority with either integral or selective metering. You can shoot with the camera hand-held or mounted on a tripod – in the former case using the Universal Handgrip with Shoulder Stock is advisable.

Leica Reprovit-R

To achieve as accurate a photograph as possible of a given object, the subject plane and the film plane must be parallel. Moreover, the subject has to be evenly lit and the camera mounted on a sturdy tripod. All these requirements are met by the Leica Reprovit-R which is a repro stand with a 90cm column and an adjustable camera mount. Two 300W halogen lamps with a low-vibration cooling fan are mounted to the left and right of the column on the 46x50cm baseplate to guarantee even

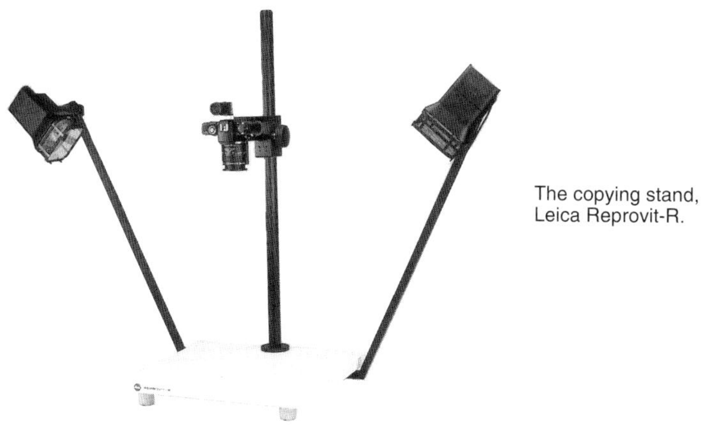

The copying stand,
Leica Reprovit-R.

subject illumination. The Reprovit-R is suitable not only for reproduction of flat subjects, but also for close-up photography.

The camera is aligned in parallel with the subject plane by means of the camera mount, and can be used with the 50mm,f/2, 60mm,f/2.8, 90mm,f/2, 90mm,f/2.8, 100mm,f/2.8 Apo, and the 100mm,f/4 lenses, as well as with the bellows.

The colour temperature of the halogen lamps is between 3200 and 3400 kelvin and is therefore geared towards artificial-light colour slide film. If black-and-white film is to be used the film speed has to be reduced by about one stop. The lamps can be exchanged for two flash units for working with daylight colour film.

With flat subjects especially, the exposure should be metered on a grey card with a reflectance value of 18%. The exposure is adjusted via the shutter speed because you will usually work with a constant aperture of f/8 or f/11.

The Anglefinder R makes for easier viewfinder access and focusing. In repro photography filters are often used to improve the reproduction quality. For colour reproductions, such as of oil paintings, a polarizing filter can eliminate reflections and achieve greater colour saturation. Stains on documents become invisible on black-and-white film if a yellow or orange filter (depending on the colour of the stains) is used. The blue lines of graph paper can also be eliminated on black-and-white film by using a blue filter.

Other accessories

Databack DB2 Leica R

The Databack DB2 is used to imprint exposure data directly onto the film, namely in the lower right-hand corner. One of the following sets

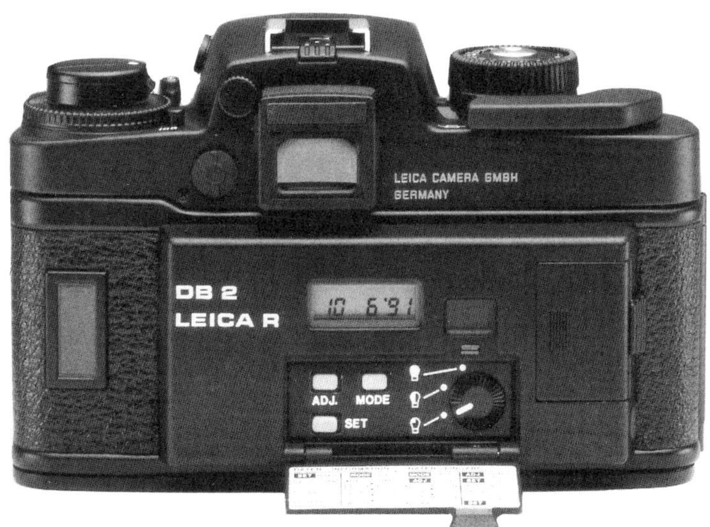

The Databack DB 2 Leica R with the back panel open revealing the operating controls.

of data can be imprinted onto an area of 0.65x4.6mm in three groups of two figures: day-hour-minutes, day-month-year (in any order), different numbers up to 99 99 99, and frame numbering (ascending or descending). All data can be set via three buttons, and are indicated on the LCD panel on the back. Once an imprint has taken place, **PRINT** appears on the display. The Databack is attached to the camera in place of the standard back and is powered by two silver oxide button cells of 1.5V – the same as those used in the Leica R7. One set of batteries can imprint data on about 100 rolls of film. The automatic calendar is pre-programmed until the year 2099.

The intensity of the imprint can be adjusted to the film speed in two steps. The data is imprinted onto the film from behind, ie through the protective layer on the back of the film. This can cause flare on the imprinted characters, particularly on higher-speed films – if this is the case, select the lower setting. On colour positives the data is reproduced in yellow, and in white on black-and-white film. Because of this it is particularly important in the portrait format to ensure that the imprint area does not fall on a bright portion of the subject. In addition, you should remember that with thick films such as Kodachrome 25 or 64, as well as some slow Polaroid slide films and infra-red films, the data cannot be imprinted perfectly.

The Databack is particularly useful for documentary photography in the fields of science and technology, or for the marking of test photographs. You can, of course, use it to date your holiday snaps, but in pictorial photography the imprinted data can appear intrusive. It can be useful for archival purposes to date the first frame of a film if several films are sent off for processing at the same time. Whether a databack is a worthwhile investment is ultimately a decision for each individual photographer.

Universal Handgrip with Shoulder Stock

The Universal Handgrip with Shoulder Stock is a versatile accessory. As a 'pistol' handgrip with an individually adjustable shoulder stock it improves the camera position, especially if used hand-held with tele-photo lenses or the bellows. If the shoulder stock is attached the other way around, the handgrip becomes a handy table-top tripod. The electric release available as an extra makes for easier handling if the Winder or Drive are used. The Universal Handgrip can be supplied as standard with the rapid-focusing lenses Telyt-R 400mm,f/6.8 and 560mm,f/6.8, but is also available as an accessory and can, of course, be used with other long focus lenses or with the bellows for hand-held macropho-tography.

Table-top Tripod and Ball and Socket Head

The table-top tripod will fit in any jacket pocket when it is folded up. As an 'ever-present' tripod it can replace a heavy tripod in certain photo-graphic situations. In low light, if you want to achieve great depth of field with low-speed films, in the close-up and macro range, and even with telephoto work this mini-tripod can be a valuable help, provided you can find a surface at the right height to rest it on. With a little practice you can also use it as a chest stock, or it can be pressed against a wall.

The easiest way to use the Leica table-top tripod is with the ball head. This head can be locked very easily in any position.

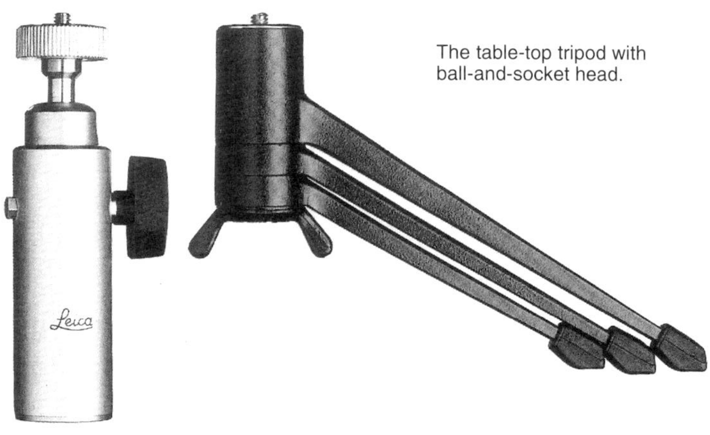

The table-top tripod with ball-and-socket head.

154

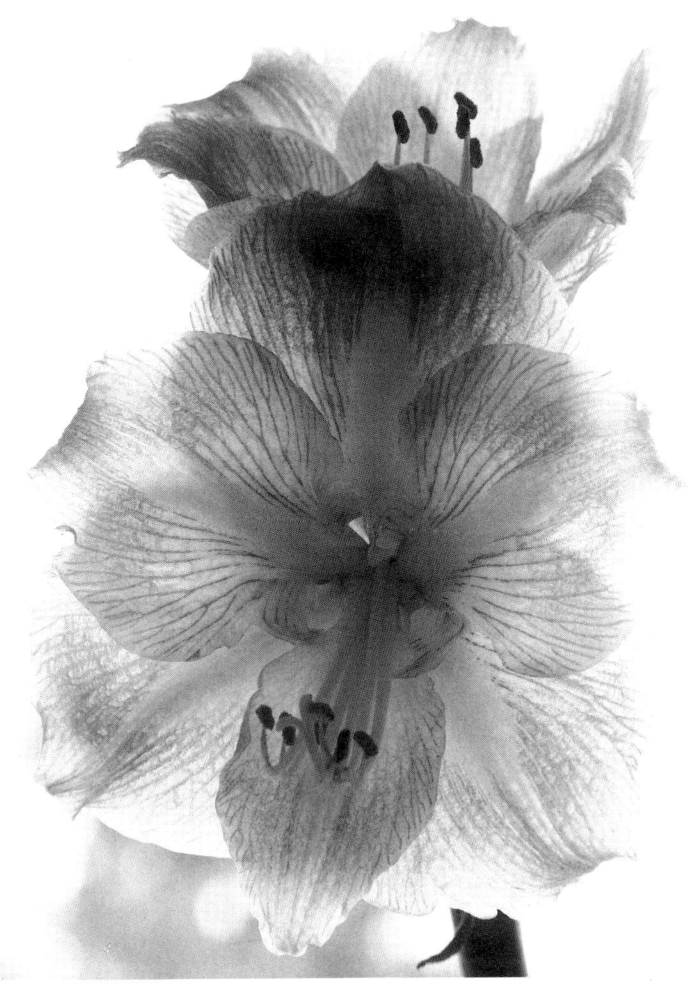

The table-top tripod with ball-and-socket head is useful when extreme stopping down to achieve greater depth of field results in slow shutter speeds.

Cases

The value of cases should not be underestimated. They protect your expensive Leica outfit against knocks, dust, sand, rain, and even humidity, and therefore help to ensure the continued functioning of the equipment. Cases should also provide quick access to camera, lenses, and accessories and distribute their weight evenly to provide comfortable carrying. Cases should also be fairly restrained in terms of colour and shape – to make sure you don't frighten off wild animals or attract thieves.

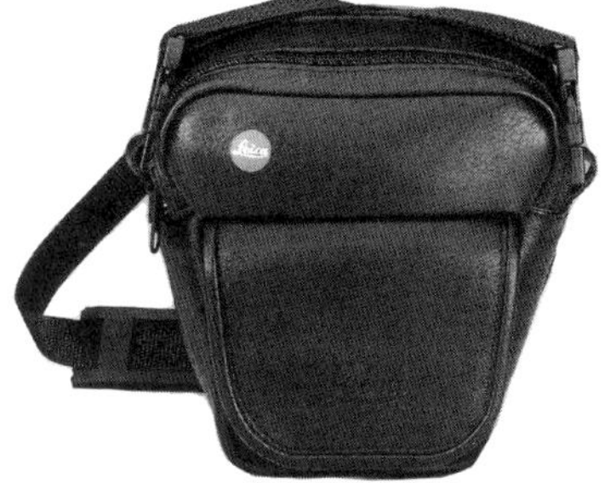

One of the Leica photo bags made from black calf nappa leather.

Leica offer several cases which fulfil these requirements: the small and large Combi-Bag R, the Universal Bag R, and the Reporter Bag. The quality of these cases, made from black nappa leather of understated elegance, reaches the proverbial Leica standard. In addition, the Leica range includes three ever-ready cases – but these are generally not as practical as their name would suggest.

The Leica R lenses are supplied in a leather case, although the Apo-Telyt-R 280mm,f/2.8, the Apo-Telyt-R 400mm,f/2.8, and Telyt-S 800mm,f/6.3 come with an aluminium case.

For particular purposes or individual preference you can, of course, buy bags and cases from independent manufacturers. But if you do, always go for high-quality products which are at least partially designed for professional use. Landscape and animal photographers may decide on a photo rucksack. These are available in different sizes and can be enlarged by several exterior pockets to accommodate larger outfits. Apart from the car, these are the most comfortable way of carrying heavy photographic equipment. However, getting at your equipment is anything but fast as the rucksack has to be taken off first. Photo waistcoats, used by many sports, action, and press photographers, offer the easiest access. Aluminium cases provide the best protection for valuable photographic equipment, especially for travelling and storage; they are shock-proof, and some are also waterproof. If a professional tripod needs to be extended to its full length, you can even stand on your aluminium case, but carrying it about is anything but easy.

A large photographic outfit is best kept in a cupboard. Professional or semi-professional photographers have several methods of transporting their gear and assemble the right equipment for each photographic occasion. Consider carefully whether a case, bag, or rucksack is best suited to your equipment and preferred applications. If no single one suits your needs you may need two or more.

System compatibility

Leica attaches great importance to system compatibility. You can use many lenses and large numbers of accessories for all Leicaflex and Leica

R models with your Leica R7, although the camera functions may be restricted by some combinations. Damage to the Leica R7 from SL or older R accessories is only possible in exceptional cases. If you are worried about the compatibility of older accessories, always check back with the Leica factory in Solms – writing in English is no problem. The address is as follows:-

Leica Camera GmbH
Kunden- und Informationsdienst
Postfach 1120
Oskar-Barnack-Strasse 11
6336 Solms
Germany
Tel. 6442 208 189

9. Filters

Filters should be part of the standard equipment of every advanced photographer. They can increase the appeal of a photograph, producing exciting pictures of average subjects, but they can also help to achieve a realistic rendering of tonal values and colours. So, depending on the application, there are different kinds of filters, for black-and-white photography, for colour photography, for special effects, and for technical work. The most important filters and their applications are described in the following pages, but before making a decision about one or other filter, a number of basic principles need to be taken into account.

Filters are made from coloured glass or plastic and (apart from integral filters which are part of the optical construction of a lens) are attached in front of the front element. Therefore the use of filters creates additional air-glass or plastic-glass interfaces which absorb light and, depending on the optical quality of the filter, refract the incident light to a greater or lesser degree. A consequence of this is a loss of light and a reduction in sharpness and contrast.

The loss of light depends on the filter type and is stated by the manufacturer as the filter factor, usually engraved on the metal mount. The TTL metering system of the Leica R7 usually takes the filter factor into account automatically. When working with a manual exposure meter the metered exposure value has to be multiplied by the filter factor; alternatively you can hold the filter in front of the exposure meter so that the filter factor is automatically taken into account. But this method is not recommended when using graduated filters or with some effects filters, because the exposure also depends on the position of such filters.

Amongst other things, the filter factor also depends on the colour temperature of the light used to make the exposure. The stated factor normally refers to medium daylight (5500 kelvin) so it will not be correct for photographs taken early in the morning, in the evening, under very overcast skies, at great altitude, or with artificial light. Depending on the filter colour and the spectral composition of the light, the filter factor can be increased or reduced. Normally this is taken into account in TTL metering, but – especially with filters for black-and-white photography – the transfer to tones of grey can cause certain subject colours to be reproduced under- or overexposed. Be especially careful with contrast-increasing filters with fairly high density colours, such as orange and red.

A further cause of incorrect exposure is the different spectral sensitivity of the different types of metering cell, which can fluctuate further due to manufacturing tolerance. This applies both to external and TTL

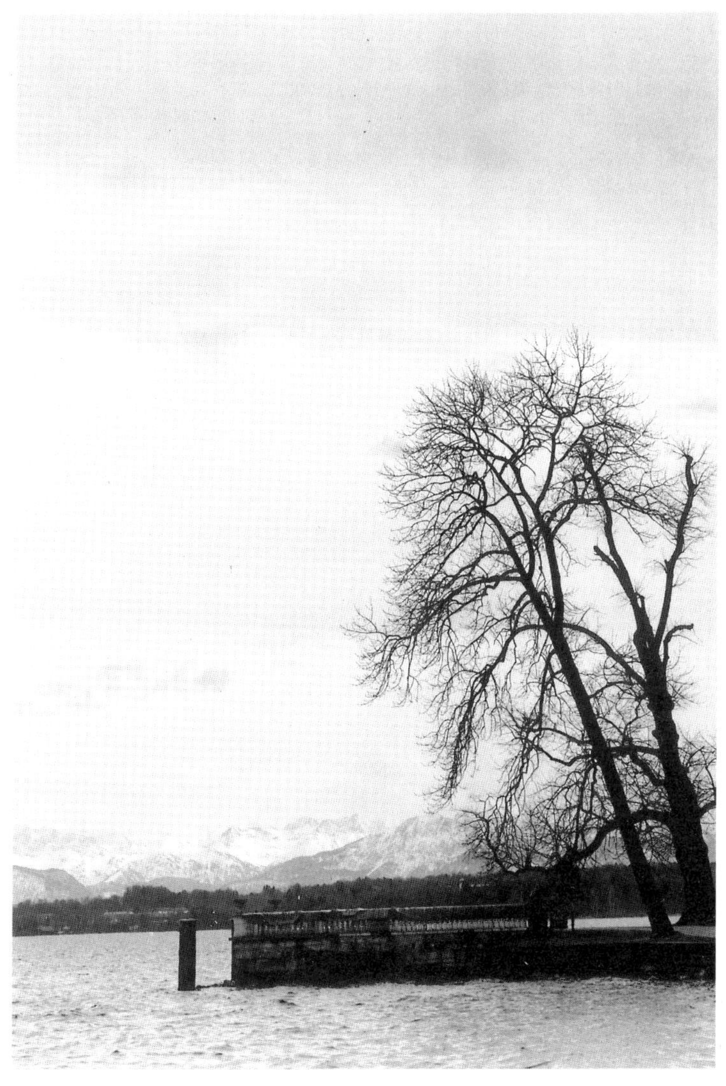

Filters need to be of high quality to maintain the reproduction quality of the lens as far as possible (picture taken with orange filter).

meters. Leica and the other manufacturers have tried to tackle this problems in recent years by providing the relevant correction (filters in front of the metering cells), but complete correction is as yet not possible. Depending on the filter colour, the spectral composition of the subject, and the light, deviations towards over or underexposure can occur.

The fact that films are not sensitized to the same extent for all colours of the spectrum can also lead to deviations in tonal value and colour.

A further point to consider is that different factors, for example if several filters are used simultaneously or if the barrel of the lens has been extended, are not added together but are multiplied. If, on the other hand, the separate factors have already been converted into light values, the light values need to be added together. Great care needs to be taken if several filters are used simultaneously. If you combine filters from different groups, such as red and green, they can cancel out each other's effect. Nor does it make sense to use several filters from the same group, such as yellow and red, together, as this does not increase the effect – only the stronger filter makes a difference.

So even a sophisticated TTL metering system requires some input from the photographer when filters are used. Your best bet is to concentrate on a few filters and familiarize yourself with their effects on the exposure meter and the final image by making test exposures. Concentrating on a few filters is also a good safeguard against overdoing it, because – advertising notwithstanding – the excessive use of effects filters does not necessarily make for creativity.

The following filters can be recommended: polarizing filters, neutral graduated filters, UV block filters in certain cases, and, for black-and-white photographers, red, yellow or orange, and yellow-green or green filters.

Screw-on filters are not part of the construction of a lens, but once fitted they become part of its optical system. This is why, when choosing filters for Leica lenses, you should always look for quality. The best optical properties are provided by dyed-in-the-bulk glass filters ground plane-parallel, with one or several layers of coating, depending on the filter type. The Leica filters are way ahead in meeting these quality requirements. As with Leica lenses, the coating is applied depending on the application of each filter. Leica filters are loosely mounted so that surface strains cannot affect the plane-parallel surface of the filter. High-quality filters from Leica or other manufacturers are inevitably not cheap. This is why many photographers buy filters for their lens with the greatest diameter filter mount and attach these to other lenses by means of adapter rings. One argument against this is that the lens hood can no longer be clipped on or extended and as plane-parallel filters are particularly sensitive to light reflections, this can affect the contrast. Moreover, adapter rings can cause vignetting with extreme wide-angle lenses.

Filter holders, which accept plastic or gelatin filters, offer an inexpensive solution. The filter holder can be attached to almost all lenses via different adapters. Commonly used systems are those from Cokin and Kodak (Wratten, CC-filters), both of which provide a wide range of filters. These filter types, because of the nature of their holders, facilitate more easily the use of more than one filter at a time. Plastic and gelatin filters are of good quality but don't reach the level of quality of coated glass filters. In addition they are easily scratched and tend to attract dust.

UV block filters (0-Haze)

With clear skies the level of ultraviolet light can be fairly high, particularly in mountains, at sea, with snow, and even in landscapes around towns. The human eye cannot see ultraviolet light, but most films (except some with a UV block layer) are sensitive to it. Taking into account the fact that lenses focus UV rays in front of the image plane (because of their wavelength), it is immediately clear why a high proportion of ultraviolet rays can lead to lack of sharpness. The UV block filter reduces the amount of UV radiation reaching the film so that the unsharpness and atmospheric haze are suppressed (hence the name haze filter). On colour photographs the blue colour cast caused by UV radiation is also eliminated. UV filters have a factor of 1 (ie the exposure does not have to be increased).

However, the Absorban-cement layers in Leica lenses block UV radiation anyway, so the use of a UV filter is superfluous. But photographic literature still often recommends that the front element of expensive lenses should be protected with a UV filter. This would certainly make sense in potentially hazardous environments, but otherwise the use of a UV filter as a 'transparent lens cap' is questionable. In normal use and moderate climatic zones there will be little danger to the front element, and with extreme wide-angle lenses external filters cannot be used anyway because of vignetting. However high the quality of a screw-on UV filter may be, it can still affect the image sharpness.

Skylight filters

Skylight filters are available in two versions, 1A and 1B, 1B being the stronger. They are considered standard filters for colour work as they remove the blue colour cast, especially apparent with photographs taken around midday. They also partially suppress UV radiation and consequently atmospheric haze. But the Absorban-cement layers in the Leica R lenses have the same effect, so these filters, like the UV Block filters, are superfluous.

No filter factor has to be taken into account with skylight filters, so many photographers leave them on the lens permanently to protect the front

element. But as with UV filters, this only makes sense in tough conditions, otherwise Leica photographers are better off without skylight
filters for the reasons stated above. But there is an additional reason
for not using skylight filters with Leica lenses. The filters have a slight
pink tinge which causes a warmer colour rendering and falsifies the
strictly neutral colour characteristics of the Leica lenses.

Polarizing filters

The polarizing filter is perhaps the most important filter in professional
and ambitious amateur photography. For this reason we will cover the
various factors that are important with polarizing filters in greater detail.

It is commonly known that polarizing filters can remove reflections from
non-metallic surfaces such as water, glass, shiny plastic, polished
wood, lacquered surfaces, wet pavements, and reflective green leaves
in the sun. Less commonly known are the laws of physics behind polarization, although knowing these is vital for the correct use of polarizing
filters. So let's start with a brief and simplified explanation of the polarization theory.

Light consists of electromagnetic waves which oscillate within a certain
amplitude and perpendicular to the direction of the rays. If a light ray
is only oscillating in one plane, it is called linear-polarized light. If a
light ray is oscillating in two planes, perpendicular to each other, it is

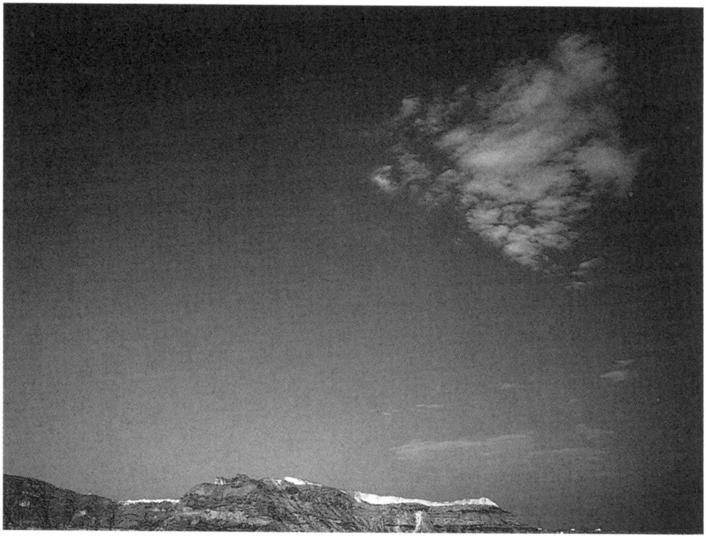

The wide angle of view of extreme wide-angle lenses captures large portions of
the sky, which often show different polarization. This is why the sky in this picture
taken through a polarizing filter has not been darkened evenly.

eliptically or circularly-polarized light. It is elliptical polarization if the amplitudes of the two waves are different, and they also have a phase difference of ¼ of the wavelength. With circular polarization the amplitudes of the two waves are the same. The projection of circular-polarized light can be pictured as the simultaneous straight and turning motion of a corkscrew. For the sake of completeness we should also mention that there is left- and right-handed elliptical- or circular-polarized light.

Light refracted, or partially reflected, or diffused has a reduced number of oscillation planes. If natural light falls onto a partially permeable medium, such as glass or water (except running or moving water), part of the light is refracted when entering the medium (due to a reduction in the speed of its movement), whilst the remainder is reflected. The reflected ray of light is subject to full linear polarization at an angle of 90°. This means that the polarization angle is dependent on the refractive index of the medium. A complete elimination of reflections by the polarizing filter is only possible at this angle. The more the shooting angle deviates from the polarization angle, the smaller the reduction of reflections. A linear-polarizing filter reduces or eliminates the linear-polarized light and linear-polarizes natural light. A circular-polarizing filter reduces linear-polarized light (to a greater or lesser degree depending on the shooting angle and position of the filter) and circularly-polarizes natural light. The shooting angle at which polarization is largely eliminated usually lies between 30° and 40°, depending on the medium and the direction of the light.

Reflections such as those which can occur on the surface of chrome-plated metal cannot be eliminated with a polarizing filter. This is because the reflected light in this case is not polarized, owing to the total reflection and the lack of refraction. For studio photographs of highly-polished metal objects, or in repro photography, the studio lighting is polarized instead by means of polarizing foil that is placed in front of the lighting reflectors. A polarizing filter in front of the lens can then eliminate reflections.

As well as being polarized by refraction and reflection, light can also be polarized by diffusion, in which case the diffusion effect is greatest at a perpendicular axis to that of the direction of the light rays. This is particularly noticeable in landscape photography. For example, if the shooting direction is at a right-angle to the direction of the sun, even a slight turn of the polarizing filter is sufficient to suppress the diffused light and to reproduce the sky darker. Incidentally, this is the only way of darkening the blue of the sky in colour photography without changing the other colours (grey graduated filters simply compensate for the contrasts between sky and landscape). But note when taking landscape photographs with wide-angle lenses and polarizing filters that the wide angle of view of the lens often captures large portions of sky, which usually differ in their amount of polarization. In such cases the sky in the photograph will not be darkened evenly, as can be seen from our example.

A polarizing filter does not just reduce the stray light, but also the reflections which occur in vegetation and on the surfaces of different objects in the landscape. As a consequence the other colours are also reproduced with more clarity, brilliance, and saturation (good polarizing filters do not cause a colour cast). For these reasons polarizing filters are very important in professional landscape and travel photography.

On cameras such as the Leica R7, where the metering cell is located behind a partially permeable mirror, only circular-polarizing filters should be used because linear polarizers will lead to incorrect measurements. The effect of the polarizing filter can be viewed directly in the viewfinder, while the filter is turned until the desired effect appears. With Leica polarizing filters in the standard mount, make sure the yellow dot is pointing towards the camera.

Despite TTL metering, particular attention needs to be given to the exposure. The operating instructions for Leica R cameras tell us that the exposure value metered with circular-polarizing filters can be used. Many people also think that the filter factor with polarizing filters does not change with the position of the filter. The reason given for this is the constant density of the filter. But in practical TTL metering, and the Leica R7 is no exception here, you will find that you can see very plainly that the exposure value does change with the position of the polarizing filter. The extent of the change depends on the proportion of polarized light and on its angle in relation to the filter. The more polarized light the filter blocks, the darker reflecting, non-metallic surfaces will appear in the photograph. The TTL metering system sets a more generous exposure for the seemingly darker subject, which means that the photograph will be overexposed to a greater or lesser extent, which in turn reduces the effect of the filter.

So in photographic practice you cannot always rely on the exposure value determined by the TTL exposure metering system. Therefore proceed as follows when using a circular polarizing filter: first set the filter to the position where its effect is least pronounced and a shorter exposure is indicated. This light value is the one to use for the subsequent exposure and so needs to be locked or recorded. The polarizing filter can then be turned to the desired position, ignoring the value for a more generous exposure that is now indicated. For ease of use when working with polarizing filters it is advisable to set the Leica R7 to manual exposure mode or aperture priority with selective metering and exposure lock. If you want to use integral metering you can, ideally in shutter priority mode, determine the shutter speed and then set it manually in **m** mode; alternatively switch to the automatic program, shutter, or aperture priority with integral metering and set the previously metered value by means of exposure compensation.

Provided you work accurately, polarizing filters can improve the final result in both black-and-white and colour photography. But used thoughtlessly, polarizing filters can ruin the mood of a scene, for example by removing the shine from a wet cobbled street or eliminating significant highlights. Sometimes only partial elimination of reflections can also be very effective.

Graduated filters

Ambitious landscape photography requires graduated filters. These have one half dyed and the other half clear, but with one merging into the other so that there is a fading from colour to clear without a sharp edge. There are both neutral (grey) and coloured graduated filters. Whereas neutral grey graduated filters can be used for almost any subject in landscape photography, great care needs to be taken when using colour graduated filters as their effect can quickly become tiresome and predictable. The neutral graduated filters can be used for both black-and-white and colour photography. They can help, for example, to compensate for excessive contrast between foreground and sky, or prevent underexposure of the foreground. This is particularly important with landscape photographs on slide film, because the subject contrast is often greater than the exposure tolerance of the film. Neutral graduated filters are also useful for making clouds more visible, for reducing the intensity of light sources in interior photographs or, with flash photographs, to prevent overexposure of objects close to the camera.

I would not recommend the purchase of screw-on graduated filters because the transition between the two halves would run exactly through the centre. This almost forces the photographer to place the horizon in the centre of the frame, which generally does not make for good picture composition. I would recommend the square type which are placed in a filter holder, such as that by Cokin. It's best to go for the medium size (P), which allows greater flexibility for moving the filter within the filter holder. The filter holder is also equipped with a screw mount, so that the linear colour transition can be placed in almost any position of the image area. Moreover, the larger size reduces the danger of vignetting when using wide-angle lenses. The neutral grey graduated filters from Cokin are available in two densities.

The effect of graduated filters is greatest in the wide-angle range and with the lens stopped down. The depth of field pre-view lever is useful for checking the effect. However, you should not stop down below f/8, otherwise the transition may appear too abrupt. The centre-weighted integral metering system of the Leica R7 generally delivers correct results when graduated filters are used, because contrasts are largely compensated for. When using graduated filters for the first time, take a number of test photographs with different exposures at different focal

lengths, aperture settings, and filter positions to familiarize yourself
with their effect in different conditions.

Neutral-density filters

Grey neutral-density filters, also called ND filters, are colour-neutral
filters which absorb the entire visible spectrum (plus the UV) to the
same extent. They therefore reduce the amount of light reaching the
film and can be used in both black-and-white and colour photography.
ND filters are generally available in three different densities: 2X reduces
the light intensity by one light value, 4X by two light values and 8X by
three light values. They can be used for both technical and creative
purposes. For example, they allow slower shutter speeds, in order to
reproduce speed-blurred or flowing movement (waterfall, a mountain
stream), or wider apertures for a shallower depth of field. ND filters
can also be used if there is too much light, if the metering range of the
exposure meter is exceeded or the film is too fast.

Filters for black-and-white photography

Polarizing filters, neutral graduated filters and ND filters can be used
in both black-and-white and colour photography. But there are other
filters which are designed for the specific requirements of black-and-
white. They can achieve a correct, exaggerated or a very differentiated
transfer of the subject colours into grey tones. Basically, this type of
filter reproduces its own colour more brightly and the complementary
colour darker by passing the former and blocking the latter. The most
important filters for black-and-white photography are as follows.

Yellow

The yellow filter is most commonly used for landscape photographs.
It slightly darkens the blue of the sky, emphasizes the clouds a little
and reduces the atmospheric haze slightly. With snow landscapes the
yellow filter achieves a more brilliant and three-dimensional reproduction of the snow. Skin tones are also reproduced lighter. Some manufacturers offer as many as three different yellow filters: light, medium
and dark yellow. The filter factor is around 1.5 to 3.

Orange

The orange filter has a similar effect to the yellow filter, but more
intense: the sky is darkened a little more strongly, clouds will stand
out, and suppression of haze is better. The orange filter is very well
suited to landscape photography, but can also be used to achieve high
contrast results in architectural photography. The orange filter is also
utilized in portrait photography, particularly in artificial light, in order

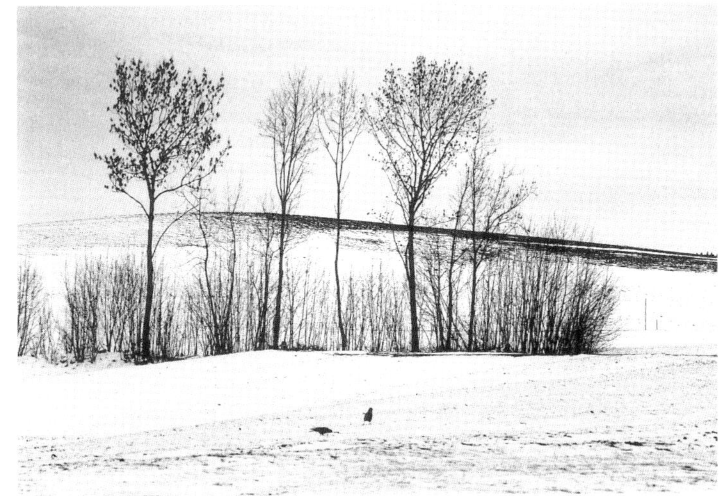

to provide a smooth rendering of the skin. Generally a yellow-orange and a red-orange filter are offered, the latter having a stronger effect. The filter factor varies between 3 and 5.

Red

With a red filter you can achieve landscape photographs which have a dramatic mood. The effect of the yellow and orange filters is substantially increased. The blue sky is rendered almost black (moonlight effect, thunderstorm mood), the increase in contrast between clouds and sky reaches a maximum, and atmospheric haze is almost completely suppressed. With portrait photographs a red filter can render freckles and red blotches on the skin invisible. Light and dark red filters are available, and the stated filter factor is 8, although you might have to allow as much as 25 in some situations. Even with TTL metering an exposure compensation of +1EV is often required for a correct exposure. The effect of the light red filter is usually sufficient. The use of red filters should be considered carefully, exaggeration should not become an end in itself but has to correspond to the intended effect of the photograph.

Yellow-green

The yellow-green filter causes a lightening of green vegetation and a slight darkening of the blue sky, which is why it is most commonly used in landscape photography. Skin tones, too, are rendered darker, particularly out of doors. Red blotches and freckles, on the other hand, are emphasized a little more strongly. The yellow-green filter can also

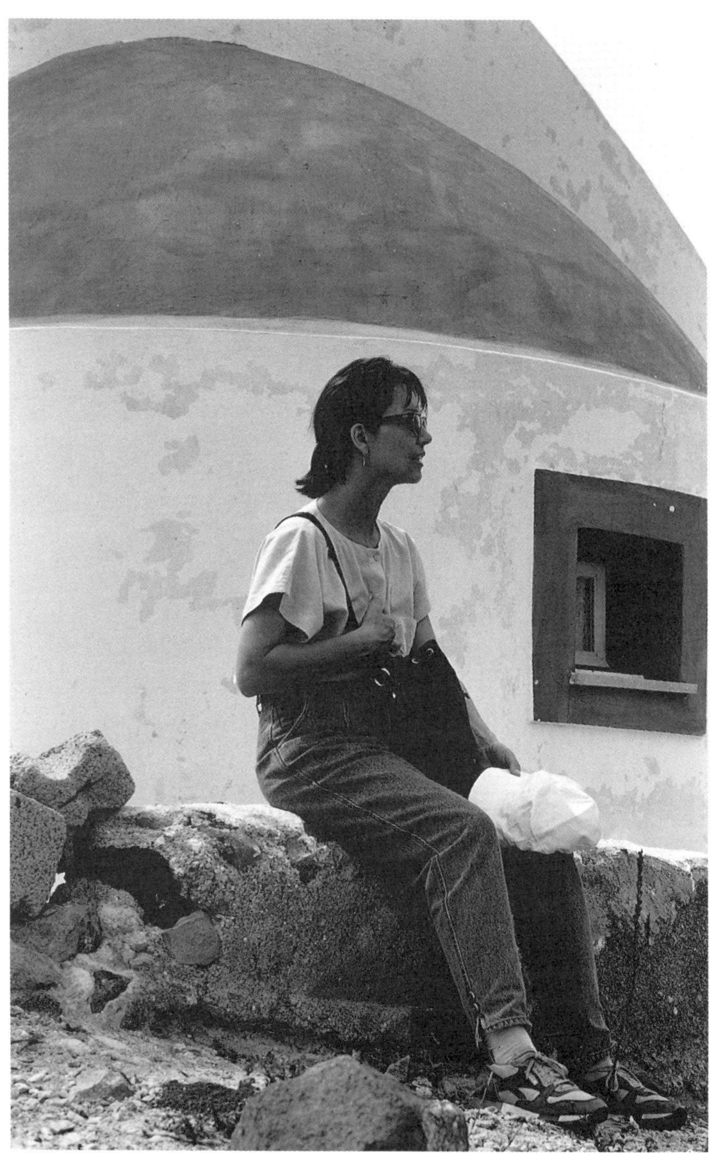

An orange filter leads to contrasty results.

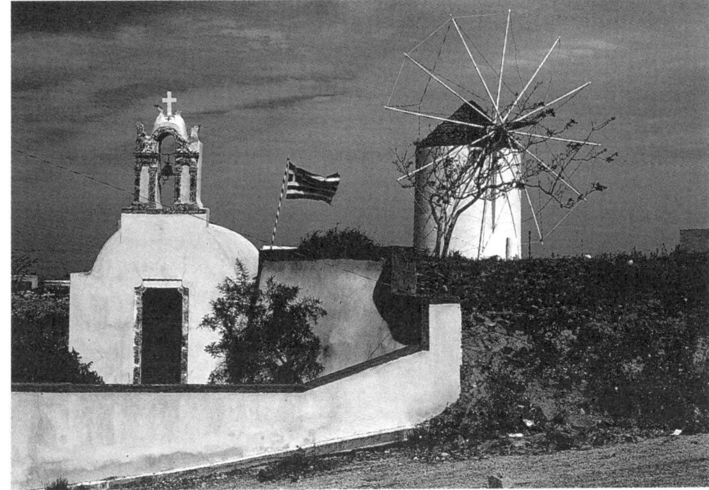

The red filter produces an even more substantial increase in subject contrast.

be helpful with panchromatic film in artificial light. The filter factor is around 2.

Green

The green filter has a more pronounced effect than the yellow-green filter. Green vegetation is rendered substantially lighter – at least in theory. In practice most panchromatic films are less sensitive to green, so that the lightening effect is often less than expected. Blue sky and red tones, on the other hand, are actually darkened. The filter factor varies between 3 and 4.

Blue

The blue filter reproduces the sky lighter and slightly emphasizes atmospheric haze. Skin and red tones are rendered slightly darker. The blue filter is suitable for portrait and glamour photographs in artificial light – note, however, that not only the skin but also red blotches and freckles are darkened and emphasized. Daylight or flash photographs with blue filters cause panchromatic films to react in the same way as orthochromatic film. Apart from the blue filter, a medium blue filter is also available. The filter factors are between 1.5 and 2.

Conversion filters

Conversion filters can be used to adjust the colour temperature of the light to the colour sensitivity of the film. Both the colour temperature and the spectral sensitivity of films is given in kelvin (K). With slide

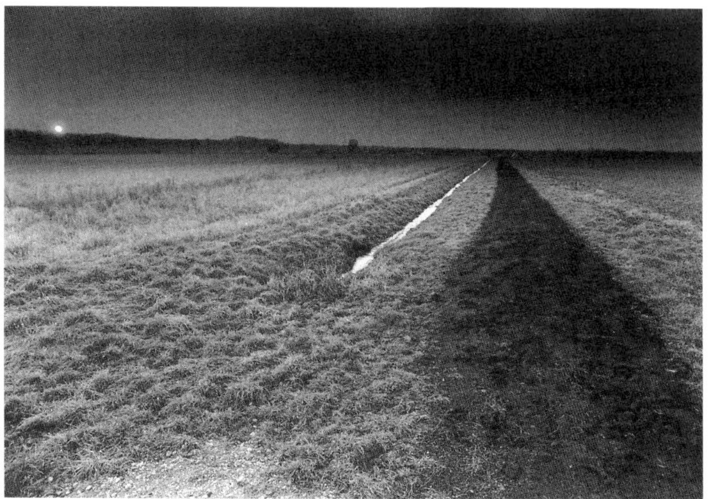

A daylight shot with moonlight effect caused by using a dark red filter.

material in particular, colour temperature and colour sensitivity need to be the same, otherwise a colour cast will occur. Conversion filters are used to achieve correct colour rendering in professional or semi-professional photography. Conversion filters are available in two tones: reddish conversion filters (KR) reduce, and bluish conversion filters (KB) increase, the colour temperature. The conversion value of the filter is given in decamired after the relevant letter for the colour tone (Kodak uses a different nomenclature for Wratten filters). The colour temperature of the light can be measured with a colour temperature meter. Standard colour temperature meters compare the proportions of blue and red light of the light source and therefore only provide information about part of the spectrum. The colour temperature determined in this way is indicated in kelvin. On newer models you can also read off the filter value (in decamired). The standard examples for the use of conversion filters show the two major applications. If you want to shoot with daylight film in artificial light, you need to use a KB filter (blue), and to shoot in daylight on artificial light film a red filter (KR) is required. To get an overview of the available conversion filters and their exact filter values, it's best to check in the catalogues and brochures of the manufacturers (Kodak, B+W, Hoya, Rowi etc).

Compensation filters

Reciprocity failure can occur with very fast or very slow shutter speeds. Depending on the emulsion type, reciprocity failure can appear in colour photography from shutter speeds of ½ sec. (and slower) and $\frac{1}{1000}$ sec. (and faster). Reciprocity failure can have different intensity in the three colour layers, so that a slight colour shift becomes visible.

170

Compensation filters can restore the colour balance on the film and are available in the six primary colours (subtractive and additive): yellow (Y), magenta (M), cyan (C), blue (B), green (G), and red (R). The density of the filter is indicated in front of or behind (depending on the manufacturer) the letter for the colour. Unfortunately the name for compensation filters varies: Kodak calls them CC-filters (colour compensating filters), while B+W simply call them colour correction filters. Data on the values of compensation filters can be found in the manufacturers' tables and manuals.

10. The Quality Chain

A chain can only be as strong as its weakest link, and the same applies to the chain that leads from the exposure to the finished picture. The important thing is that the excellent image quality of photographs taken with the Leica R7 and Leica R lenses should not be reduced by low-quality reproduction. It is therefore vital that only products that meet the demands of Leica quality are used for projection or enlargement.

Leica offers a good range of slide projectors. The smallest unit, the Leica P 150, is very compact, provides even illumination and is very good for first-time buyers of Leica projectors. The Leica P 155 and Leica P 255 offer optimum illumination right into the image corners as well as easy handling. The Leica P 155 slide projector is equipped with a 150W bulb, while the Leica P 255 has a 250W bulb. Both projectors are available in three variants, these are a standard version, one with an infra-red remote control, and one for dissolve projection. The Leica P 2000 Pradovit slide projector is designed for professional requirements. Sophisticated technology and robust construction make slide projection with the Leica P 2000 a real adventure. Thirteen high-quality projection lenses with focal lengths between 35 and 300mm are available for the Leica P 2000.

Excellent projection lenses are a must to achieve sharp and brilliant projection right into the image edges, and Leica's offerings in this area

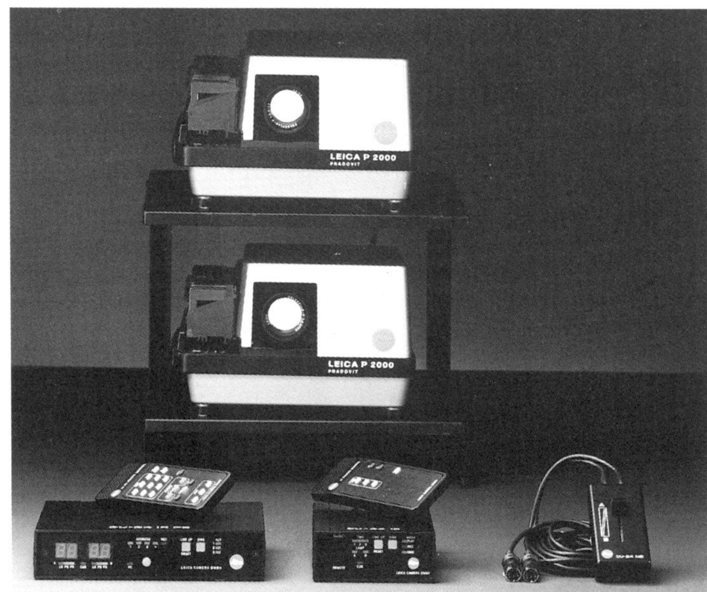

Dissolve projection of the highest quality is obtainable by using Leica projectors.

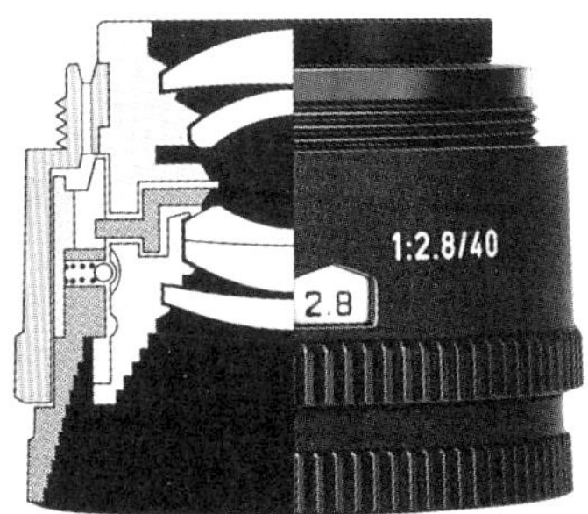

The high-quality enlarging lens WA-Focotar 40mm,f/2.8

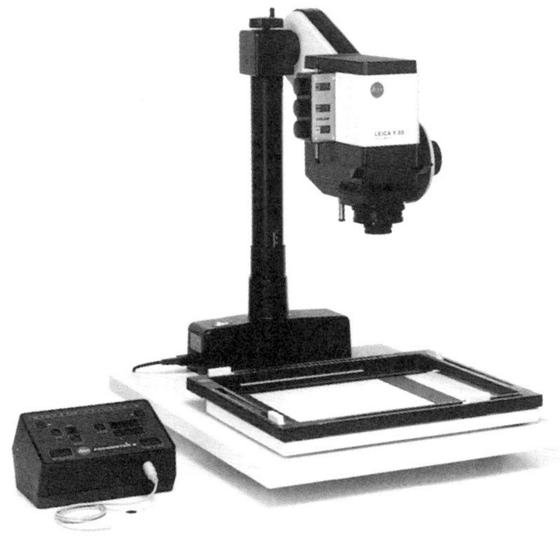

The autofocus enlarger Leica V 35 Focomat.

are considerable. The Colorplan-P2 90mm,f/2.5 and the Colorplan-P2 CF 90mm,f/2.5 can be used with all Leica projectors. The 'CF' stands for 'curved field' and means that the lens compensates for the curvature in slides not mounted between glass. For glass-mounted slides one of the Leica non-CF lenses is required. The new star amongst the Leica projection lenses, the Super-Colorplan-P2 90mm,f/2.5, can be used with the Leica projectors P 155, P 255 and P 2000.

If you prefer prints, you will be well served by the Leica V35 enlarger. The robust and maintenance-free unit offers autofocus convenience in the range from 3x to 16x magnification. Used in conjunction with the WA-Focotar 40mm,f/2.8 high-quality lens, the Leica V35 guarantees excellent image quality even with enlargements of only a portion of the negative. The Leica V35 can be equipped with a colour module, or for black-and-white work with either a module for normal black-and-white printing papers or a Variocontrast module for multigrade papers.

Maintenance and service

The Leica R7 is a robust and reliable camera, which stays fully functional even in adverse conditions. But even with the most robust and reliable equipment damage is possible. In case of breakdown a high-quality camera such as the Leica R7 should not be taken to the nearest backstreet repair shop, but to the service department of the relevant Leica agency.

Index

Page numbers in *italics* refer to illustrations